A FIELD GUIDE TO

FERNS

AND THEIR RELATED FAMILIES

NORTHEASTERN AND CENTRAL

NORTH AMERICA

THE PETERSON FIELD GUIDE SERIES®

A FIELD GUIDE TO

FERNS

AND THEIR RELATED FAMILIES

NORTHEASTERN AND CENTRAL NORTH AMERICA
SECOND EDITION

BOUGHTON COBB
AND
ELIZABETH FARNSWORTH
AND CHERYL LOWE
FOR THE NEW ENGLAND
WILD FLOWER SOCIETY

Illustrations by
LAURA LOUISE FOSTER *and*
ELIZABETH FARNSWORTH

SPONSORED BY
THE NATIONAL WILDLIFE FEDERATION,
THE ROGER TORY PETERSON INSTITUTE, AND
THE NATIONAL AUDUBON SOCIETY

HOUGHTON MIFFLIN COMPANY
BOSTON   NEW YORK   2005

Visit our Web site: www.houghtonmifflinbooks.com

PETERSON FIELD GUIDES and PETERSON FIELD GUIDE SERIES
are registered trademarks of Houghton Mifflin Company.

Library of Congress Cataloging-in-Publication Data

Cobb, Boughton.
A field guide to ferns & their related families of northeastern and
central North America / Boughton Cobb, Elizabeth Farnsworth and Cheryl
Lowe ; illustrations by Laura Louise Foster and Elizabeth Farnsworth.
p. cm. — (The Peterson field guide series)
"Sponsored by the National Wildlife Federation,
and the Roger Tory Peterson Institute."
Includes bibliographical references and index.
ISBN 0-618-39406-0
1. Ferns—United States—Identification.   2. Ferns—Canada—
Identification.   3. Ferns—United States—Pictorial Works.
4. Ferns— Canada—Pictorial Works.   I. Title: Field Guide to
ferns and fern allies of northeastern and central North America.
II. Title: Ferns & their related families of northeastern and central
North America.   III. Title: Ferns and their related families of
northeastern and central North America.
IV. Farnsworth, Elizabeth.   V. Lowe, Cheryl.   VI. Title.   VII. Series.

QK525.C749 2005
587'.3'097—dc22   2005042793

Book design by Anne Chalmers
Typeface: Linotype-Hell Fairfield; Futura Condensed (Adobe)

Printed in Singapore

TWP 10 9 8 7 6 5 4 3 2 1

 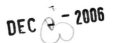

to
Aaron
from Elizabeth

to
Chuck, Anne, and my dad
from Cheryl

CONTENTS

ACKNOWLEDGMENTS

The revision of this Field Guide would not have been possible without the guidance and assistance of many amateur and professional botanists. Crucial to this effort was the input of more than a dozen reviewers across North America, each of whom is expert in a particular group of plants. We thank the following people.

Ray Abair for introductory field courses on ferns.

David Barrington for reviews of *Dryopteris* and *Polystichum*.

Bill Brumback for loans of obscure references from deep in his bookshelves.

David Conant for reviews of *Athyrium, Deparia, Diplazium, Onoclea,* and *Thelypteris.*

David DeKing for inspiration and encouragement.

Heather Driscoll for review of *Phegopteris.*

Marylee Everett, Gray Wexelblat, and Leslie Duthie for beta testing keys in the field.

Donald Farrar for reviews of *Trichomanes, Vittaria,* the Ophioglossaceae, and *Woodwardia,* providing a new key for *Botrychium* species, and donating photographs.

Art Gilman for expertise on the Ophioglossaceae and for putting us in touch with other experts in the field.

Nick Gotelli for musical input.

Arthur Haines for excellent advice on constructing keys, for sharing his New England keys for many taxa, and for reviews of *Selaginella* and Lycopodiaceae.

Jim Hickey for his insightful critique of the Morphology section, his suggestions to include new species of *Isoëtes,* reviews of *Gymnocarpium,* and perspectives on Lycopodiaceae.

Chad Husby for review of *Equisetum.*

Don Lubin for his careful reading of the manuscript, clear teaching of the ferns, and excellent suggestions for differentiating species in the field.

Malcolm Meltzer for reading many of the sections.

Robbin Moran for review of *Cystopteris*.

Catherine Paris for review of *Adiantum*.

Tom Ranker for review of *Asplenium*.

Lucinda Swatzell for review of *Cheilanthes*.

Frances Tenenbaum and Lisa White of Houghton Mifflin for recognizing the need to update this guide and for the invitation to write it and Beth Kluckhohn for artful layout.

Michael Windham for review of *Cryptogramma, Pellaea, Polypodium, Pleopeltis, Woodsia,* and *Cheilanthes*.

We took their input into account whenever possible, but any errors or omissions are our responsibilities.

INTRODUCTION

Almost fifty years ago, Boughton Cobb, the original author of the *Peterson Field Guide to Ferns,* wrote:

> To those interested in nature and to those who perhaps want to specialize in one of the fields of the natural sciences, the ferns and their allies offer a good springboard for study. The ancient lineage of ferns, their interesting biology, the comparatively few numbers of…genera and species…and the presence of ferns in nearly all ecological systems make them objects of special interest to the scientist as well as to the layman.
>
> Wherever we go, or wherever we are, in any part of the world except in the arid deserts or on the high seas, we are likely to find ferns…on the tops of mountains and in low swamps; in dimly lit, moist, cavelike crevices and in sunny open fields; on high, dry, and windswept cliffs; in and on still waters of ponds or lakes; along highways, in towns and villages; and even in the cities, commonly displayed in florists' windows.

The relatively small number of species in our area (just over 100) makes it possible to find them all, although the rare species do present a challenge. For both professional and amateur users of this Field Guide, however, the search is usually not about numbers of different fern species seen, but about the pleasure of the journey, of discovering and appreciating ferns in diverse habitats and in all their various forms.

The intent of this Field Guide is to be brief and simple, yet as accurate as possible, using drawings, photos, and text, but keeping the general layout of the original book. It is pocket-sized and uses as few botanical terms as are needed in order to avoid ambiguity. We retained most of the original drawings, which were faithfully and artfully rendered from mature, living specimens by Laura Louise Foster, with all parts of the plants illustrated. We were fortunate to be able to locate and rescan the original beautiful drawings thanks to the curators of the Hunt Institute for Botanical Documentation. Elizabeth Farnsworth has added drawings where needed.

AREA COVERED

This Field Guide covers northeastern and central United States and adjacent Canada, as indicated on the map on page ii.

NEW INFORMATION IN THIS REVISION

Since the last edition of this guide, researchers have uncovered fascinating new information about ferns and fern allies, their evolution, and their relationships, which has led to numerous changes in botanical names. This includes changes in our understanding of the term "fern allies," which we use interchangeably with "fern relatives." See "The Place of Ferns and Fern Relatives in the Plant Kingdom" (page 9). If a species' scientific name has changed, we list the former name (called a synonym) under the new species and index both names. Common names can be confusing, because several names are sometimes used for one plant. This Field Guide lists one or two of the more familiar common names of each species. Our primary source for nomenclature is the *Flora of North America,* Volume 2 (1993), although we consulted other botanical journals as well, especially the *American Fern Journal.* In addition, we are grateful for the extensive guidance and information provided by numerous scientists currently conducting research in this field (see Acknowledgments).

We have updated the bibliography and also present a new section on "Fern Habitats and Conservation," a glossary of botanical terms, and new information on fern gardening and uses ("Ferns in Cultivation and Culture").

ORGANIZATION OF THE GUIDE

FERNS AND FERN RELATIVES

This Field Guide is divided into two broad groups: "true ferns" and "fern relatives." Plants in both groups reproduce by spores instead of seeds and have vascular systems to transport fluids through roots, stems, and leaves. (Mosses, algae, and liverworts also produce spores but do not have a true vascular system.) The section on ferns, Part Two, covers most of the familiar species with leaflike structures (fronds), well-developed veins, and spores that are contained in capsules (sporangia) on the fronds. Part Two also includes the Moonworts, Grape Ferns, and Rattlesnake Fern (*Botrychium* and *Ophioglossum* species), which are also true ferns. The section on fern relatives, Part Three, covers plant families related to ferns. In contrast to the true ferns, the spore-bearing structures of these plants are not borne on a frond. Some of these plant families are much more closely related to ferns than others, but for simplicity's sake we have grouped them together.

KEYS AND DESCRIPTIONS

The general keys at the beginning of the book use verbal descriptions and illustrations of distinguishing characters to guide the reader to the correct genus of fern or fern ally. As with flowering plants, it is often essential to observe the reproductive structures when using a key, but these are not always present throughout the growing season. Therefore, we provide alternative characteristics to look for when reproductive parts are not available, and we offer a simple silhouette key. The general keys take the reader to a genus description. Under each genus is a key to the species. In writing this guide and researching the taxonomy of ferns, we discovered that much disagreement still exists about the fern families and which species are included in which families. To avoid confusion, we chose not to organize the descriptions of individual species under particular families, as the previous edition of this Field Guide did. Rather, we organized the ferns and fern allies alphabetically by genus within broad groups, with species listed within the genus.

Full-page, illustrated descriptions of species provide information on the overall form, growth habit, habitat, range, and diagnostic characters that distinguish the species. A photograph or drawing illustrates useful diagnostic traits whenever possible, with pointers to highlight unique characters. Species or hybrids that are rare, obscure, or seen only occasionally in our area receive less detailed descriptions, but we mention them here to encourage readers to discover these lesser-known groups. Interested readers can find more information on them in sources like the *Flora of North America*.

FIELDS OF EXPLORATION

Field guides are one of many tools we use to understand more about the natural world, and exploration is a way to learn more. For the casual nature lover, exploring ferns might mean simply stopping to carefully observe the design of a frond, inspect the beautiful patterns made by the sori hidden underneath, or admire the way the plants spread through the forest. For the amateur botanist, learning the names and habits of these ferns might start with this Field Guide, but observing how a species varies in form, habit, or preference from one site to another takes the amateur to a higher level of understanding. For the advanced botanist or professional researcher, it is always a pleasure to discover species that were previously unknown in our area, to contribute new observations on the life of ferns, and to work for the conservation of ferns and their habitats. We hope this is an informative Guide that can be used readily by a wide range of fern enthusiasts.

The legacy of America's great naturalist, Roger Tory Peterson, is preserved through the programs and work of the Roger Tory Peterson Institute of Natural History. The RTPI mission is to create passion for and knowledge of the natural world in the hearts and minds of children by inspiring and guiding the study of nature in our schools and communities. You can become a part of this worthy effort by joining RTPI. Just call RTPI's membership department at 1-800-758-6841, fax 716-665-3794, or e-mail (webmaster@rtpi.org) for a free one-year membership with the purchase of this Field Guide.

LIFE CYCLE OF A FERN

Unlike flowering plants, ferns and related species reproduce from spores, not seeds. Until the sixteenth century, people knew that all plants grew from seeds, but were unable to figure out how ferns reproduced. In the context of the times, magical, invisible seeds were the only explanation. Now, with the power of electron microscopes, both the spore and its intricate pattern and shape are visible. We also now understand that ferns and fern allies undergo two radically different developmental stages (alternating generations) before a new plant recognizable as a fern appears: a nearly invisible gametophyte stage, which is the sexual phase of a fern's life; and the familiar, leafy sporophyte stage, which is the spore-producing phase.

The various characteristics of spores and other reproductive structures are the basis for organizing ferns and fern allies into taxonomic orders, families, and genera, but the life cycle for all these plants is basically the same. We use Marginal Wood Fern (*Dryopteris marginalis*), a common fern, as an illustration.

If you look at the underside of a frond of Marginal Wood Fern in mid-summer, you will see tiny, round, greenish to tan dots near the pinna margin. By late summer, these dots, called sori, have turned dark brown. Sori are actually masses of tiny spore cases, called sporangia, and on the Marginal Wood Fern the sori are covered by a thin round membrane or protective shield called an indusium. The presence and shape of the indusium varies from one species to another.

Pinna with sori

Side view of indusium covering sori

All the mature fronds of Marginal Wood Fern look similar and sori are found on almost every frond, but this is not true for all ferns. Some species have separate sterile and fertile fronds; sori are produced only on fertile fronds. Some fertile fronds, such as those of the Cinnamon Fern (*Osmunda cinnamomea*), look completely different from the sterile ones (see page 172).

The sporangia clustered in the sori are small, spherical capsules mounted on a tiny stalk and composed of a single layer of cells. A ring or band of special, thickened cells, called the annulus, runs vertically three-quarters of the way around the spherical capsule. (In some ferns, the annulus is transverse, running along the equator of the sphere.) When the sporangia of the Marginal Wood Fern are ripe and begin to dry, the thin layer of cells becomes brittle and tension builds. The cell walls of the annulus are thicker and stronger than the rest of the sporangium capsule, so when the sporangium finally splits, it is pulled open by the central "spine" of the annulus. The annulus pulls back slowly at first, but then, as water tension in the cells is suddenly released, the annulus snaps rapidly forward, catapulting the spores away from the fern. In dry conditions, even the smallest air currents can easily carry the microscopic spores a significant distance.

Sporangium dispersing spores

Those spores fortunate enough to land in a moist, shady place begin developing into a *gametophyte* (sometimes called a prothallus), the stage in which the fern's sexual organs are formed. The gametophyte starts as a one-celled body and promptly puts down a tiny rootlike hair to anchor itself to the soil. It then develops into a flattened, green, heart-shaped body about one-quarter inch in diameter. More rootlike hairs develop to absorb and transport nutrients and water to the cells. The notched end of the "heart" is several times thicker than the apex, forming a sort of cushion. The male organs, or antheridia, are near the apex, and the female organs, or archegonia, are near the notch. Both male and female organs are microscopic in size. The female organ consists of a neck or chimneylike tube with its base embedded in the cushion part of the gametophyte. The base holds a single egg. There are often 20 or more archegonia on one gametophyte. The antheridia, more numerous than the archegonia, are short, bulbous organs, and each contains several sperm.

Gametophyte: early stages (left); mature form (right)

When the gametophyte is fully mature and the sex organs fully developed, the thin shell of each antheridium bursts when it comes in contact with water. The sperm, shaped like corkscrews with many hairs (flagellae) at one end, swim through the water to reach the archegonia. The sperm might go in any direction, so archegonia often exude a chemical attractive to the sperm, enticing them to swim toward the open tubes, enter, and fertilize an egg. Once an egg is fertilized, the tube closes, as do the tubes of the other archegonia, so only one plantlet develops from each gametophyte.

Once fertilized, the egg divides and grows, forming a new sporophyte. At first, the growing sporophyte is anchored to the gametophyte. Then it sends a root down into the soil and a stem upward. From the stem grows the first tiny leaf. Nutrition from the cushion lasts only long enough to sustain the developing root and leaf until the sporophyte can support itself.

Archegonium (top right); corkscrew-like sperm (lower right); antheridium (left); young sporophyte (bottom)

In ideal conditions, the spores of Marginal Wood Fern develop into gametophytes in about 2 weeks, and gametophytes develop into young, new ferns in approximately $3^{1}/_{2}$ months. This developmental period varies tremendously under different weather, temperature, and site conditions. It also varies greatly by species.

With the archegonium and antheridium so close together, one might assume that self-fertilization is common. Ferns, however, use some of the same mechanisms to avoid self-fertilization that flowering plants use. In many species, male and female organs mature at different times so that the gametophyte is functionally unisexual at a given moment. Sometimes the archegonia arch away from the antheridia. One mechanism of avoiding self-fertilization is unique to ferns: in many species, mature female gametophytes secrete chemicals, antheridiogens, that suppress formation of archegonia and stimulate antheridial development on adjacent gametophytes. Self-fertilization, however, does sometimes happen.

In theory, each spore, and thus each gametophyte, has half the number of chromosomes of the parent fern. When fertilization occurs, the chromosome number returns to the original number of the parent fern. Living systems are wonderfully creative and complex, so they do not always follow the rules: ferns may and often do hybridize; they produce polyploid offspring (i.e., with more than two sets of chromosomes); and occasionally they produce individuals without fertilization. For example, hybrids are produced when two species in the same genus synchronize gametophyte development in the same tiny bit of moisture and one species fertilizes another. Although the resulting sporophyte plant might grow to maturity, a large percentage of spores produced by that plant will be sterile. Hybrids are fairly common in Spleenworts (*Asplenium* spp.), Wood Ferns (*Dryopteris* spp.), Bladder Ferns (*Cystopteris* spp.), and Christmas, or Holly, Ferns (*Polystichum* spp.), among others.

Chromosome numbers can multiply when mitotic cell division during spore formation is atypical, producing diploid spores (spores with two sets of chromosomes instead of the usual one). This results in polyploidy, a situation in which multiple sets of chromosomes are present in the sporophyte. Maidenhair Spleenwort (*Asplenium trichomanes*) and Fragile Fern (*Cystopteris fragilis*), for example, occur as both diploid (with 2 sets) and tetraploid (with 4 sets) sporophytes. Hybrids may become new fertile, stable species if polyploidy occurs. Sometimes a sporophyte arises vegetatively from a gametophyte without fertilization, a process known as apogamy. Since sperm transport requires water, apogamy occurs more often in ferns of dry habitats, such as Lip Ferns and Cliffbrakes (*Cheilanthes* and *Pellaea*).

A single fern can produce millions of spores—each sporangium of a Marginal Wood Fern, for example, usually contains 64 spores; 30–50 sporangia are clustered in a sorus; 50–100 sori on each pinna; 30–40 pinnae on each fertile frond; and more than 10 fronds on a full-grown Marginal Wood Fern. That adds up to 67 million spores. Spores are viable from a few days to a few months, but only a handful of those spores land in a propitious spot, and even fewer en-

Dryopteris marginalis sori and indusia. *(Photo by John Lynch)*

counter all the conditions conducive to full gametophyte development, fertilization, and growth of the young sporophyte.

In reality, ferns reproduce by vegetative means more often than by spores. Rhizomes branch out and develop new fronds and roots. As the older portions of the rhizome die, the branches become separate plants. Hay-scented and Bracken Ferns (*Dennstaedtia punctilobula* and *Pteridium aquilinum*) produce massive colonies this way, with fronds emerging along the spreading rhizome. In Ostrich Fern (*Matteuccia struthiopteris* var. *pensylvanica*), crowns of new plants appear several feet from the parent plant; fronds emerge in a circular cluster from the ends of long slender rhizomes. Rhizomes are an effective device to claim new territory, but for cliff-dwelling ferns, pushing rhizomes through solid rock is a tough assignment. Instead, the Bulblet Fern (*Cystopteris bulbifera*) develops pealike formations on the frond, which drop off, roll down to a new crevice, and grow into new plants. Walking Fern (*Asplenium rhizophyllum*) takes a different approach, developing new roots at the tip of its small, arching, slender fronds—a successful mode of travel around its cliff habitat. Some ferns, like Hart's-tongue (*Asplenium scolopendrium*), occasionally produce small plantlets on the blade surface that

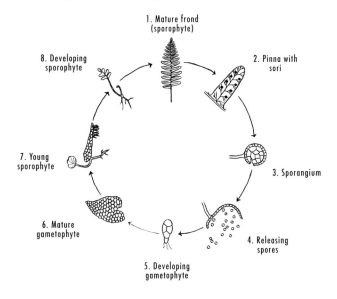

FIGURE 1. LIFE CYCLE OF A TRUE FERN

1. Mature frond (sporophyte)
2. Pinna with sori
3. Sporangium
4. Releasing spores
5. Developing gametophyte
6. Mature gametophyte
7. Young sporophyte
8. Developing sporophyte

drop off and become new plants. Adder's-tongue Ferns (*Ophioglossum* species) develop special buds on their roots, which produce new fronds and then new roots for the nascent plant.

LIFE CYCLES OF FERN RELATIVES

The life cycle of fern relatives differs slightly from that of true ferns. Sporangia are not produced on the undersides of the fronds, but at the base of special, sometimes modified leaves called sporophylls, or in conelike structures called strobili, or in special stalked cases called sporocarps. (Water ferns, like *Azolla* and *Marsilea*, are true ferns but also produce sporocarps.) Gametophytes come in a range of shapes and might be large, long-lived subterranean bodies or delicate, filamentous ones. We summarize the differences here. More detailed descriptions appear in the introductions to the various groups of fern relatives.

Clubmosses (*Dendrolycopodium, Diphasiastrum, Huperzia, Lycopodiella, Lycopodium, Pseudolycopodiella, Spinulum*): Strobili; one type of spore; a gametophyte with both male and female sex organs.

Firmosses (*Huperzia*): No strobili; sporangia at base of evergreen sporophylls; presence of gemmae; a gametophyte with both male and female sex organs.

Horsetails (*Equisetum*): Sporangia produced in a cone composed of small, umbrellalike structures; one type of spore; separate male and female gametophytes.

Quillworts (*Isoëtes*): Two types of sporangium (male and female) borne in basal cavities of leaves; two types of spore.

Spikemosses (*Selaginella*): Strobili or modified terminal leafy zones; two types of spore; two types of sporangium.

THE PLACE OF FERNS AND FERN
RELATIVES IN THE PLANT KINGDOM

EVOLUTION OF FERNS

Ferns and their allies are clearly unique in the modern plant world and differ in many ways from the flowering plants. Fernlike plants occupy a thick slice of the fossil record; this varied group of plants includes some of the oldest species extant on the planet. They evolved from the earliest vascular plants that made their way onto land, and fossil evidence of their existence can be traced back more than 350 million years to the Devonian Period.

A few sample fossils tell the story of fern evolution. *Rhacophyton,* one of the most ancient Devonian forms, bore little resemblance to modern ferns except in the fine structure of its vascular tissue and rhizomes. *Stauropteris,* appearing about 20 million years later in the Carboniferous Period, displayed an elaborate filigree of branching fronds comparable to later ferns. At the same time, an intriguing group known as the "seed ferns" was experimenting with new shapes and lifestyles. For example, one sapling-sized seed fern, *Trigonocarpus,* produced peanut-sized seeds on its fronds. Seed ferns were an abortive lineage, and they are long extinct; evolution is rife with false starts. Nevertheless, the evolutionary innovation of the "seed" would be reinvented later among the angiosperms and gymnosperms—seed-bearing plants that have come to dominate the earth.

The Carboniferous Period (360–286 million years ago) was the heyday of ferns and their allies, when they became the predominant plant group in the sultry tropical forests that covered much of the equatorial landmasses of the planet. A uniform, warm climate provided luxurious growing conditions. Clubmosses attained the size of great trees, a formidable 100 feet or more in height and 5 feet in girth. Horsetails resembled giant, bushy bamboos. Tree ferns similar to today's species proliferated during this time. While ferns basked in tropical temperatures, cycles of glaciation proceeded apace at the poles and caused large fluctuations in sea level. Seas periodically inundated the Carboniferous forests, burying large amounts of slowly decomposing plant debris in layers that, later subjected to heat and pressure, formed the famous coal deposits that are exploited for "fossil" fuels today. These fossils in the coal strata yield glimpses into the diversity of ferns that thrived during this period.

Toward the end of the Carboniferous Period, continental collisions and glaciation with attendant climate and sea-level changes contributed to the extinction of numerous plant groups; for unknown reasons, the Clubmosses were particularly hard-hit. With a drying trend and the emergence of more terrestrial habitat, ferns and Horsetails flourished, but most species appearing in the Carboniferous Period declined by the Permian Period (286–245 million years ago). Ever resilient, however, fern species rebounded in the Mesozoic Era (245–146 million years ago), which witnessed the rise of many fern genera that are still around today. By the latter end of the Mesozoic Era, in the Cretaceous Period when dinosaurs ruled (about 120 million years ago), flowering plants began their evolutionary ascendancy. It was traditionally thought that ferns began to decline in sheer numbers during the stiff competition of the time, but new evidence from molecular studies tells a different story: a major evolutionary radiation occurred among ferns in the Cretaceous Period, producing many of today's contemporary species. In fact, a unique chemical receptor (phy3), which allows ferns to take advantage of many wavelengths of light in the shadow of the angiosperms (i.e., the dark understory of flowering plant forests), may have been a critical evolutionary innovation that allowed ferns to diversify during this time. Today, some 11,000 species of ferns and fern relatives in 300 genera occupy every corner of Earth, from mountaintops to deserts to coastal swamps.

Globally, most species of ferns show a broader geographic distribution than even the most cosmopolitan angiosperms. It is interesting to note that many of the ferns of eastern North America are related to species of temperate eastern Asia; indeed, ten or more species, including *Onoclea sensibilis* (Sensitive Fern), *Cryptogramma stelleri* (Slender Cliff Brake), and *Asplenium rutamuraria* (Wall Rue), are native to both regions. During the Tertiary Period (66–26 million years ago), a land bridge across what is now the Bering Strait (from Alaska to Russia) once joined the North American and Asian continents. Great exchanges of flora and fauna proceeded across this land bridge—most likely with ferns leading the charge.

Ferns recolonize the site of a recent volcanic eruption near Pu'u Huluhulu, Hawai'i. (Photo by Elizabeth Farnsworth)

With lightweight spores, ferns traverse distances easily and are often among the earliest colonizers of newly available habitats. In fact, in modern times, ferns were among the first plants to recolonize Mount St. Helens following the massive volcanic eruption in 1980, and the spores of at least one species wafted in from Japan. For the same reason, nearly half of the ferns and fern allies described in this book also occur in Europe and the British Isles. Thus, the versatile ferns are some of the most inveterate travelers of the plant kingdom.

THE RELATIONSHIPS OF FERNS

To understand where ferns and their relatives fit in the modern plant world (and contemporary systems of plant classification), we first take a brief step back to understand the plant kingdom as a whole. Biologists have traditionally divided the plant kingdom into two large groups, or subkingdoms: the thallophytes (the al-

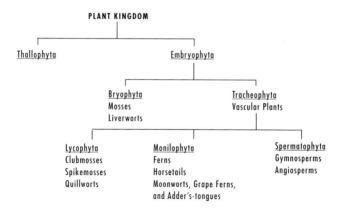

FIGURE 2. FERNS AND THE PLANT KINGDOM

gae), which do not form embryos, and the embryophytes, which do. The thallophytes form only a mass of tissue (a thallus) lacking true roots, stems, or leaves. The embryophytes are divided into the Bryophyta (liverworts, mosses, and hornworts), with no vascular tissues, and the Tracheophyta (the plants that produce vascular tissues for transporting water and nutrients). The Tracheophyta are divided into the Spermatophyta (the angiosperms and gymnosperms), the Monilophyta, and the Lycophyta.

Botanists have traditionally referred to two groups, the "Ferns" (the familiar leafy ferns and the Moonworts, Adder's-tongues, and Grape Ferns) and the "Fern allies" (a large group that includes the Horsetails, Clubmosses, Spikemosses, and Quillworts). The loose term "Fern allies" is problematic because it encompasses a group of plants that are only distantly related to true ferns and to each other, including the Horsetails, which are more closely related to ferns than to any other of these "allies." It is more useful to refer to the fern and fern-related groups as Monilophyta (true ferns and horsetails) and Lycophyta (Clubmosses, Spikemosses, and Quillworts). Both groups are distinct from the spermatophytes because they do not form seeds. *A fern is a vascular plant that has large, complex leaves with branching venation and that reproduces by spores.* The Lycophyta are also vascular plants that reproduce by spores, but they diverged early in evolutionary time from the Monilophyta and are not as closely related to the true ferns as botanists once thought.

The Monilophyta consists of five main groups:

> Horsetails: a single genus, *Equisetum*
> Leptosporangiate Ferns: our familiar leafy ferns
> Grape Ferns, Moonworts, and Adder's-tongues
> Whisk Ferns (a single ancient genus, *Psilotum,* found in southern and tropical areas)
> Marattioid Ferns: predominantly tropical ferns

The Lycophyta consist of

> Clubmosses and Firmosses: *Dendrolycopodium, Diphasiastrum, Huperzia, Lycopodiella, Lycopodium, Pseudolycopodiella,* and *Spinulum*
> Spikemosses: one genus, *Selaginella*
> Quillworts: one genus, *Isoëtes*

Leptosporangiate ferns produce small, stalked sporangia with capsule walls only one cell layer thick, and (usually) a special ring or annulus that aids in spore dispersal. In the spring, the leptosporangiate ferns unfurl from coiled fiddleheads, exhibiting a pattern of growth called "circinate vernation." The diverse leptosporangiate ferns consist of the many genera we think of as typical ferns—*Osmunda, Thelypteris, Dryopteris*, and so on. Eusporangiate ferns produce large sporangia (>¹⁄₃₂ in. wide) with thick capsule walls that consist of several layers of cells, and which contain several spores. These ferns do not emerge as fiddleheads in the spring; they spring up erect or bent from the ground. Figure 3 (below) illustrates the relationships for the ferns and fern allies in our area. The complex relationships among species in these groups are still being investigated and are the subject of much intensive study.

coiled

bent

Fiddleheads

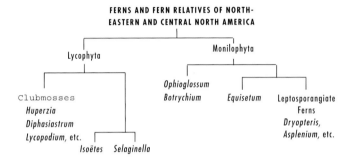

FIGURE 3. RELATIONSHIPS BETWEEN FERNS AND FERN ALLIES

How have botanists figured out all these relationships? Students of ferns (pteridologists) look carefully at a number of features—frond shape, sori, sporangia, spores, and so on—and delineate groups of related species based on the characters they share. Today, as methods of genetic analysis become easier and more sophisticated, botanists also frequently examine the sequence of amino acids in the plant's DNA; each species has a unique genetic code, and more closely related species share more of their code, in the same sequence, than distantly related species. (Evolution, after all, is accomplished by changes in the genetic code that are manifested in the myriad physical forms of species.) Botanists also note if ferns share specific enzyme proteins in their cells; the presence and absence of these can help detect fine-scale relationships of groups within species and can help identify which parent species give rise to particular hybrids. Equipped with these new tools, contemporary research on ferns is proceeding at a feverish pace, and new varieties, subspecies, and species are being discovered, named, and revised all the time.

NAMES OF FERNS

All species are given a two-part Latin name (always written in italics) consisting of a genus name (always capitalized) and a species epithet (not capitalized). The names or nomenclature of fern species reflect the relationships among them; closely related species are grouped in one genus, much as a last name is shared by human family members. In tribute to the botanist who first officially "names" a species by publishing a technical description and name that is accepted formally as part of the International Code of Botanical Nomenclature, his or her name is placed as the "authority" beside the Latin name of the species. Abbreviations of these "authorities" are given with the species epithet in the species descriptions in this book. We also furnish common names (the colloquial English names used to refer to particular species), which are sometimes descriptive and useful for remembering identities. However, these names often change over time or by personal preference and may sometimes refer to several species. Thus, the Latin nomenclature is the more reliable and consistent way to refer to ferns.

The names of genera and species of ferns have remained relatively stable as new data on their origins and taxonomy accrue, but their larger-scale affiliations at the plant family level have been more difficult to determine. Various taxonomic treatments have ascribed the many species of ferns to between 14 and 20 families. Currently, taxonomists tend to "lump" the genera into fewer (14 or so) families, with the family Polypodiaceae being the most diverse in terms of species. Because the nomenclature of fern families is in flux, we place the emphasis in this Field Guide on identifying fern genera and species, downplaying the somewhat malleable family affiliations.

Some species are split into smaller groups— subspecies or varieties—in recognition of fine- and finer-scale (respectively) differences in several traits. It is assumed that such infraspecific groups can interbreed, given the opportunity, but may be at the threshold of diversifying

The common name for Denn-staedtia punctilobula (Michx.) T. Moore is "Hay-scented Fern." (Photo by William Cullina)

Dryopteris celsa (Log Fern) is a fertile hybrid of D. goldiana *(Goldie's Fern) and* D. ludoviciana *(Southern Wood Fern). (Photo by David Stone/NEWFS)*

into new species as they adapt to new environments or become reproductively isolated from their kin.

A major factor complicating relationships of the ferns and fern allies, and sometimes frustrating to our ability to identify plants in the field, is hybridization. As discussed in "Life Cycle of a Fern" (page 3), two closely related species occasionally interbreed to produce offspring that may show characteristics of both parents. Hybrids are most often sterile because of mismatches in their chromosome pairings. If these sterile hybrids are particularly frequent or widespread, they are sometimes assigned a new name, with an "×" written before the species epithet to indicate that they are a cross between two different parental species. For example, *Asplenium × clermontae* is a rare, sterile hybrid resulting from a cross between *A. ruta-muraria* (Wall Rue) and *A. trichomanes* (Maidenhair Spleenwort). Occasionally, a doubling or further multiplication of the chromosomes of hybrids occurs during spore formation, which allows chromosomes to pair up properly and produces viable spores. This process, known as polyploidy, has played a significant role in the evolution of new taxa of ferns and fern allies. Fertile hybrids that now exist as separate species from their parents are usually given a new species epithet without the customary "×" prefix. *A. pinnafitidum* (Lobed Spleenwort), for example, is a hybrid originally produced from a cross between *A. montanum* (Mountain Spleenwort) and *A. rhizophyllum* (Walking Fern). It is a tetraploid (with 4 sets of chromosomes), and is reproductively competent. It exhibits characteristics of both parents. To confuse matters still further, it can also backcross with at least one of its parent taxa, Mountain Spleenwort. Thus, hybridization and polyploidy are forces that shape the evolution of ferns and fern allies in complex ways.

FERN HABITATS
AND CONSERVATION

Ferns can tell you a lot about a place. They can be choosy about where they live, inhabiting only specialized environments or restricting their range to a narrow sector of a region. As such, several species are considered ecological specialists, and can even serve as indicators of important habitat conditions such as the type of bedrock present and soil moisture. The northeastern quadrant of the United States encompasses a variety of habitats, from rolling hills and coastal plains to the Appalachian Mountains to the prairies. Glaciers have left their marks in the North with dunes, ponds, and rocky soils. By contrast, the mid-Atlantic states and the parts of Illinois, Wisconsin, Iowa, and Minnesota that escaped direct glaciation have older, weathered soils, deposits of fine wind-blown soil, or gravelly outwash emanating from distant ice fields. Bedrock types in our area range from easily eroded calcareous marbles to tough, weathered acidic granites. The ferns of this region reflect this diversity of landform and climate, from the northern species characteristic of sub-Arctic forests to more southerly denizens of the mid-Atlantic states. A long history of colonial settlement, with clearing of forests for pasture and planting, has also left its signature in the presence of "weedy" ferns such as Bracken, even where forest cover has rebounded dramatically in the past century.

Asplenium trichomanes (*Maidenhair Spleenwort*) *prefers calcium-rich rock outcrops. (Photo by Cheryl Lowe)*

Ferns and fern allies can be found just about everywhere in our area; however, certain habitats are particularly rich in species and are excellent places to search for the more unusual species. The following habitats harbor especially diverse assemblages or unusual types of fern.

Limestone or marble rock outcrops: These rocks have a wealth of calcium and/or magnesium and they weather easily to a rich soil that is often near-neutral in pH. Calcium and magnesium buffer acidity and make nutrients more readily available to plants. Several fern species are almost totally restricted to calcareous rock types, including Walking Fern (*Asplenium rhizophyllum*), Slender Cliffbrake (*Cryptogramma stelleri*), Hart's-tongue Fern (*Asplenium scolopendrium*), Wall-rue (*Asplenium ruta-muraria*), Maidenhair Spleenwort (*Asplenium trichomanes*), and Bulblet Fern (*Cystopteris bulbifera*). If you come upon these ferns on a dripping cliff face, you are almost certainly in a calcium-rich area, which is also likely to support a diverse array of flowering plants. Other bedrock types, such as basalt, are also relatively rich in calcium or magnesium, and, especially if the associated soils are seepy or wet, they may support a diverse collection of ferns, including Goldie's Fern (*Dryopteris goldiana*), Ebony Spleenwort (*Asplenium platyneuron*), and Blunt-lobed Woodsia (*Woodsia obtusa*).

Xeric cliffs and outcrops: Certain species of fern adapt well to the absence of water during the drier parts of the late summer, or a severe drought. The Rock Polypody (*Polypodium virginianum*), Appalachian Polypody (*Polypodium appalachianum*), and Resurrection Fern (*Pleopeltis polypodioides* var. *michauxiana*) are quite tolerant of dry conditions because of the tough cuticle on their fronds. These "resurrection ferns" curl up and appear quite dead during long bouts of desiccation, only to return to life when water next becomes available. Other drought-resistant species, such as the Lip Ferns (*Cheilanthes* species), are endowed with densely hairy or woolly fronds that hold water close to the leaf surface and shade the underlying tissue from the hot, drying rays of the sun.

Freshwater wetlands: Certain ferns have their feet wet

Cheilanthes lanosa (*Hairy Lip Fern) is a drought-resistant fern of rocky slopes and dry soils. (Photo by Cheryl Lowe)*

(Left) Osmunda regalis (*Royal Fern*) *grows in saturated soils.* (*Photo by Dorothy Long/NEWFS*) (Above) Marsilea quadrifolia (*Water Shamrock*) *lives exclusively in water.* (*Photo by NEWFS*)

all the time, are regarded as frequent inhabitants of wetlands, and serve as very useful indicators of saturated soil. Among the ferns frequently found in wetlands are Cinnamon Fern (*Osmunda cinnamomea*), Netted Chain Fern (*Woodwardia aureolata*), Virginia Chain Fern (*Woodwardia virginica*), Sensitive Fern (*Onoclea sensibilis*), Marsh Fern (*Thelypteris palustris*), and Royal Fern (*Osmunda regalis*). Many of the Horsetails bear common names that attest to their preferences for damp places, including Marsh Horsetail (*Equisetum palustre*) and Water Horsetail (*Equisetum fluviatile*).

Aquatic habitats (lakes, ponds, and streams): Some ferns and their relatives live exclusively in water, including many of the Quillworts (*Isoëtes* species), the Water Shamrock (*Marsilea quadrifolia*), and the Mosquito Fern (*Azolla caroliniana*). Although some of the Quillworts may be flooded only temporarily, most of these species can be considered truly aquatic plants. Several Quillwort species are very sensitive to changing water quality; some have disappeared from European lakes that have become polluted in recent years, and may be disappearing here also.

RARE FERNS AND THEIR CONSERVATION

Ferns have long excited the attention of amateur and professional botanists, artists, horticulturalists, and collectors. Our affection for ferns, however, has nearly led to their demise, and we must be vigilant in our conservation efforts if a rich array of species is to persist in North America. Ferns have been a focus of concern for conservationists for more than a century. Some ferns we consider common today were on the brink of extinction not so long ago; they have recovered as a result of successful campaigns to educate the public. Writing as early as 1901, the eminent botanist George E. Davenport observed: "the *Osmundas,* the Ostrich Fern, and some of the Shield Ferns are in greater danger of being exterminated on account of the more exposed condition of their rootstocks and frond-buds, and as they are among the most useful and showy of our native ferns they should be protected in every possible way." Davenport lamented that the Royal Fern (*Osmunda regalis*) had almost been extirpated from England by zealous collectors, while "the *Woodsias,* Spleenworts, the Bladder Ferns, and the Oak Ferns [were] becoming extremely rare" in northeastern North America. Davenport implored fern lovers to restrict their collecting to late in the season when the next year's crosiers had been set and to leave the rhizome intact. With this practical advice, we could be assured that "the plants themselves will continue to live as long as the habitats remain in existence."

By 1910 the imperative for conservation was even stronger, as ferns were being systematically harvested on a huge scale for use in floral displays. According to an issue from that time of the *Pittsfield Journal* of western Massachusetts, there were some 50 million ferns in cold storage at one facility that employed hundreds of workers to harvest them from the Berkshire Mountains. The *New York Times* documented in 1914 that more than 60 million wild ferns were imported to New York City alone to supply the florist trade. As ferns became less common, however, the law of diminishing returns and an emerging

Botanical collecting and commercial harvesting seriously endangered the existence of species like Asplenium trichomanes *(left) and* A. platyneuron *(right). (Photo by David Stone/NEWFS)*

conservation ethic pushed both hobbyists and industries to develop methods for propagating desirable ferns. The British Pteridological Society, the American Fern Society, the New England Wild Flower Society, the Hardy Fern Foundation, and other organizations founded around that time and since continue to advocate for the conservation of ferns.

Today the most immediate threat to ferns is destruction of their habitat. In Massachusetts alone, more than 40 acres of land per day are lost to development for housing and industry—think of all the ferns bulldozed under to accomplish this! About a third of the species of ferns and fern allies in Massachusetts are state-listed (Watch-list, Special Concern, Threatened, or Endangered); a handful of others are now regarded as gone from the state altogether—statistics that broadly reflect the situation throughout northeastern and central North America. Some species were rare to begin with, inhabiting types of habitat that are uncommon in the region. Others have disappeared with the draining of wetlands or with the conversion of forests to agriculture in past centuries. But many more will decline in the region without concerted efforts to protect their vanishing habitats.

A full list of species that are rare is beyond the scope of this book, and in any case, the list is always changing. Before beginning to study ferns in earnest, take some time to learn which species are rare or declining in your state. An easy way to do this is to visit the Web site of your state's Natural Heritage Program to obtain a list of the rare plant species in your area. Familiarize yourself with these species, and be on the lookout for them during your field forays. Refrain from collecting them, but take pictures and copious notes if you do come across any of these species. Report your sightings to the Natural Heritage Program to help them keep track of the locations and health of rare fern populations.

Because ferns cannot produce new areas of actively growing tissues in the same growing season once the fiddleheads have emerged, picking is particularly damaging and difficult to recover from. Collect only if necessary to definitely identify a species (usually your own field observations of the living plant will suffice), and harvest only the minimum amount of tissue needed. Above all, be careful not to damage a fern permanently when collecting any part of it.

Best of all, cultivate a profound appreciation for these species and educate other people about them.

MORPHOLOGY OF A FERN

(MORPHOLOGY — THE STUDY OF FORM)

Botanists use several specialized terms to describe the anatomy of a fern. The terms that are particularly useful in field identification are defined in detail below (with English pronunciations and synonyms for certain technical terms in parentheses) and are defined briefly in the Glossary. Some of these terms have several synonyms, which we identify; however, throughout this Field Guide, we consistently use one term for each structure whenever possible. The terms are arranged from bottom to top, that is, from the underground rooting structures to the aboveground leafy parts.

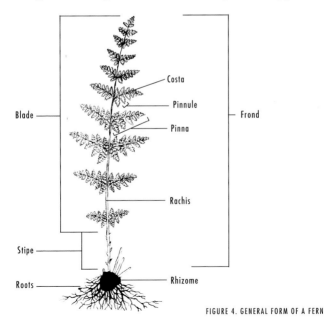

FIGURE 4. GENERAL FORM OF A FERN

RHIZOME (Synonyms: rootstock, trunk, stem): Technically, the stem of the fern, usually horizontal but sometimes vertical, that produces roots below and frond above. Rhizomes can be short, thick, and almost completely buried or they can be long, narrow, or thin, growing horizontally below or along the ground's surface. Rhizomes are perennial, remaining alive even when the fern fronds die at the end of the growing season. They are often covered with scales or hairs.

ROOTS: Organs that grow from the sides and undersides of the rhizome and absorb nutrients from the soil, sometimes forming dense mats. Usually thin, wiry, black, forking, and shallow-growing in ferns.

Scaly stipe   Hairy stipe

STIPE (Synonyms: stalk, stem, petiole): Part of the frond arising aboveground from the rhizome, below the point where the leafy blade is produced. It is usually flat, concave, or grooved in front with a rounded back, and may be covered with distinctive hairs or scales. The stipe can be many colors, from green to brown to black; colors can change as the fern matures. In certain cases, colors are diagnostic characters for a species.

FROND (Synonym: leaf): The entire, aboveground, visible fern leaf, including the blade and stipe. Depending on the species, fronds can emerge individually or in pairs, rings, or tufts. Some fern species produce fertile and sterile fronds of different sizes and shapes. Fertile fronds bear, usually on the underside, the spore-bearing sporangia in clusters called sori.

BLADE (Synonym: lamina): The green, leafy, expanded part of the frond. Blade shapes vary widely among species, from simple, undivided forms to complex, compound, lacy forms. The accompanying figures show the basic architecture of a blade and the terms we use to describe fern blades. Many ferns are distinguished by the finer details of the blade and how it is divided, and descriptions of fern blades can seem complicated and frustrating to the beginner. There are two common approaches. The first is to describe how many times a blade is "divided": not divided at all, or once-, twice-, or thrice-divided (or once-, twice-, or thrice-cut). Some people find it useful to draw lines delineating the divisions of the blade as in figure 5. The problem with this approach is that sometimes a blade is not fully divided into pinnae or the pinnae are lobed but not quite fully cut in pinnules (i.e., they are ¾-cut or 1½-cut).

The other approach is to use more technical but more fully descriptive terms. (Numbers in parentheses refer to figure 6 on page 24.) In this approach, a blade that is not divided at all is called

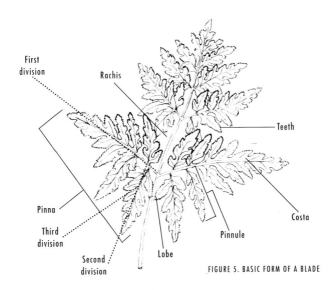

First division · Rachis · Teeth · Pinna · Costa · Third division · Pinnule · Second division · Lobe

FIGURE 5. BASIC FORM OF A BLADE

"simple" or "entire" (1). A blade that is lobed, but not fully cut to the rachis into discrete pinnae, is called "pinnatifid" (2). A blade that has distinct pinnae joined separately to the rachis at a narrow connection is called "pinnate" (3). A blade with pinnae that are lobed but not cut all the way to the costa is "pinnate-pinnatifid" (4). A blade with pinnae that are fully divided into separate pinnules is called "bipinnate" (5). A blade with pinnules that are lobed but not fully separate is called "bipinnate-pinnatifid" (6). A blade with pinnules that are fully divided into separate "pinnulets" is called "tripinnate" and the fern typically has a very lacy appearance (7).

The pinnae on any given blade are often quite variable in shape from the base to the tip of the blade. We recommend always examining the most mature pinnae, i.e., the ones produced lowest on the blade.

RACHIS ("ray-kiss"): Central axis (midrib) of the blade that bears the pinnae. Together the rachis and the stipe make up the whole axis of the frond.

PINNA ("pinn-ah"): plural, pinnae ("pinn-nee") (Synonym: leaflet): Fully separate subdivision of the blade that is attached to the rachis. This term applies when the blade is fully divided (i.e., pinnate), not just lobed.

PINNULE ("pinn-yule") (Synonym: subleaflet): Fully separate subdivision of the pinna. This term applies when the pinna is fully divided (bipinnate), not just lobed.

(1) Simple

(2) Pinnatifid

(3) Pinnate

(4) Pinnate-pinnatifid

(5) Bipinnate

(6) Bipinnate-pinnatifid

(7) Tripinnate

FIGURE 6. KINDS OF BLADE

COSTA: Midvein of the pinna.

SCALE: Small membranous or papery tissue resembling a loose fish scale that can be found on the rachis, rhizome, stipe, costa, or blade. The color, size, density, and translucency of scales can help distinguish species.

Scale   Hairs

HAIR (Synonym: trichome ["try-comb"]): A thin projection, only one cell thick and one or more cells long, that can be found along the rachis, rhizome, stipe, costa, or blade, giving some fern species a downy appearance. Like scales, hairs may protect the fern from excessive light or herbivores. Some hairs terminate in a sharp tip; others have a bulblike glandular tip that secretes waxy or volatile compounds. (These are referred to as glandular hairs.)

VEINS: Elongate cells, most visible on the leafy parts, that transport essential nutrients and sugars. Most North American fern species have "free" veins that extend from the main midvein of the pinna or pinnule to the edges without uniting with other veins. Sometimes these veins fork (once or several times) before they reach the pinna margin.

Free veins

A few distinctive groups of ferns (e.g., the Chain Ferns [*Woodwardia* species]) have more complex networks of netted veins that divide repeatedly and unite with each other, resembling the intricate patterns of veins visible when you hold a tree leaf up to the light.

Netted veins

FIDDLEHEAD (Synonym: crosier ["crozee-er"]): Unfurling young frond of most ferns, loosely resembling the ornate, curled end of a fiddle. The first visible structures to emerge aboveground early in the growing season.

REPRODUCTIVE STRUCTURES

The following terms refer to some of the reproductive structures that are seen when examining the fern blade. These structures can be very useful for distinguishing among species and are best examined with a hand lens or microscope.

SPORE: The minute offspring of a fern or fern ally, containing half the complement of chromosomes of the parent plant. Spores have

Left to right: *Dryopteris filix-mas* sori (photo by William Cullina); sporangium with annulus releasing spores; false indusium of *Adiantum*.

distinctive roundish, kidney, or tetrahedral shapes that are often diagnostic for a species; they are best seen under a strong hand lens or microscope.

SPORANGIUM ("spore-an-jee-um"); plural sporangia. (Synonym: spore case): A small, thin-walled, usually stalked capsule that bears the spores.

SORUS ("sore-us"); plural sori ("sore-eye"). (Synonym: fruit dot): A cluster of sporangia, usually borne on the underside or margins of the pinnae or pinnules. Sori are often brown at maturity and may appear confluent (massed together) or remain spread apart on the pinna. The shapes and arrangement of sori are good diagnostic features for ferns.

INDUSIUM ("in-doo-see-um"); plural indusia: Specialized, protective flap of tissue covering the sorus that protects the developing sporangia. In some ferns, part of the pinna or pinnule margin folds over the sorus to form a "false" indusium, as in *Adiantum* species.

TERMS UNIQUE TO FERN ALLIES AND AQUATIC FERNS

Equisetum cone

CONE: Upright reproductive structure of Horsetails (*Equisetum* species) with lateral branches ending in flat plates that hold the sporangia.

GEMMA ("jem-ma"); plural gemmae: A tiny plantlet produced by vegetative reproduction that is genetically identical to the parent plant. Gemmae are most commonly associated with *Huperzia* (Firmoss) species, which produce them on the upper portion of the stem. However, genera such as *Trichomanes* (Filmy Fern) and *Vittaria* (Shoestring Fern) can also produce gemmae as part of the gametophyte generation.

MEGASPORE: Large "female" spore produced by heterosporous (producing two types of spore) species such as *Isoëtes* (Quillworts),

The strobilus of Lycopodiella in-undatum *(Bog Clubmoss). (Photo by Frank Bramley/NEWFS)*

Selaginella (Spikemosses), *Marsilea* (Water Shamrock), and *Azolla* (Mosquito Fern). Megaspore size and surface texture are particularly helpful traits for distinguishing among the Quillworts. See page 361 for illustrations of megaspores.

MICROSPORE: Tiny "male" spore produced by heterosporous species.

SPOROCARP: The structure that contains the microspores and megaspores. Sporocarps may be soft and thin-walled (as in *Azolla* species) or very hard and thick-walled (as in *Marsilea* species).

SPOROPHORE ("spore-o-four"): The upright, nonleafy structure that bears the sporangia in Moonworts, Grape Ferns (*Botrychium* species), and Adder's-tongues (*Ophioglossum* species).

Sporophyll

SPOROPHYLL ("spore-o-fill"): A specialized leaf that is associated with the sporangia in Firmosses, Clubmosses, *Selaginella* species, and *Isoëtes* species.

STROBILUS ("strow-bulus"); plural strobili: A specialized upright cylinder (usually resembling an upright yellowish catkin) that is produced on the tip of upright shoots of certain Clubmosses (e.g., *Lycopodium, Diphasiastrum*) and Spikemosses (*Selaginella*). This structure bears the sporangia on whorls of sporophylls. (See photo above.)

TROPHOPHORE ("tro-fo-four") (Synonyms: blade, leaf): The green, leafy, vegetative part of the Moonworts, Grape Ferns (*Botrychium* species), and Adder's-tongues (*Ophioglossum* species).

TROPHOPHYLL ("tro-fo-fill"): The vegetative, photosynthetic leaves of Firmosses, Clubmosses, *Selaginella* species, and *Isoëtes* species.

GENERAL CHARACTERISTICS
TO EXAMINE ON FERNS

Ferns and their relatives exhibit many helpful characteristics that enable you to reach a positive identification reasonably quickly in the field. The keys in this guide ask you to examine these features closely and a 10× hand lens will be useful for some of these characteristics. The full species accounts also mention characteristics that might require greater magnification, particularly if they are important for distinguishing among species of the more challenging groups (e.g., the Quillworts [*Isoëtes* species]). However, because this is a guide for use in the field, we emphasize visible, macroscopic features wherever possible. Note that we do not advise looking at belowground features such as roots, because this would entail damage to the fern.

It helps to examine ferns and related families at the height of their reproductive seasons, especially when the fronds are fully expanded and the spores are maturing. Examine many plants if possible; they will vary in some characteristics and it is valuable to get a general impression of many individuals. Here are some of the diagnostic features to notice first about a fern you encounter in nature:

- The overall height of the fern frond and its shape or outline; specifically, where it tapers (toward the base or toward the tip or both). With fern allies, look at overall shape of the plant.
- The growth form: prostrate, upright, clumped, or spread out.
- For ferns, how dissected the blades are: entire, pinnatifid, pinnate, pinnate-pinnatifid, bipinnate, bipinnate-pinnatifid, or tripinnate. Note: Pinnae within a single frond are often variable in form; often the lower pinnae are more dissected while the upper pinnae or pinnules sometimes appear to fuse to a tapering tip. It is best to examine fully mature pinnae below the middle of the frond when determining how dissected your fern specimen is.
- Color of the fern stipe.
- Presence and types of scales or hairs on various parts of the plant.
- For ferns, the shape of the pinnae, lobes and/or teeth on their edges, vein patterns, position opposite each other along the rachis, hairiness, and whether they hug close to the stem (are "sessile") or whether their bases are stalked (as with leaves on petioles).
- Presence of reproductive parts on specialized fronds or structures that differ from sterile ones.
- On ferns, arrangements of the sori: scattered throughout the pinnae, on margins, along midvein, and so on.
- On ferns, presence and shape of a true or false indusium.
- Vegetative reproduction by proliferation on a rhizome or production of gemmae, tiny offspring that are genetically identical to the parent.
- Latitude and features of the habitat including bedrock type and presence of water.

How to Use This Field Guide

A key, as used in botany, is a tool in which groups of plants (genera, species, subspecies, or varieties—generally known as "taxa") are progressively distinguished from one another by combinations of unique traits, using a process of elimination. Each juncture or step of a key (like a step in a flow chart) presents a set of choices listing one to many, usually mutually exclusive, characters. The botanist determines which set of traits most accurately describes the fern specimen in question. Proceeding through increasingly narrow sets of choices, the botanist eventually arrives at the only taxon in the key that shares the relevant suite of characters with the specimen.

This Field Guide uses botanical keys to help you identify the species of fern you see. Each key assumes that you have a specimen of a mature fern, and in many cases, a sample of good-quality reproductive material. Knowing that you will not always have the luxury of seeing a "textbook" specimen, we have tried to offer as many types of diagnostic characters as possible, including vegetative traits, overall form, habitat, and characteristics of the sori and indusia. It is advisable to have a 10× handlens with you in the field to see some of these characters.

The large key at the beginning of the guide will aid you in identifying a plant to the genus level. This key uses both verbal descriptions and images (sketches and silhouettes) to illustrate the diagnostic characters mentioned in the key or to give an overall "gestalt" of the fern. To begin using any key in this guide, read both (or all, if more than two are given) of the choices numbered "1." Make sure you understand the terminology (a Glossary of terms is provided, p. 391). Choose the description that fits your fern most closely. In certain cases, that choice will bring you directly to the genus. In other cases, the choice will lead you to a second couplet of choices, numbered "2," or will instruct you to

GO TO PAGE "X" to view another set of choices. Choose the most applicable set of characters from this set, and proceed to "3" or the next indicated page, and so on. A key is a bit like a maze; one wrong choice and you can end up in a dead end. Therefore, be sure that you read all choices carefully; the first one may seem satisfactory until you read the second or third. Between the pictorial and verbal descriptions, you will know quickly if you are proceeding down the wrong path. If necessary, you can easily backtrack and try another route.

Once you have correctly identified the specimen's genus, proceed to the page that contains an overview description of the genus. Read this synopsis thoroughly as it often provides very valuable information about unique traits and memory devices for recognizing a genus of ferns or fern allies consistently in the field. Following the genus summary is a key to all the species of that genus covered by the Field Guide. Once again, we have tried to keep these keys as simple but descriptive as possible. Some groups, such as the Moonworts and Quillworts, demand more complex keys, and you may want to refer to other, more technical works on these groups to make a definitive identification.

You will make a final, and usually positive, identification of the fern or fern ally under consideration by turning to the pages with the full description. The left-hand page describes not only the growth form (or habit) of the species and its ecology but also detailed features such as pinnae, rachis, stipe, sori, strobilus, and so on. The right-hand page, facing the page of description, is a detailed drawing of the complete plant. This section may also mention certain species or hybrids of similar form that differ in their combinations of characteristics. Drawings showing details of specific characters are arranged as marginalia on this page. In addition, diagnostic arrows emphasize the key characteristics of the species. Each illustration has been drawn from a living specimen, and may not look exactly like your fern. Photographs are provided whenever possible to illustrate the species or structures more clearly. For species that are occasional or at the edge of their ranges in our region, we provide shorter verbal descriptions without many accompanying figures. If you are interested in learning more about these taxa (which we hope you will be!), we encourage you to consult many of the excellent technical texts listed in the bibliography.

In the past decade, new information about ferns and their relatives has been discovered, based on increasingly sophisticated studies of morphology and genetics. We have learned much more about the evolutionary relationships among the many species, causing some ferns to be renamed and some species to be divided into subspecies. Such name changes can confound the aspiring botanist (do not despair!), but they reflect the ever-changing state of the science and our best knowledge at the time. Likewise, we also now recognize that many ferns are hybrids (descendants from the cross of two species), which may exhibit characters that are intermediate among the parents and are thus challenging to identify using keys. And, of course, no two ferns are identical, even within a population of close relatives; all show some variation in morphology due to differences in growing conditions and genetic profiles.

Thus, the keys, drawings, and photographs in this Field Guide can offer only a description of a typical fern or fern relative. The plants illustrated and described here represent plants that are of average adult size; the fronds of young ferns are often nondescript and very similar in form among disparate species. Also, plant growth is influenced by environment, but the illustrations and descriptions represent plants in their most typical habitat. As you gain practice with identifying the ferns in your region, you may wish to annotate the keys and species descriptions here with your own hints for identification.

PART I

1A. Terrestrial (non-aquatic) ferns with leafy blades.
GO TO PART II of the key (PAGE 34).

1B. Plants without leafy blades; with cylindrical, hollow main stems, with or without whorls of thin, wiry branches.
Equisetum, Horsetails (PAGE 333)

1C. Plants with tiny (less than $1/2$ in. long), crowded, pointed leaves or scalelike leafy parts. **GO TO PART III of the key (PAGE 48).**

1D. Plants with leafy parts shaped like thin ribbons, wires, threads, or grasses (less than $1/4$ in. wide).
GO TO PART IV of the key (PAGE 50).

1E. Plants entirely aquatic, floating, submerged, or with leafy parts borne at or above water's surface.
GO TO PART V of the key (PAGE 50).

1A. Terrestrial ferns with leafy blades

1B. *Equisetum*, Horsetails

1C. Plants with tiny, pointed leaves

1D. Plants with ribbonlike leaves

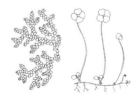

1E. Aquatic plants

PART II: TERRESTRIAL FERNS
WITH LEAFY BLADES

1A. Climbing, vinelike plants with lobed pinnae shaped like hands (palmate). **Lygodium, Hartford Fern (PAGE 156)**

1B. Ferns not like vines; pinnae not shaped like hands. Go to 2.

    2A. Leafy parts with free veins that run straight to the leaf margin or, if branching, do not form netted patterns. Go to "Leafy Parts Without Netted Veins," page 36 of the key.

    2B. Leafy parts with netted veins (best seen under hand lens or on leaf held up to light). Go to 3.

        3A. Unfernlike plants with leafy portions usually not more than 4 in. tall; with an oval, entire, fleshy blade overtopped by a slender spore-bearing spike containing beadlike sporangia (resembling a rattlesnake's tail). **Ophioglossum, Adder's-tongue (PAGE 271)**

        3B. Fernlike plants taller than 6 in. with blades divided into pinnae and/or pinnules. Go to 4.

            4A. Pinnae on sterile frond with lobes; fertile frond with no leafy tissue; sori globe-shaped and enclosed by hardened, beadlike pinnules. **Onoclea, Sensitive Fern (PAGE 166)**

            4B. Pinnae of sterile frond with wavy or finely toothed edges, or divided into pinnules; fertile frond with narrower pinnae than sterile frond; sori narrow and in chainlike rows paralleling the midvein of the pinnae or pinnules. **Woodwardia, Chain Ferns (PAGE 235)**

1A. *Lygodium*

2A. Leafy parts with free veins
(e.g., *Asplenium* [left] and *Adiantum* [right])

2B. Leafy parts with netted veins
(e.g., *Onoclea* [left] and *Ophiogolossum* [right])

3A. *Ophioglossum*

4A. *Onoclea*

4B. *Woodwardia*

1A. Plants usually shorter than 12 in. tall (with the exception of *Botrychium virginianum,* Rattlesnake Fern), with triangular or trowel-shaped fronds divided into (often fleshy) pinnae or pinnules; beadlike sporangia, separate from each other, not covered with an indusium or inrolled leaf margin, borne on a specialized fertile stalk that diverges at or well above ground level from the sterile leafy portion.

Botrychium, Moonworts and Grape Ferns (PAGE 240)

1B. Plants with dainty, narrow, long-tapering fronds usually shorter than 15 in., variable in shape from entire to lobed and lacy; sori elongated, straight, and narrow, attached along one side of a vein (not along margins of pinnae).

Asplenium, Spleenworts (PAGE 59)

1C. Ferns with fronds of various shapes and sizes, sori and indusia mostly not linear (except *Athyrium* or *Diplazium,* which can have linear to J-shaped indusia) and borne on leafy tissue (except *Osmunda*). Go to "Blades Pinnatifid," page 38 of the key.

LEAFY PARTS WITHOUT NETTED VEINS

1A. Genus *Botrychium*
(e.g., left to right: Grape Ferns, Rattlesnake Fern, Moonworts)

1B. Genus *Asplenium*
(e.g., left to right: Hart's-tongue Fern, Walking Fern, Wall Rue, Bradley's Spleenwort)

1B. (cont'd). Genus *Asplenium*
(e.g., left to right: Ebony Spleenwort, Lobed Spleenwort, Mountain Spleenwort)

BLADES PINNATIFID

Hint: examine the lower, fully-formed pinnae.
Ferns with the blade lobed but not quite divided to the rachis (not separate pinnae, at least in the central part of the frond). If blade has pinnae or pinnules, go to "Blades Pinnate" in next section of the key.

1A. Blades densely scaly on the underside; deeply embedded sori create bumps on surface of fertile blade; plants often grow on other living plants or logs.

Pleopeltis, **Resurrection Fern (PAGE 190)**

1B. Blades without scales; sori do not create bumps on surface of fertile blade; plants often grow on rocks.

Polypodium, **Polypody (PAGE 192)**

BLADES PINNATE

Hint: examine the lower, fully-formed pinnae.
Ferns with the blade fully cut once into separate pinnae that are entire with teeth or only partially lobed, not divided further into pinnules. If the pinnae has many deep lobes or is divided into pinnules, go to "Blades Pinnate-Pinnatifid or Bipinnate" on page 40 of the key.

1A. Stipe and rachis densely covered with dense scales; pinnae with distinctly eared lobes at the juncture with the rachis; indusia round and attached at their centers to the pinna like a shield or funnel.   *Polystichum* **in part, Holly Fern (PAGE 197)**

1B. Stipe and rachis with no or very sparse scales; pinnae without eared lobes and sharply tipped at ends; indusia elongated.

Diplazium, **Glade Fern (PAGE 122)**

BLADES PINNATIFID

1A. *Pleopeltis*

1B. *Polypodium*

BLADES PINNATE

1A. *Polystichum* (in part)

1B. *Diplazium*

BLADES PINNATE-PINNATIFID
OR BIPINNATE

Hint: examine the lower, fully-formed pinnae.

Fronds with separate pinnae divided into deep lobes or pinnules (but the lobes or pinnules are not further lobed or divided). If the separate pinnae are divided into pinnules that have lobes or are further divided into pinnulets, go to "Blades Bipinnate-Pinnatifid or Tripinnate" on page 44 of the key.

1A. Sterile and fertile fronds dissimilar in shape. Go to 2. If you cannot tell (i.e., the fern has no sori or sporangia), read the species descriptions in their entirety and if they do not describe your fern, go to 1 B.

> **2A.** Blades widest at middle, and often arising in large, vase-shaped clusters from a stout rhizome that is very stubbly with old, withered stipes; sporangia not covered by leaf margin or an indusium, borne on a distinct fertile frond or on separate fertile pinnae within or toward the tip of the frond. *Osmunda* **(PAGE 170)**

> **2B.** Blades widest above the middle, gracefully arching, tapering to the bottom; sporangia enclosed by leafy tissue, borne on a fertile frond that is stiff with hardened inrolled pinnule margins enclosing the sori. *Matteuccia,* **Ostrich Fern (PAGE 162)**

> **2C.** Blades widest at bottom, small (less than 12 in. long) and delicate; fertile fronds look very narrow relative to the sterile pinnules; inhabits rocky outcrops or talus slopes. *Cryptogramma* **(PAGE 99)**

1B. Sterile and fertile fronds roughly similar in size and shape (fertile fronds or pinnae sometimes appear slightly more constricted than sterile fronds). Go to 3.

> **3A.** At least the upper pinnae winged or fused at their connection with the rachis; lower pinnae symmetrical and widest toward the middle; rachis and stipe with few to many scales; indusium absent. *Phegopteris,* **Beech Ferns (PAGE 184)**

> **3B.** Rachis without obvious wings or fused tissue at juncture of pinnae. Go to 4.

> > **4A.** Stipe dark reddish brown or purple-black throughout, slender or wiry; pinnules longer than wide; fertile fronds with sori lining the edges of pinnules and the margins of the pinnules rolled slightly inward over them; ferns of calcareous cliffs, exposed sites, or rock outcrops. *Pellaea,* **Cliffbrakes (PAGE 178)**

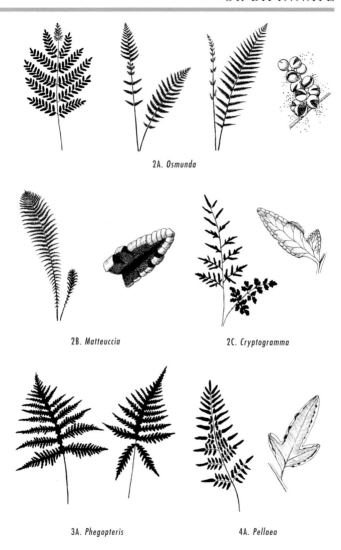

2A. *Osmunda*

2B. *Matteuccia*

2C. *Cryptogramma*

3A. *Phegopteris*

4A. *Pellaea*

4B. Stipe green, straw-colored, or brown or dark only at base. Go to 5.

5A. New fronds often surrounded by stubble of jointed older stipes (you can feel these at the base of the fronds); indusium consisting of multiple lobes or strands that enfold the sori like a fist (becoming obscured by the enlarging sori as they mature).
Woodsia, Cliff Ferns (PAGE 224)

5B. Clusters of stubbly older stipes not present. Go to 6.

6A. Stipe and blade densely covered with whitish hairs; stipe swollen at base; indusium silvery and rigid; sori straight or slightly curved, arrayed in a herringbone pattern.
Deparia, Silvery Glade Fern (PAGE 118)

6B. Stipes slender, with few or no scales; blades with minute, sharp hairs; indusium kidney-shaped.
Thelypteris (PAGE 208)

6C. Stipes stout and scaly; pinna margins of some species with small teeth; indusium kidney-shaped; dark green ferns of shaded woods.
Dryopteris in part, Wood Ferns (PAGE 126)

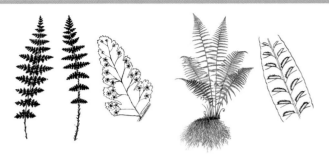

5A. *Woodsia*

6A. *Deparia*

6B. *Thelypteris*

6C. *Dryopteris* (in part)

BLADES BIPINNATE-PINNATIFID OR TRIPINNATE

Hint: examine the lower, fully formed pinnae.
Ferns with separate pinnae that are divided into pinnules that have lobes or are further divided into pinnulets.

1A. Lowest pair of pinnae much larger than the upper pinnae, giving the frond a triangular form. Go to 2.

    2A. Fronds delicate, <18 in. long; indusia absent; growing in moist, cool, shady woodlands, often on rocky talus.
      Gymnocarpium, Oak Fern (PAGE 150)

    2B. Fronds leathery, often 36 in. or more long; rachis and stipe stout and green to brown; sori forming infrequently; forms vigorous colonies in disturbed, open areas.
      Pteridium, Bracken (PAGE 203)

1B. Lowest pair of pinnae not disproportionately larger than pinnae above them. Go to 3.

    3A. Lower pinnae asymmetric because pinnules on upper side of costa are shorter than corresponding pinnules on lower side of costa; stipes scaly and stout; sori with kidney-shaped indusia; dark green ferns of shaded woods.
      Dryopteris in part, Wood Fern (PAGE 126)

    3B. Lowest pinnae symmetrical about the costa. Go to 4.

      4A. Dainty, light green, translucent ferns of damp, acid, dark grottoes of sandstone cliffs, rocks, or shallow caves.   **_Trichomanes boschianum,_ Filmy Fern (PAGE 216)**

      4B. Blades not translucent; ferns not restricted to dark, damp habitats. Go to 5.

        5A. Pinnules with bristly teeth; stipe and rachis densely scaly; indusia round and attached at their centers to the pinnules.
          Polystichum braunii, Braun's Holly Fern (PAGE 200)

        5B. Pinnules without bristly teeth. Go to 6.

          6A. Ferns without hairs on pinnae, rachis, or stipe. Go to 7.

            7A. Rachis and stipe delicate and polished dark brown or black, not hairy or scaly, slender, often arching; pinnules wavy or incised but not toothy; sori covered by inrolled pinnule margin.   **_Adiantum,_ Maidenhair Ferns (PAGE 54)**

2A. *Gymnocarpium*

2B. *Pteridium*

3A. *Dryopteris* (in part)

4A. *Trichomanes boschianum*

5A. *Polystichum braunii*

7A. *Adiantum*

7B. Scales present on the lower portion of the stipe; pinnules with teeth but not bristly; indusium present, attached to long side of linear or J-shaped sori.

Athyrium, Lady Fern (PAGE 85)

6B. Ferns with sparse to dense hairs present on pinnae, rachis, or stipe. Go to 8.

8A. Rachis and stipe purplish to dark brown; densely hairy at least on rachis; fertile pinnules tiny with margins folded over the sori; of dry, rocky areas.

Cheilanthes, Lip Ferns (PAGE 92)

8B. Rachis green. Go to 9.

9A. Fronds grow in tufts or clumps; indusia thin, arching over sorus like a pocket, sori produced in interior of pinnule; mostly of calcareous rock outcrops or moist, rich, rocky woods.

Cystopteris, Bladder Ferns (PAGE 103)

9B. Fronds not in tufts, produced on long rhizomes; blades tacky to the touch with glandular hairs, which cover pinnae, stipe, and rachis; cup-shaped indusium produced on pinnule margin; forms vigorous terrestrial colonies in open, disturbed areas.

Dennstaedtia, Hay-scented Fern (PAGE 115)

7B. *Athyrium*

8A. *Cheilanthes*

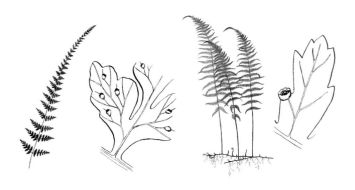

9A. *Cystopteris*

9B. *Dennstaedtia*

PART III: PLANTS WITH TINY LEAVES

1A. Plants 2 in. tall or smaller, usually creeping and mosslike.
Selaginella, **Spikemosses (PAGE 371)**

1B. Plants more than 2 in. tall, usually upright, often proliferating by runners along the ground. Go to 2.

2A. Plants like miniature trees, with upright main stems bearing several spreading branches. Go to 3.

3A. Strobilus (upright, conelike, spore-bearing structure) sessile (not on a stalk), branches roundish in cross-section and more than ¹/₄ in. wide.
Dendrolycopodium, **Tree Clubmoss (PAGE 285)**

3B. Strobilus borne on a stalk (very short or indistinct in *D. sitchense*), branches flattened (somewhat rounded in *D. sitchense*) or quadrangular in cross-section and ¹/₄ in. or less wide. *Diphasiastrum,* **Ground Cedar (PAGE 292)**

2B. Plants not treelike, upright stems usually produced singly (if these are branched, branches are also upright, like a candelabra or antlers). Go to 4.

4A. Plants without strobili (sporangia are found in distinct zones on the upper portion of the stem); often produce gemmae (tiny plantlets) near upper end of the stem.
Huperzia, **Firmoss (PAGE 303)**

4B. Plants with strobili; without gemmae. Go to 5.

5A. Strobili borne on long, distinct stalks.
Lycopodium, **Clubmoss (PAGE 320)**

5B. Strobili sessile (not on a stalk). Go to 6.

6A. Plants with visible annual constrictions (zones of smaller leaves on the stem); leaves have tiny, firm, sharp, spinelike tip.
Spinulum, **Bristly Clubmoss (PAGE 328)**

6B. Plants without annual constrictions; leaves without distinct bristle. Go to 7.

7A. Stems below the strobilus with very few or no leaves.
Pseudolycopodiella, **Slender Bog Clubmoss (PAGE 326)**

7B. Stems below the strobilus covered with leaves. *Lycopodiella,* **Bog Clubmoss (PAGE 313)**

1A. *Selaginella*

2A. Clubmosses
(in part)

3A. *Dendrolycopodium*

3B. *Diphasiastrum*

4A. *Huperzia*

5A. *Lycopodium*

6A. *Spinulum*

7A. *Pseudolycopodiella*

7B. *Lycopodiella*

PART IV: GRASSLIKE PLANTS

1A. Ground-dwelling plants of bogs and swamps; fronds upright, wiry, and curly like a pig's tail.

Schizaea, **Curly Grass Ferns (PAGE 206)**

1B. Plants that resemble chives or tufts of grass with bulbous bases that house the sporangia; most species dwell at water's edge.

Isoëtes, **Quillworts (PAGE 360)**

1C. Tiny plants with thin leafy parts ¼ to 1 in. long, found in dark crevices of acidic rock outcrops and caverns.

Vittaria, **Shoestring Ferns (PAGE 221)**

1D. Tiny, threadlike plants resembling algae and intertwining to produce feltlike mats that coat the interior of grottoes and crevices of acidic bedrock.

Trichomanes intricatum, **Weft Fern (PAGE 220)**

PART V: ENTIRELY AQUATIC FERNS

1A. Plants with leafy parts that resemble a four-leaf clover 1–2 in. across.

Marsilea, **Water Shamrock (PAGE 158)**

1B. Plants with leafy parts composed of tiny (¼ in. wide) pinnae in two overlapping rows.

Azolla, **Mosquito Fern (PAGE 89)**

PART IV: GRASSLIKE PLANTS

1A. *Schizaea*

1B. *Isoëtes*

1C. *Vittaria*

1D. *Trichomanes intricatum*

PART V: ENTIRELY AQUATIC FERNS

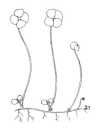

1A. *Marsilea*

1B. *Azolla*

TRUE FERNS

GENUS *ADIANTUM*: MAIDENHAIR FERNS

(Greek: *a*, "without," + *diainem*, "to wet"; referring to how leaves shed water)

Maidenhair ferns are one of the most beautiful, graceful, and easily recognized genera of ferns. Typical for this genus are the thin, polished, dark purple to black stems (stipe, rachis, and costa) that support arching pinnae with fragile, delicate, fan-shaped or oblong, often overlapping pinnules. Sterile and fertile fronds are the same. In this genus the pinnule margins curl over the sori to form false indusia. The veins are free, forking many times but not forming networks. Fronds are clustered together, but not in a circle.

Adiantum is a large and widely distributed, mostly tropical genus, with 150–200 species recognized worldwide, and 9 species in North America. In our area, we have only one common species, *Adiantum pedatum* (Northern Maidenhair Fern), and three species that are uncommon to rare and are described only briefly below. *A. capillus-veneris* (Southern Maidenhair Fern) is an edge-of-range species for our area; disjunct populations of *A. aleuticum* (Western Maidenhair Fern) are uncommon in our area; *A. viridimontanum* (Green Mountain Maidenhair), a recently described species (1991), is found only in serpentine outcrop habitats in Vt. and Que. This species, being somewhat variable in appearance, is sometimes difficult to distinguish from its parents.

ADIANTUM KEY

1A. Individual pinnules fan-shaped to roundish with lobes of various sizes; dark color of costa extends into base of pinnules. Va. and Ky., primarily south of our area on moist calcareous cliffs. **A. capillus-veneris (Southern Maidenhair Fern)**

1B. Pinnules oblong or somewhat triangular, at least twice as long as they are broad. Go to 2.

> **2A.** Pinnules ± oblong, blades arching and relaxed; lobes on pinnules separated by shallow incisions; rich, mesic forests. **A. pedatum (Northern Maidenhair Fern)**

> **2B.** Pinnules ± triangular, blades stiffer and more upright than above; of serpentine soils and talus. Go to 3.

>> **3A.** Pinnule petiole less than 1 mm long; length of pinnule margin forming the false indusium ⅛ in. ± long; lobes on pinnules generally separated by wider incisions. Rare in our area. **A. aleuticum (Western Maidenhair Fern)**

3B. Pinnule petiole longer than 1 mm; length of pinnule margin forming the false indusium ⅛–¼ in. long; only in Vt. and Que.

A. viridimontanum (Green Mountain Maidenhair Fern)

Adiantum aleuticum (left) *(Photo by Arthur Haines) and* Adiantum pedatum (right) *(Photo by Bob Kelley/NEWFS)*

Adiantum capillus-veneris

Adiantum viridimontanum *(Photo by William Cullina)*

NORTHERN MAIDENHAIR FERN

Adiantum pedatum L.

HABIT: Blades graceful, fan-shaped, arch in a horizontal or slightly pendulous manner, borne on slender, erect branched stipes.

ECOLOGY: Rich, deciduous woodlands and rocky (talus) slopes, often on limestone. Grows in a range of soils, most abundant and more luxurious in moist, rich, neutral to slightly alkaline soil.

RANGE: N.S. south to n. Ga., west to n. Tex., north to Minn. and Ont.

FRONDS: 16–26 in. long. Erect stipes bearing horizontal or slightly drooping, bright green blades, 6–16 in. wide; sterile and fertile fronds the same.

BLADE: Semicircular, fan-shaped; blade formed by division of rachis into two rachis branches; usually 5–6 pinnae develop on outer side of each branch.

PINNAE: Elongate, smooth, 2–7 in. long. Longest pinnae borne closest to point of branching; divided into 12–20 pinnules.

PINNULES: Alternate, very short petiole, variable shape. Varies from oblong to fan-shaped at tip of pinnae; margin entire on edge closest to center of blade but outer edge more or less incised. Veins several times forked.

RACHIS: Smooth, slender, black to purple-brown.

STIPE: 20 in. ± long. Shining black or purple-brown, smooth except for scales at very base. Slightly longer than blade; stipes often conspicuous on ground after fronds die back.

RHIZOME: Creeping, with gray-brown, bronzy scales near the growing tip.

SORI: Elongate; on outer margins of pinnules. Reflexed margin of pinnule is false indusium.

NOTES: Crosiers delicate, wine red, emerge in early spring.

MARGINALIA: *A. Underside of fertile pinnule of* Adiantum aleuticum.
B. Underside of fertile pinnule of A. pedatum.

DIAGNOSTIC ARROWS: *1. Rachis branched; blade semicircular and horizonal to slightly drooping. 2. Shining, dark, slender stipe. 3. Pinnules oblong in* A. pedatum. *4. Pinnule incisions wider in* A. aleuticum.

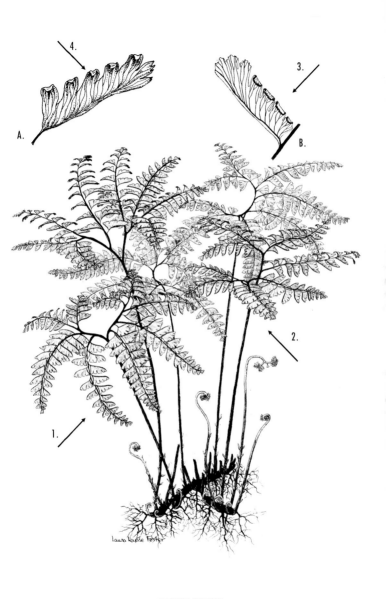

ADIANTUM PEDATUM
NORTHERN MAIDENHAIR FERN

WESTERN MAIDENHAIR FERN
(ALEUTIAN MAIDENHAIR FERN)
Adiantum aleuticum (Rupr.) Paris
Synonym: *Adiantum pedatum* L. var. or ssp. *aleuticum*

Primarily a w. U.S. species, from Alaska to Ariz. and scattered throughout the Rocky Mts. Also in scattered, disjunct locations in Nfld., Que., Me., Md., Pa., and Vt. Restricted in the northeast to serpentine outcrops and talus slopes. Similar to *Adiantum pedatum* (Northern Maidenhair Fern) but pinnae are more erect and rigid (less horizontal to pendulous), blade is more funnel-shaped than semicircular; foliage more blue-green (glaucous), incisions in the pinnules are generally wider. Blade tissue is more leathery and stems are stiffer than those of Northern Maidenhair Fern.

GREEN MOUNTAIN MAIDENHAIR FERN
Adiantum viridimontanum Paris

This is a hybrid descendant of *Adiantum pedatum* (Northern Maidenhair Fern) and *A. aleuticum* (Western Maidenhair Fern), with four sets of chromosomes. Restricted to serpentine outcrop habitats in Vt. and Que. Can be distinguished from the latter parent by longer pinnule petioles and slightly longer sections of pinnule margin that form the false indusia. Distinguished from Northern Maidenhair Fern by its more erect habit, more triangular pinnules, and longer petiole of pinnules. This species has a more upright growth habit in sun than in shade; most often found in sunny, disturbed sites.

SOUTHERN MAIDENHAIR FERN
Adiantum capillus-veneris L.

This species slips into the southern edge of our area in Va. and Ky., on moist limestone cliffs. Range from Ky. south to Fla., west to Colo., Utah, and Calif., but also south through Central America to Venezuela and Peru, and in warm regions of Eurasia and Africa. Rachis is not branched; individual pinnules are nearly round (not oblong) and more fan-shaped than those of *Adiantum pedatum* (Northern Maidenhair Fern), with lobes of various sizes. Pinnules are more widely spaced, giving it a lacier appearance; costae in a soft zigzag pattern.

GENUS *ASPLENIUM:* SPLEENWORTS

(Greek: *a,* "without," + *splen,* "spleen"; in reference to supposed medicinal properties)

Spleenworts are delicate ferns that grow from short, creeping, erect or ascending rhizomes with slender, usually dark, wiry, and tough stipes. Many *Asplenium* species grow on rocks or in rocky places, with delicate fronds dangling from crevices and cracks between ledges. Their fronds usually grow in clusters with various degrees of dissection into pinnae, depending on the species. Indusia are narrow, usually straight, and attached to one side of a vein. Veins are simple or forked and do not reach the margins. *Asplenium* species also have translucent, lattice-like ("clathrate") scales on the rhizome, which loosely resemble stained-glass windows. These can be difficult to see without excavating the whole fern and damaging the plant.

Sori on pinna

The uniqueness of *Asplenium* species has led some taxonomists to segregate them into their own single-genus family, the Aspleniaceae, while others prefer to include them in the broad family Polypodiaceae. There are approximately 700 species in the genus *Asplenium,* most of which are tropical. Thirteen species, including 2 subspecies, occur in our area.

Asplenium platyneuron (*Ebony Spleenwort*) *blades* (left) *and sori* (above) (*Photos by Arthur Haines*)

Many of the species crossbreed and produce hybrids, some of which have been given species-level rank by taxonomists. Eight of the Spleenworts in our area represent so-called parental taxa: *Asplenium septentrionale* (Forked Spleenwort), *A. trichomanes-ramosum* (Green Spleenwort), *A. trichomanes* (Maidenhair Spleenwort), *A. ruta-muraria* (Wall Rue), *A. rhizophyllum* (Walking Fern), *A. platyneuron* (Ebony Spleenwort), *A. resiliens* (Black-stemmed Spleenwort), and *A. montanum* (Mountain Spleenwort). The following figure illustrates many of the hybrids—some fertile (shown with black dots), some sterile—that have resulted from crosses between these parents. Hybrids in small type do not tend to occur in our area. Many of these hybrids show features that are intermediate between the parental taxa.

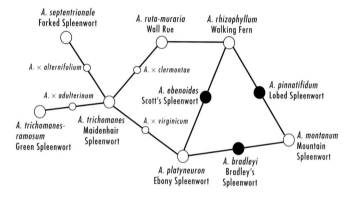

Asplenium Key

1A. Blades simple (straplike or grasslike), or lobed but not cut all the way to the rachis. Go to 2.

    2A. Blades less than $1/4$ in. wide; forking, leathery, unlobed, grasslike, restricted in our area to W. Va. region.

           A. septentrionale (Forked Spleenwort)

    2B. Blades wider than $1/2$ in.; not restricted to W. Va. Go to 3.

        3A. Blades irregularly lobed or cut almost to rachis; a few distinct pinnae may be present near base of blade. Go to 4.

            4A. Rachis purplish and lustrous; ferns typically on limestone or conglomerate rock.

                A. ebenoides (Scott's Spleenwort)

4B. Rachis green; ferns grow on acidic rocks.
A. pinnatifidum (Lobed Spleenwort)

3B. Blades not lobed. Go to 5.

5A. Blades frequently produce new plantlets at tip, narrow and smoothly tapering to a long tip; widespread. **A. rhizophyllum (Walking Fern)**

5B. Blades not producing new plantlets at tip; blade wide and tip blunt; extremely rare and local.
A. scolopendrium (American Hart's-tongue Fern)

1B. Blades with true pinnae throughout at least half of the blade length. Go to 6.

6A. Pinnae not further divided into pinnules; ferns grow in a wide range of terrestrial habitats, less commonly on rocks or cliffs. Go to 7.

7A. Pinnae alternate along rachis; fertile fronds erect and larger than sterile, more prostrate, fronds; stipe dark reddish brown; wide-ranging throughout our area.
A. platyneuron (Ebony Spleenwort)

7B. Pinnae opposite along rachis; fertile and sterile fronds the same and both erect; stipe dark brown to black; found only from Del. south.
A. resiliens (Black-stemmed Spleenwort)

6A. Pinnae toothed, lobed, or divided into pinnules; ferns growing mainly in crevices of rocks, boulders, and cliffs. Go to 8.

8A. Pinnae deeply lobed or divided into pinnules. Go to 9.

9A. Pinnae irregularly and deeply lobed almost to costa or cut into bright green, narrow, sessile pinnules; stipe brown near base; growing on acidic rock.
A. montanum (Mountain Spleenwort)

9B. Pinnae with distinctly fan-shaped, long-stalked, dull green pinnules; stipe green throughout; grow on alkaline rock types, occasionally masonry.
A. ruta-muraria (Wall Rue)

8B. Pinnae not divided into distinctly separate pinnules. Go to 10.

10A. Pinnae with distinctly toothed margins, with protruding basal lobe (sometimes cut); many rust-colored sori at maturity; upper portion of rachis green, lower part darker; on acidic cliffs; rare and local, N.Y. south. **A. bradleyi (Bradley's Spleenwort)**

10B. Pinnae not toothed; more rounded with smooth or slightly indented margins. Go to 11.

11A. Rachis purplish brown to black throughout. Go to 12.

12A. On acidic basalts or sandstones; ranges north to Nfld. ***A. trichomanes* ssp. *trichomanes* (Maidenhair Spleenwort)**

12B. On basic limestones, ranges only to s. Me. and n. Vt. ***A. trichomanes* ssp. *quadrivalens* (Maidenhair Spleenwort)**

11B. Rachis green throughout; limestone cliffs and boulders; ranging north from n. N.Y. ***A. trichomanes-ramosum* (Green Spleenwort)**

Asplenium ebenoides, *an uncommon species*

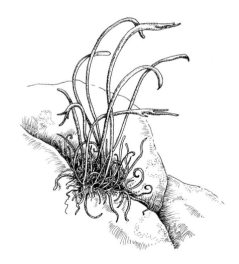

Asplenium septentrionale, *an uncommon species*

(Above) Asplenium pinnatifidum (*Lobed Spleenwort*). (*Photo by David M. Stone/NEWFS*) (Right) Asplenium scolopendrium (*American Hart's-Tongue Fern*). (*Photo by L. A. Duthie, Norcross Wildlife Sanctuary*)

(Below) Asplenium trichomanes (*Maidenhair Spleenwort*). (*Photo by William Cullina*) (Right) Asplenium trichomanes-ramosum (*Green Spleenwort*). (*Photo by William Cullina*)

Asplenium bradleyi D. C. Eaton

HABIT: A small, lustrous, brown-stemmed, evergreen, rock-loving fern that grows erect in tufts; blades cut once into pinnae with prominently toothed edges and wide, lobed bases.

ECOLOGY: High, dry, steep, bare cliffs of acidic rock such as granite or sandstone.

RANGE: Rare and local; not abundant. From N.Y. to Ala., inland to the Ozark region of Okla., Ky., Ill., and Mo., north to Ohio.

FRONDS: 1–11 in. ± long. Sterile and fertile fronds the same.

BLADE: Oblong (longer than wide), broader toward base, tapering to tip, once-cut into 5–15 pairs of pinnae; very variable in shape.

PINNAE: ½–2 in. long. Oval-oblong or triangular; often lobed asymmetrically at base; edges deeply toothed. Lower pinnae distinctly stalked, upper pinnae not stalked.

RACHIS: Lower half shiny dark green or purple-brown, upper half lighter green.

STIPE: ⅓–¾ as long as the blade. Dark lustrous reddish or purple-brown throughout, long, erect, wiry.

RHIZOME: Short, creeping, nearly erect, occasionally branched, with numerous black scales.

SORI: Numerous (3–many per pinna), rusty or dark brown, mid-way between margin and midvein, separate throughout growth. Indusium ample and membranous.

NOTES: Bradley's Spleenwort is a hybrid derived from a cross between *Asplenium montanum* (Mountain Spleenwort) and *A. platyneuron* (Ebony Spleenwort). Similar species: Mountain Spleenwort has deeply indented pinnae not lacy-cut; stipe is dark at base and green above, and pinnae have prominent stems.

MARGINALIA: *A. Underside of fertile pinna.*

DIAGNOSTIC ARROWS: *1. Pinnae eared and lacy-cut. 2. Pinnae with very short stems. 3. Dark stipe throughout.*

ASPLENIUM BRADLEYI
BRADLEY'S SPLEENWORT

MOUNTAIN SPLEENWORT

Asplenium montanum Willd.

HABIT: Small, delicate, bluish green fern, grows in tufts, usually in crevices of overhanging rocks. Stipe can be almost as long as the blade, giving a wispy and sometimes drooping appearance to the plant.

ECOLOGY: Shaded and sheltered crevices of silica-rich sandstone, gneiss, and shale, where there are tiny pockets of acid soil.

RANGE: Quite widely distributed in acid soil of the Appalachian Mts. belt, becoming rare in New England. From s. Vt. south to Tenn., W. Va., and Ky. Isolated populations in Mo. and Ind.

FRONDS: 4–8 in. long. In tufts; evergreen; sterile and fertile fronds the same.

BLADE: Oblong (longer than wide) and widest at base, slightly leathery, more drooping than erect, cut into 6 or more pairs of pinnae, which are deeply lobed or cut again.

PINNAE: Ovate-oblong; narrow, distinctly stalked, with coarsely and irregularly indented lobes; veins few, free, forked, or simple.

RACHIS: Broad, flat, green; sparse hairs throughout.

STIPE: $1/3$ to equal the length of the blade. Slender, fragile, dark brown to purplish black at base, green above; smooth with a few narrow scales only at very base.

RHIZOME: Short, usually creeping.

SORI: Few, mostly elliptical or narrow, often massing together at maturity, 1–15 per pinna. Indusium thin and fragile.

NOTES: The species roughly resembles *Asplenium ruta-muraria* (Wall Rue), but the stipe of Wall Rue is green throughout, the pinnae are much more triangular and long-stalked, and it prefers basic rock types. A young *Cystopteris fragilis* (Fragile Fern) could be confused with this species, given its affinity for rocks, but Fragile Fern has true pinnules, a more scaly stipe, and oval rather than narrow sori.

MARGINALIA: *A. Underside of fertile pinna. B. Underside of fertile pinnule.*
DIAGNOSTIC ARROWS: *1. Distinctly stemmed, widely spaced pinnae. 2. Long stipes dark at base, green above. 3. Pinnules indented, not lacy-cut.*

ASPLENIUM MONTANUM
MOUNTAIN SPLEENWORT

LOBED SPLEENWORT

Asplenium pinnatifidum Nutt.

HABIT: A creeping, rock-loving fern with long, tapering, and pointed simple fronds that are bright green and crinkled.

ECOLOGY: Rocky, usually inaccessible crevices containing acid soil, usually in sandstone.

RANGE: Locally frequent from N.J. inland along the Appalachians, south to n. Ala., west to Okla., north to Wisc. and Ind.

FRONDS: 1–12 in. long. Sterile and fertile fronds the same.

BLADE: Broadest at base, tapering gradually to a long and pointed tip; lower half distinctly and deeply lobed, upper half less deeply lobed or merely wavy; lustrous, sparsely hairy, somewhat leathery, evergreen. Considerable differences in size, shape, and number. Veins forked, fan-shaped.

RACHIS: Green and smooth.

STIPE: $^1/_{10}$–$1^1/_2$ times the length of the blade (highly variable). Dark brown at base, becoming green toward the blade.

RHIZOME: Short and erect.

SORI: Variable in shape even within a blade, from the typical *Asplenium* linear shape to a semirounded form; often massing together as they age. Indusium distinct and long-lasting.

NOTES: This fern is a hybrid derived from a cross between *Asplenium rhizophyllum* (Walking Fern) and *A. montanum* (Mountain Spleenwort); some plants are sterile, but others are fertile tetraploids (with 4 sets of chromosomes). It can resemble Walking Fern, but the fronds are lobed, with long stipes, and more upright. Scott's Spleenwort (*A. ebenoides*) has pinnae irregular in shape and size; long pointed tips usually point upward.

MARGINALIA: *A. Underside of fertile pinna.*

DIAGNOSTIC ARROWS: *1. Rather uniformly lobed pinnae. 2. Long pointed tips usually curling downward.*

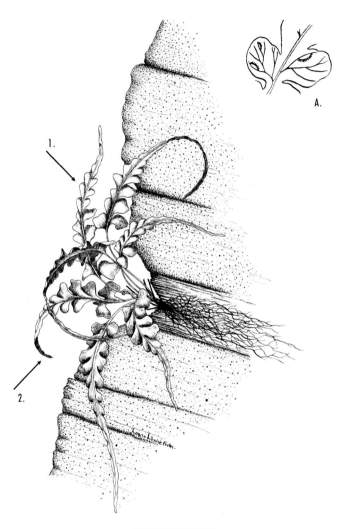

1.

2.

A.

ASPLENIUM PINNATIFIDUM
LOBED SPLEENWORT

EBONY SPLEENWORT

Asplenium platyneuron (L.) Britton

HABIT: One of most widespread and tallest Spleenworts in our area. In summer, its vaselike clusters of fertile fronds with dark stipes stand out in undergrowth of rocky fields or woods. On some plants, buds proliferate on the stipe, which sprout into clumps of new fronds. Somewhat inaccurately called "ebony" spleenwort for the dark stipe and rachis, which are actually deep lustrous brown, not ebony-black.

ECOLOGY: Throughout the area in shaded woods, fields, talus slopes, along banks, bases of rocky ledges, walls or fences in all kinds of well-drained, rocky soils or hummocks of humus, even in full sun, if reasonably moist though not wet. More tolerant than other Spleenworts of disturbed sites.

RANGE: S. Me., Ont., and Que. to n. Fla., west to Tex., north to Neb. and Mo. Highly disjunct populations also in South Africa.

FRONDS: Fertile fronds 12–20 in. long. Erect, sinuous, narrow, tapering to top and bottom. Sterile fronds shorter, spreading, sometimes flat on ground. Fertile fronds dark green and semi-evergreen; sterile fronds more numerous, lighter green, and evergreen. Both cut into 18 or more pairs of pinnae.

PINNAE: Fertile pinnae narrow-oblong, pointed, notably eared at base, with toothed or serrated edges, distinctly spaced and not opposite. Sterile pinnae variable in shape, more rounded, closer together, and only slightly eared, with less toothy edges than fertile pinnae. Veins free and forked.

RACHIS: Dark reddish brown, smooth, shining throughout.

STIPE: Dark reddish brown, smooth. Short, stiff, erect and brittle for fertile fronds; shorter and spreading for sterile fronds.

RHIZOME: Thick, usually erect; few scales.

SORI: Short, straight, often mass together, numerous (1–12 pairs per pinna). Indusium silvery when young, soon withering.

NOTES: Could be confused with *Polystichum acrostichoides* (Christmas Fern), but the fronds of that species are much wider, more densely clumped, and the greenish (not brown) stipe bears numerous scales. In the South, fertile fronds of Ebony Spleenwort can grow to heights of 20 in.; in the North, they are usually about a foot tall.

MARGINALIA: *A. Sterile pinna. B. Fertile pinna. C. Pinnae variation.*
DIAGNOSTIC ARROWS: *1. Pinnae eared; not opposite. 2. Tall and erect fertile fronds. 3. Short and pendent sterile leaves. 4. Sterile pinnae more rounded and crowded together.*

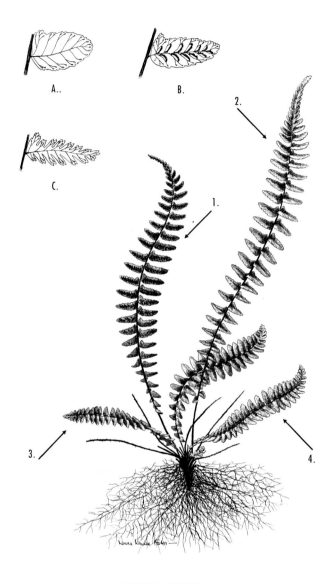

A..

B.

C.

1.

2.

3.

4.

ASPLENIUM PLATYNEURON
EBONY SPLEENWORT

Asplenium resiliens Kunze

HABIT: A southern fern that probably should bear the common name of "Ebony" Spleenwort because its stipe and rachis are black. Produces evergreen, erect tufts of both fertile and sterile fronds.

ECOLOGY: Locations similar to that of *Asplenium platyneuron* (Ebony Spleenwort) at bases of rocks and stones in semishaded fields, woods, and cliffs. Has a particular affinity for limestone and other rocks with more basic pH.

RANGE: Patchy distribution from Del. south to n. Fla., west through inland Tex. to Ariz. and Mexico, north to Mo. and Kans.

FRONDS: 8 in. long. Fertile and sterile fronds similar; all stiffly erect; evergreen, tufted.

BLADE: Narrow, tapering to top and bottom, dark green, cut into 20–40 pairs of distinctly spaced pinnae.

PINNAE: Mostly opposite, blunt-tipped, sometimes with shallowly toothed edges, slightly eared at base, nearly sessile; lower pinnae reflexed and spaced wide apart.

RACHIS: Distinctly dark brown, almost black, smooth, shiny.

STIPE: Short, stiff, brittle, dark brown or black.

RHIZOME: Short, creeping or half erect, with stiff, black scales.

SORI: Oblong, nearer margin than midrib, prominent, often mass together as they age; 2–5 pairs per pinna.

NOTES: Closely resembles Ebony Spleenwort, but its pinnae are more rounded and more opposite and the stipe is very dark. Pinnae similar to those of *A. trichomanes* (Maidenhair Spleenwort) but more widely spaced and subtly "eared."

MARGINALIA: *A. Underside of fertile pinna.*

DIAGNOSTIC ARROWS: *1. Pinnae opposite, semi-eared, and oblong.*
2. Black-stemmed throughout. 3. Lower pinnae usually wide-spaced.

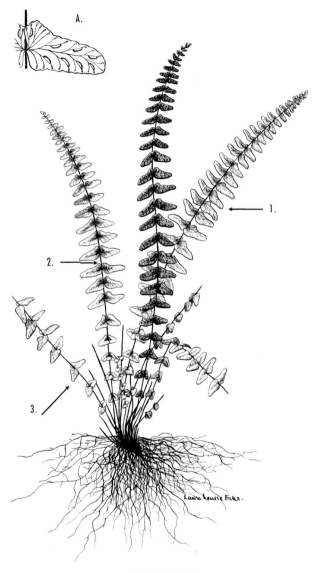

A.

1.

2.

3.

ASPLENIUM RESILIENS
BLACK-STEMMED SPLEENWORT

WALKING FERN

Asplenium rhizophyllum L.
Synonym: *Camptosorus rhizophyllus* (L.) Link

HABIT: An interesting little evergreen fern that "walks." Long, narrow, fine-pointed, arching leaves radiate from the rhizome. Tips touching the ground can sprout new plants; occasionally, sprouts arise from the basal lobes of the frond. Often, old plants are surrounded by a dense family of attached plantlets. Fronds grow in star-shaped tufts; young plants are flat to the ground while older plants have semi-erect and/or arching fronds. The Latin name, *rhizo* ("root") + *phyllum* ("leaves"), refers to this unusual mode of spread.

ECOLOGY: Shaded, moss-covered faces of limestone or other basic cliffs, rocks, and boulders; edges, cracks, and crevices of moist outcroppings; usually northerly exposure. Sometimes on ground or fallen logs. Rarely on sandstone.

RANGE: Quite rare and local, reported from all areas in our region where limy soil exists, from s. Me. and Que., south to Ga. and Ala., west to Ark., Okla., and Mo., north to Mich. and s. Ont.

FRONDS: 1–15 in. long, 1–2 in. wide at base. Fertile fronds can be somewhat larger than sterile fronds.

BLADE: Evergreen, slightly leathery, shiny green above, paler below, smooth, usually heart-shaped or somewhat eared at base, triangular, tapers to a long, thin point. Variable form with margins wavy or indented, but always narrow, long, and pointed when mature. Veins sometimes netted near the midrib.

STIPE: Slender, flattened, and grooved face; dark brown at base, green and smooth above.

RHIZOME: Short, slender, erect.

SORI: Often numerous and scattered irregularly throughout blade at junctures of veins. Indusium inconspicuous.

NOTES: A highly distinctive fern within the genus that was formerly segregated into its own genus, *Camptosorus* ("mounded sori"). This species frequently hybridizes with other *Asplenium* species, however, indicating it is closely related to them. *A. pinnatifidum* (Lobed Spleenwort), for example, derives from a cross between Walking Fern and *A. montanum* (Mountain Spleenwort) and can look like a very lobed version of Walking Fern.

MARGINALIA: *A. Base of fertile blade and sori.*
DIAGNOSTIC ARROWS: *1. Plantlet growing from tip. 2. Blade with heart-shaped based and long, narrow tip. 3. Jumbled and scattered sori.*

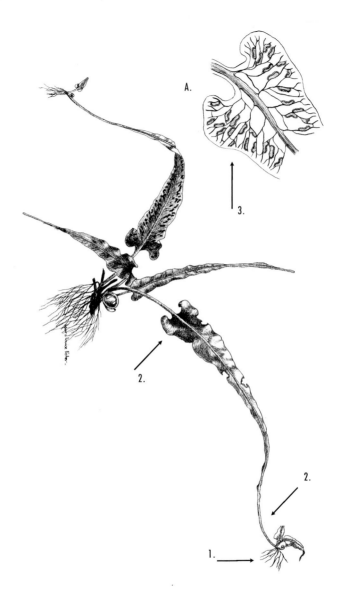

A.

3.

2.

2.

1.

ASPLENIUM RHIZOPHYLLUM
WALKING FERN

Asplenium ruta-muraria L.

HABIT: Delicate, feathery, light green, uncommon fern with branched clusters of small, distinctly stalked pinnae with stalked and fan-shaped pinnules; often growing flat on mossy surfaces in crevices of rocky cliffs.

ECOLOGY: On sheltered cliffs, in the smallest seams and crevices of limestone or other calcareous rock outcroppings, in shade or semishade.

RANGE: W. New England, Ont., and Que., south to the interior Appalachian Mts. of Tenn.; isolated pockets in Mich. and Mo. Also Europe, e. Asia (although relationships with European counterparts are still not clear).

BLADE: 3–7 in. long. Bluish green or olive green; slightly leathery; smooth; evergreen; oval, feathery.

PINNAE: Widely spaced, not opposite, distinctly stalked, with 2–7 widely spaced pinnules.

PINNULES: Variable but mostly fan-shaped on distinct stalks; edges toothed, indented, or fringed.

RACHIS: Smooth, green, dull, grooved in front, delicate, with very sparse, tiny hairs.

STIPE: Up to 3 1/2 in. ± long. Usually longer than blade, very slender, somewhat rigid, grooved in front, smooth and green except at very base, where it is dark brown and somewhat scaly.

RHIZOME: Creeping or, more commonly, ascending, short, with many old dead stipes attached; covered with many tiny, pointed, dark brown scales hidden among roots.

SORI: Short, narrow; often mass together to cover underside of pinnule completely. Indusium whitish, delicately membranous, with hairy edges.

NOTES: Could superficially resemble *Asplenium montanum* (Mountain Spleenwort), but is found on basic, not acidic, rocks and has much broader, long-stalked pinnae.

MARGINALIA: *A. Fertile pinna.*

DIAGNOSTIC ARROWS: *1. Stemmed pinnule. 2. Palm-shaped pinnule. 3. Widely spaced and stemmed pinnae.*

A.

1.

2.

3.

ASPLENIUM RUTA-MURARIA
WALL RUE

AMERICAN HART'S-TONGUE FERN

Asplenium scolopendrium L. var. *americanum* (Fern.) Kartesz & Gandhi
Synonym: *Phyllitis scolopendrium* (L.) Newm. var. *americanum* Fern.

HABIT: Glossy, bright green, leathery, evergreen fern with strap-shaped fronds growing upward and outward in circular tufts. Frond resembles a hart's tongue, hence the common name. ("Hart" is another word for "stag.")

ECOLOGY: Shaded, damp, rocky limestone crevices in sinkholes, cave entrances, and on talus slopes where it is cool, moist, and shady.

RANGE: Extremely rare, local. Recorded in Ont., N.Y., Mich., Tenn., and Ala.; also Mexico.

FRONDS: 4–18 in. long; 1–2 in. wide. Sterile and fertile fronds the same.

BLADE: Dark glossy green above, lighter green beneath; thick and straplike; often with wavy edges, base heart-shaped; tip bluntly pointed; veins fork and do not reach edge of blade.

RACHIS: Yellowish, becoming pale brown at base.

STIPE: Short ($1/8$–$1/4$ length of blade). Furrowed, pale brown; young stipes covered with narrow, brown scales (old stipes sometimes without scales).

RHIZOME: Very short, upright.

SORI: Elongate, various lengths, nearly perpendicular to the rachis, restricted usually to upper frond, in pairs on either side of veins with indusia opening toward each other.

NOTES: The American variety of this fern is recognized as distinct from the European variety (*P. scolopendrium* var. *scolopendrium*) because it is diploid (2 sets of chromosomes), while the European variety is tetraploid (4 sets). European plants appear to be more vigorous and readily cultivated. Could be confused with *Asplenium rhizophyllum* (Walking Fern), but the long, blunt-tipped, glossy green fronds with long, narrow sori distinguish this species.

MARGINALIA: *A. Heart-shaped base of blade. B. Underside of fertile blade, showing sori and indusium.*

DIAGNOSTIC ARROWS: *1. Tongue-shaped blade with wavy edge. 2. Irregularly elongated rows of sori.*

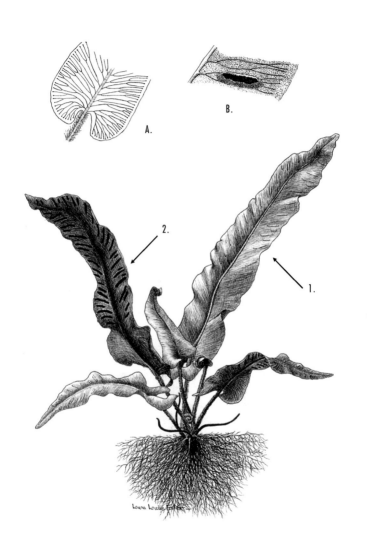

A.

B.

2.

1.

ASPLENIUM SCOLOPENDRIUM
AMERICAN HART'S-TONGUE FERN

Asplenium trichomanes L.
  A. t. ssp. *trichomanes*
  A. t. ssp. *quadrivalens* D. E. Meyer

HABIT: Spreading fronds of this dainty fern form dense rosettes on moist and shaded moss-covered surfaces of cliffs and boulders. Sterile fronds are prostrate; late-sprouting fertile fronds are erect, fresh, bright green, and spritely; both wither when winter arrives. This species is separated into two subspecies, *Asplenium trichomanes* ssp. *trichomanes* and *A. t.* ssp. *quadrivalens*, which have similar features overall but differ in habitat preference, range, spore size, and numbers of chromosomes.

ECOLOGY: Rock-loving fern of moist, shaded crevices in moss-covered outcroppings. *A. t.* ssp. *trichomanes* prefers sandstone, basalt, granite, and other more acidic rocks; *A. t.* ssp. *quadrivalens* grows on limestone or other alkaline bedrock.

RANGE: *A. t.* ssp. *trichomanes* ranges from Nfld. south to S.C., west to Okla., north to s. Ont. Another population band is found from Mexico through Ariz. north to Wyo., and others are found in the Pacific Northwest from n. Calif. to s. Alaska.

  A. t. ssp. *quadrivalens* has a smaller range in our area, from Me. south to W. Va., west to Wisc. and Mich., with isolated populations in B.C. and n. Wash. Both subspecies are noted from Europe, Asia, Africa, the Indo-Pacific.

FRONDS: 2–10 in. long. Long, narrow and tapering toward both top and bottom, dark green, cut into 20 ± pairs of pinnae. Fertile fronds upright, sterile fronds usually flat to surface of rocks.

PINNAE: $1/4$ inch ± long. Tiny; smaller toward tip of blade, rounded or slightly oval, slightly toothed margins, opposite and slightly stalked. Upper pinnae crowded, often overlapping; lower pinnae more widely spaced but close together. Veins free and forked.

RACHIS: Dark, purplish brown throughout.

STIPE: $1/3$ as long as the blade. Dark purplish brown, brittle, wiry.

RHIZOME: Short, erect or ascending, with dark brown scales.

SORI: Few (2–4 pairs per pinna), often mass together. Indusium fragile.

NOTES: Resembles *Asplenium trichomanes-ramosum* (Green Spleenwort), with which it sometimes grows, but Maidenhair Spleenwort tends to be larger with denser fronds and has a dark rachis.

MARGINALIA: *A. Underside of fertile pinna.*
DIAGNOSTIC ARROWS: *1. Opposite and rounded pinnae. 2. Short stipes. 3. Spreading rosettelike growth form.*

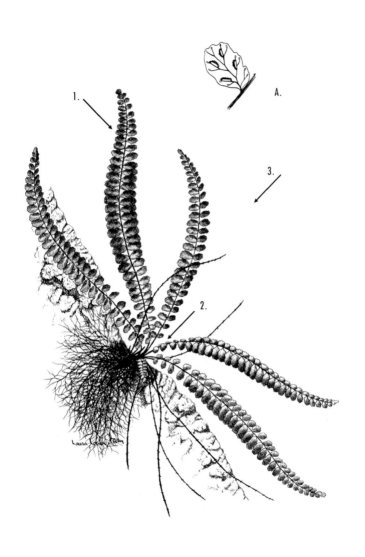

A.

1.

3.

2.

ASPLENIUM TRICHOMANES
MAIDENHAIR SPLEENWORT

GREEN SPLEENWORT

Asplenium trichomanes-ramosum L.
Synonym: *Asplenium viride* Hudson

HABIT: Rare, delicate, tiny fern with rounded, green pinnae; grows in small tufts on rocks.

ECOLOGY: Cool, moist, shaded crevices of limestone.

RANGE: Rare, only in our most northerly regions in scattered populations from Greenland south to n. N.Y., Vt., Me., west to Ont. Western populations from S.D. to B.C. south to n. Calif., Colo., and Idaho. Also Europe, Asia.

FRONDS: 2–7 in. long. Delicate, narrow, semi-erect, evergreen; fertile and sterile fronds the same.

BLADE: Cut into 12 ± pairs of pinnae, lower and middle pinnae widely spaced.

PINNAE: Rounded, wedge-shaped or rectangular, slightly indented edges; opposite or subopposite; lower pinnae with short stalks. Veins variably forked.

RACHIS: Green, delicate.

STIPE: Thin and flexible, about half as long as the blade; brown to blackish at base, green and smooth above.

RHIZOME: Short; more erect than short-creeping.

SORI: 2–4 pairs per pinna, seldom more. Indusium thin and fragile.

NOTES: Resembles *Asplenium trichomanes* (Maidenhair Spleenwort), with which it sometimes grows, but Green Spleenwort tends to be smaller and has a green rachis.

MARGINALIA: *A. Underside of fertile pinna.*

DIAGNOSTIC ARROWS: *1. Semi-erect form. 2. Widely spaced lower and middle pinnae. 3. Short stipes.*

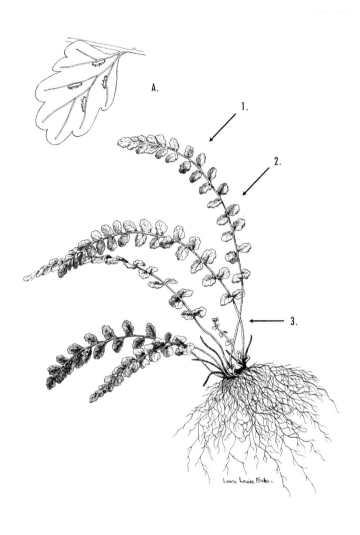

A.

1.

2.

3.

Laura Louise Foster.

ASPLENIUM TRICHOMANES-RAMOSUM
GREEN SPLEENWORT

SCOTT'S SPLEENWORT
Asplenium ebenoides Gray, B. & B.
Synonym: *Asplenosorus ebenoides* (R. R. Scott) Wherry

This species is a hybrid resulting from a cross between *Asplenium platyneuron* (Ebony Spleenwort) and *A. rhizophyllum* (Walking Fern). As such, it exhibits features of an arching, tapering Walking Fern with cut or lobed fronds 1 1/2–12 in. long, reminiscent of the Ebony Spleenwort, with many variable forms in between. The fern grows in tufts with the smaller, sterile fronds flat to the ground and the somewhat larger, fertile fronds more erect; some frond tips can give rise to new plants, as in Walking Fern. The stipe is purplish brown and lustrous throughout, shorter than the blade; the rachis is purplish, fading to green at the frond tip. This rare fern grows on boulders of limestone, sandstone, or conglomerate (often with Walking Fern); fertile individuals are known only from Ala. This was one of the first ferns to be confirmed as a hybrid, through a series of very clever crossing experiments by pteridologists Margaret Slosson in 1902 and Herb Wagner and R. S. Whitmire in the 1950s. See page 62.

FORKED SPLEENWORT
Asplenium septentrionale (L.) Hoffmann

This unique species is regarded as rare throughout its range; however, it may be overlooked because it resembles the thin blades of a grass more than a fern. The leathery, smooth blades are tiny (1/4–2 in. long) and very narrow (only up to 1/4 in. wide), borne on longer, wiry stipes up to 5 in. long that are dark reddish brown at the base and green toward the blade. Sori are sparse. Grows on cliffs of various substrates, including granite, sometimes forming mats on boulders. Known only from our area in W. Va.; more widespread in the western states of Tex., N.M., Utah, Ariz., Colo., and Calif. Also from Baja Calif., Mexico, Europe, and Asia. It can hybridize with *A. trichomanes* (Maidenhair Spleenwort) to produce a sterile hybrid, *A. × alternifolium*. See page 62.

(Greek: *a*, "without," + *thyrus*, "door"; mature sporangia barely push back the edge of the indusium, thus appearing as if the "door" did not open)

The *Athyrium* species are delicate in texture, but relatively large deciduous ferns. The thick, usually short-creeping rhizomes produce a lush, compact cluster of softly arching fronds. The blade is divided into pinnae, which in turn are cut into pinnules (or bipinnate), which are also lobed, giving it a very lacy effect. *Athyrium* species, like the genus *Asplenium* with which they were once grouped, have sori that are mostly narrow and elongate along a vein, with indusia attached lengthwise on one side.

Approximately 180 species of *Athyrium* are found worldwide in mostly temperate climates; two species are native to North America, one of which grows in our area. Our species, *Athyrium filix-femina* (Lady Fern), is common and circumboreal, extending into Central and South America, Europe, and Asia. It is separated into five varieties (considered by some taxonomists to be subspecies), with two in our area: Northern and Southern Lady Ferns — var. *angustum* and var. *asplenioides*.

One distinctive form of Lady Fern has red stems. Formerly known as *A. f.* var. *rubellum*, it is not a separate botanical variety but a color form that occurs sporadically in all botanical varieties of *A. filix-femina*.

Although the common name is a translation of *filix-femina*, to remember the name, people use several mnemonic associations, ranging from "delicate ladies with hairy legs" (referring to the scales on the stipe), to the arching sori, which resemble the eyebrows of a beautiful lady.

ATHYRIUM KEY

1A. Blades broadest at or just below middle and narrowed at base; pinnae sessile or with very short stalks; mature spores golden yellow. **A. filix-femina var. angustum (Northern Lady Fern)**

1B. Blades broadest just above base; pinnae with stalks; mature spores dark brown.
A. filix-femina var. asplenioides (Southern Lady Fern)

NORTHERN LADY FERN

Athyrium filix-femina (L.) Mertens var. *angustum* (Willd.) Lawson
Synonyms: *Athyrium filix-femina* (L.) Mertens var. *michauxii* (Sprengel) Farwell; *Athyrium angustum* (Willd.) Presl.

HABIT: Rather large, showy, vigorous fern. Lacy-cut, medium to yellow-green deciduous fronds growing in fairly compact, irregular but somewhat circular clusters.

ECOLOGY: Common throughout our area. Moist woods, swamps, thickets, and fields.

RANGE: Greenland to Man., south to N.C., west to Neb. and north to N.D.

FRONDS: 16–36 in. long; 4–14 in. wide. Sterile and fertile fronds similar. Blades broadly lanceolate with pointed tips, broadest near or just below middle. Smooth throughout, variable in form. Cut into 30–40 pairs of pinnae.

PINNAE: 8 in. ± long. Narrow pointed tips; very short or no stalk. Cut again into 12–20 pairs of pinnules.

PINNULES: Deeply cut into lobes, with toothed margins; variable; thin-pointed or blunt-tipped. Veins are forked and reach to margin.

RACHIS: Pale, smooth, sometimes with short hairs or few scales.

STIPE: Greenish to reddish, usually with scattered, elongate dark brown scales; dark red-brown base swollen with 2 rows of teeth. Usually shorter, but sometimes as long as blade.

RHIZOME: Very scaly, shallow-creeping, often branching and sometimes semi-erect. Usually with many old dead stalks attached.

SORI: Elongate; straight or sometimes hooked or horseshoe-shaped. Indusia with hairs but not glands, edge irregularly toothed and attached to long sides of sori. Spores yellowish to brownish.

NOTES: May be confused with *Dennstaedtia punctilobula* (Hay-scented Fern), but the latter has a sticky feel from its many white glandular hairs, brown scales on stipe, and does not grow in circular clusters. *Thelypteris novaboracensis* (New York Fern) is similar but does not have toothed margins on the pinnules. *Dryopteris carthusiana* (Spinulose Woodfern) is also similar but has many scales on sturdier stipes.

MARGINALIA: *A. Sterile pinnule. B. Section of fertile pinna. C. Frond of Northern Lady Fern. D. Frond of Southern Lady Fern.*

DIAGNOSTIC ARROWS: *1. Lax tip. 2. Growth form in circular clusters from horizontally creeping rhizome. 3. Cut and toothed pinnule. 4. Smooth stipe with scattered brown scales.*

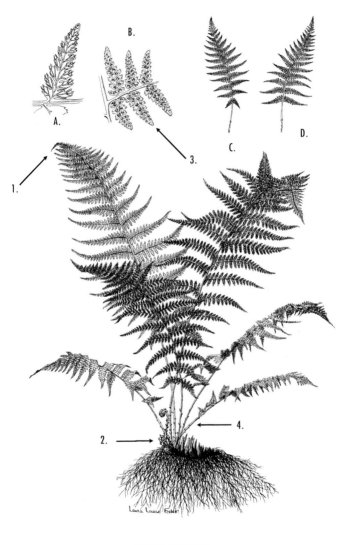

ATHYRIUM FILIX-FEMINA
NORTHERN LADY FERN

SOUTHERN LADY FERN

Athyrium filix-femina (L.) Mertens var. *asplenioides* (Mich.) Farwell
Synonym: *Athyrium asplenioides* (Mich.) Hultén

Southern Lady Fern is similar to its northern cousin, except that the blade is widest just above base or well below the middle; the pinnae have much longer pointed tips and stalks (sessile in var. *angustum*), stipe scales are lighter brown; indusia sometimes have glandular hairs; and mature spores are dark brown instead of yellow. The ranges of the two species do overlap somewhat; Southern Lady Fern is found from Mass., south to Fla., west to Tex., and north to Kans.

Lacy frond of Athyrium filix-femina *(Northern Lady Fern). (Photo by Frank Bramley/NEWFS)*

Fiddleheads of Athyrium filix-femina *(Northern Lady Fern). (Photo by Frank Bramley/NEWFS)*

GENUS *AZOLLA:* MOSQUITO FERN

(Greek: *azo,* "to dry," + *ollyo,* "to kill"; referring to fact that drought kills the species)

One species of this genus occurs in our area, *Azolla caroliniana* (Mosquito Fern). *A. caroliniana* has spread from the southern states to the middle Atlantic and midwestern states wherever the winter is not too cold. Being a tiny plant with clinging roots, *Azolla* probably is spread by waterfowl, particularly wading birds.

Like the other aquatic fern in our area, *Marsilea quadrifolia* (Water Shamrock), Mosquito Fern has two types of spore: egg-bearing megaspores and sperm-bearing microspores. Unlike Water Shamrock, each type of spore develops in a different kind of capsule, or sporocarp. In spring, when the spores have ripened but before fertilization, both kinds of sporocarps, which are equipped with "floats," break off from their stems and are carried to the water's surface. The capsule containing the microspores opens and breaks up into many spherical clusters of disclike structures called massulae. The massulae have barb-ended, hair-like appendages that they use to attach themselves to the mega-spore for fertilization. The megaspore has fine, hairlike filaments that float from its top to guide the sperm through the water to the canal that leads to the egg. The fertilized egg then grows into a new floating fern that will produce spores all over again.

Azolla species engage in a mutualistic relationship with a species of blue-green algae (cyanobacterium) called *Anabaena azollae.* It is rare to find an *Azolla* plant without *Anabaena* as tenant. *Anabaena* disperses with new pieces of fern that fragment off the parent stem, thus maintaining a permanent relationship across the generations. *Azolla* provides nutritional byproducts of photosynthesis to the resident cyanobacteria, while *Anabaena* fixes inorganic nitrogen into ammonium that is taken up by the fern. This allows *Azolla* tissues to become very rich in nitrogen, which in turn makes the species an excellent "green manure," or fertilizer, for other plants. Thus, various species of *Azolla* throughout the world are planted with crops such as rice, or are fed to livestock as a highly nutritional food source.

MOSQUITO FERN
(WATER FERN, CAROLINA POND FERN)

Azolla caroliniana Willd.

HABIT: Minute, free-floating, truly aquatic fern that looks like a tiny portion of the tip of an arborvitae leaf or like a red or green snowflake. Individual plants are only $^1/_2$–1 in. long. When well established, grows in 1–2 in.-thick mats across surface of still water in masses supposedly dense enough to smother mosquito larvae. Tiny layered leaves, which change from red in full sun to bright green in shade, give an iridescent, fall foliage character to colonies of these ferns.

ECOLOGY: Hardy; particularly abundant in still backwaters, ponds, and even in brackish bayous in temperate zones. At low water, clings to muddy banks and will creep up the wet, mossy banks of ponds several inches above water level. Readily transplanted by birds from one watery spot to another, where it multiplies rapidly if not killed by extreme cold and ice.

RANGE: Mass. south to Fla., west to Tex., north to Neb. and Mich. Known from South America, Europe, Asia.

PINNAE: Tiny, $^1/_5$–$^1/_4$ in. in diameter. Deeply cleft into pointed oval pinnules that grow from tiny fan-shaped branches, which are so fragile that disturbances along the surface of the water break off the outer edges or ends, allowing small fern plants to float free and disperse.

PINNULES: Pointed oval, delicately membranous, growing in two overlapping rows, color varies from red to dark green. Lower pinnules grow below the surface of the water; the upper ones float on the surface.

RHIZOME: Tiny, pale brown, brittle, less than 1 in. long; branches frequently; bears tiny roots.

SPOROCARPS (RARELY SEEN): Both types of sporocarp are soft and thin-walled; usually borne in pairs in the axils, or junctures, of the pinnae. One large, roundish sporocarp or capsule contains several masses of the tiny microspores; and one smaller, somewhat acorn-shaped sporocarp contains only one large megaspore. Megaspore without pits or bumps, covered with tangled filaments. Microspores globular.

MARGINALIA: *A. Mosquito Fern growth habit. B. Underside of branch with sporocarps. C. Bird's-eye view of plant.*

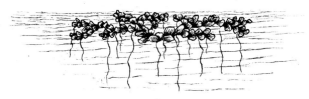

A.

B.

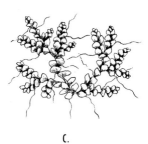

C.

AZOLLA CAROLINIANA
MOSQUITO FERN

GENUS *CHEILANTHES*: LIP FERNS

(Greek: *cheilos,* "lip" or "margin," + *anthos,* "flower"; referring to the position of the sporangia near the margin)

The Lip Ferns are lovers of dry, rocky places. Similar to other rock-dwelling ferns, they curl up and look dead during droughts but quickly recover after rain. These are sometimes referred to as resurrection ferns, though in our region the common name Resurrection Fern usually refers specifically to the southeastern species, *Pleopeltis polypodioides* var. *michauxiana.*

The Lip Ferns are small, evergreen or semi-evergreen ferns, usually hairy or woolly. The hairs help prevent water loss from transpiration. They grow in small tufts from short, compact rhizomes covered with rusty brown scales. The firm green fronds, which intermingle with dead stalks from previous years, are finely dissected with the smallest segments (pinnule lobes) often bead-like in appearance. There is little difference between the sterile and fertile fronds. Their veins are forked and almost reach the edges of the margins. Technically, the sporangia are not clustered into sori; instead they are concentrated at the ends of the veins and, in most species, are so crowded that they form a continuous line along the edges of the pinnule lobes. For the purposes of this Field Guide, however, we will call them sori. The pinnule edges curl over the sori and form a more or less continuous false indusium — typical of Lip Ferns. Lip Ferns are most easily distinguished from other small ferns by the minute, beadlike, often hairy pinnule lobes and purplish to dark brown stipe and rachis.

Approximately 150 species of Lip Fern are listed worldwide, primarily in the tropical or subtropical zones of the Western Hemisphere. Twenty-eight species are native to North America, but only *Cheilanthes lanosa* (Hairy Lip Fern) is common in our area. *C. tomentosa* (Woolly Lip Fern), *C. alabamensis* (Smooth Lip Fern), and *C. feei* (Slender Lip Fern) are at the edges of our range. Their common names are truly descriptive for each species: *C. lanosa* is very hairy; *C. tomentosa,* very woolly; *C. alabamensis,* smooth; and *C. feei,* slender.

CHEILANTHES KEY

1A. Stipe and rachis hairy or smooth, but without scales. Go to 2.

    2A. Pinna surface smooth or nearly so; rachis with many more hairs on upper than lower surface; Va. and south.

                                                C. alabamensis (Smooth Lip Fern)

2B. Pinna surface hairy; rachis with similar numbers of hairs on both sides. Go to 3.

    3A. Fronds tightly tufted; pinnule lobes nearly round; pinnules of lower pinnae fully cut to midrib; on bare rock, mostly Ill. and west.   ***C. feei* (Slender Lip Fern)**

    3A. Fronds somewhat separated at base; pinnule lobes elongate; pinnules of lower pinnae not as above; on shallow soils.   ***C. lanosa* (Hairy Lip Fern)**

1B. Stipe and rachis with both jointed hairs and flattened, long, narrow scales.   ***C. tomentosa* (Woolly Lip Fern)**

Blade of Cheilanthes lanosa *(Hairy Lip Fern). (Photo by William Larkin/ NEWFS)*

Cheilanthes lanosa *(Hairy Lip Fern) grows in dry, rocky habitats. (Photo by Cheryl Lowe)*

Cheilanthes lanosa (Michx.) D. C. Eat.

HABIT: Deep green clumps of finely dissected, fuzzy fronds on rocky outcrops. Like others of the genus, it dries up in drought but sends up new fronds after rain or heavy moisture.

ECOLOGY: Shallow soils of dry, rocky slopes and ledges, mostly acid, but also on limestone. Also in soils of open woodlands and semi-open areas.

RANGE: Conn. to s. Mo., south to Fla., west to e. Tex., north to se. Kans. Disjunct in Wisc.

FRONDS: 3–16 in. long, 1–2 in. wide. Fertile and sterile fronds similar.

BLADE: Narrow and long, broadest near base with lowest pair of pinnae slightly smaller than adjacent pair. Covered with dense, tan-gray jointed hairs throughout. Cut into 12–20 pairs of pinnae.

PINNAE: Lanceolate; crowded together near blade tips, often more widely spaced in lower portion of blade; mostly opposite at base, alternate above, slightly ascending. Dark color of rachis continues in costa. Divided into 7–14 pinnules.

PINNULES: Lanceolate to somewhat rectangular; lobed to deeply lobed but rarely cut completely to midrib; dense hairs on underside, less so on upper surface; veins forked.

RACHIS: Dark brown, covered with evenly distributed whitish hairs that turn tan-gray when mature; no scales.

STIPE: Shorter than blade, wiry, slender, brittle; dark brown to purplish black with dense hairs; no scales.

RHIZOME: Short; creeping; covered with long, slender brown scales usually without a dark central stripe.

SORI: Near end of veins; crowded to form continuous line around margin, partially covered by slightly incurved margin. No indusium.

NOTES: Might be confused with *Cheilanthes tomentosa* (Woolly Lip Fern) but Hairy Lip Fern has stipes with hairs but no scales, in contrast to the Woolly Lip Fern's stipe with both hairs and long narrow scales. The pinnule lobes of Hairy Lip Fern have sparse hairs on both sides; those of the Woolly Lip Fern are densely woolly underneath. *Lanosa* means "wool," which makes the common names of this and Woolly Lip Fern confusing, but remember the sparser *hairs* on the pinnules of Hairy Lip Fern compared to the thick, tangled mat of dense *wool* on the underside of the Woolly Lip Fern's pinnules.

MARGINALIA: *A. Upper side of sterile pinna. B. Upper side of fertile pinna. C. Underside of sterile pinnule. D. Underside of fertile pinnule.*

DIAGNOSTIC ARROWS: *1. Fronds somewhat separated at base (not tufted). 2. Widely spaced lower pinnae. 3. Hairy slender stipe.*

A. B. C. D.

2.

3.

1.

Laura Louise Foster.

CHEILANTHES LANOSA
HAIRY LIP FERN

Cheilanthes tomentosa Link

HABIT: Small, furry, tan-green tufted plant. (*Tomentosa* means "tangled, matted, woolly hairs.") Like others of the genus, it dries to a shriveled woolly brown clump in drought, but sends up new fronds after rain or heavy moisture.

ECOLOGY: Dry rock ledges and slopes, on a variety of substrates from limestone to granite.

RANGE: Primarily a southern species from Va. south to Ga., west through Mo. to s. Ariz. Disjunct population in Pa.

FRONDS: 4–14 in. long, 1–3 in. wide. Sterile and fertile fronds similar.

BLADE: Evergreen, oblong to lanceolate, clustered; densely woolly (tomentose), especially on undersides, with brownish white jointed hairs. Divided into 20 ± pairs of pinnae.

PINNAE: Widely spaced and almost opposite near base of blade; close together on upper blade; oblong with rounded tips; slightly hairy above, densely woolly beneath. Cut into 6–11 pairs of pinnules. Dark color of rachis coming into base of costa, but costa green for most of its length.

PINNULES: Deeply cut into oblong lobes.

RACHIS: Dark brown, with scattered, very narrow scales and hairs.

STIPE: Stout, short, dark brown with dark tan wool, and scales similar to rachis scales.

RHIZOME: Stout, short, shallow-creeping, most scales with a darker, central stripe.

SORI: Marginal, covered by incurved margin. No indusium.

NOTES: Fiddlehead more folded than coiled in this species. See *Cheilanthes lanosa* (Hairy Lip Fern) Notes for differences between these two species.

MARGINALIA: *A. Upper side of sterile pinna. B. Upper side of fertile pinna. C. Underside of fertile pinnule.*

DIAGNOSTIC ARROWS: *1. Stout and woolly stipes. 2. Crowded and woolly upper pinnae on hairy rachis.*

A.

B.

C.

1.

2.

CHEILANTHES TOMENTOSA
WOOLY LIP FERN

SMOOTH LIP FERN
(ALABAMA LIP FERN)
Cheilanthes alabamensis (Buckl.) Kunze

Barely comes into our region in Va. Similar to *Cheilanthes tomentosa* (Woolly Lip Fern) but lacks the scales and woolly undersurface of that species. Pinnae segments in Smooth Lip Fern are almost smooth (to slightly hairy) on both surfaces. Hairs on underside of rachis are sparse, spreading, and relatively straight but dense, appressed, and convoluted on upper surface of rachis.

SLENDER LIP FERN
Cheilanthes feei T. Moore

Barely enters the western edge of our range and is similar to *Cheilanthes lanosa* (Hairy Lip Fern). Clumps are much tighter, fronds smaller and usually bluish green, and smallest lobes of the blades are more rounded than Hairy Lip Fern, with pinnules of lower pinnae fully cut to midrib. It grows on bare rock or rock crevices, rather than shallow soils of cliff ledges preferred by Hairy Lip Fern; often found on limestone. It ranges from Ill. south to Tex., west to Calif., and north to Wash., with populations also reported in Ky. and Va.

Upper side of sterile pinna of
Cheilanthes alabamensis

Lower pinnae and pinnules of
Cheilanthes feei

GENUS *CRYPTOGRAMMA*:
PARSLEY FERNS OR ROCK BRAKES

(Greek: *kryptos,* "hidden," + *gramme,* "line"; referring to the lines of sori hidden by the overlapping margins on the fertile pinnae)

Cryptogramma species are small, rock-loving plants with fragile, delicate, smooth stipes. Sterile and fertile fronds are very different; the sterile ones are lax and spreading with flat, oblong pinnules, while the fertile fronds are stiffer and erect, with linear, inrolled pinnules. Pinnules of the fertile fronds are narrower because the margins curl under to cover the sori, creating a false indusium. The veins are forked and do not quite reach the pinnule margins.

Eight to 11 species of this genus are listed worldwide; of 4 in North America, 1 is primarily in our area. *Cryptogramma stelleri* (Slender Rock Brake) is rare and local, growing only on cool, moist, deeply shaded limestone ledges in northern areas. *C. acrostichoides* (American Parsley Fern) is a western species that occurs within our area only in n. Mich.

CRYPTOGRAMMA KEY

1A. Fronds scattered along creeping rhizome; fronds delicate, pale green; mostly calcareous habitats.
C. stelleri (Slender Rock Brake)

1B. Fronds tufted, often densely so, on erect rhizome; fronds leathery; usually noncalcareous sites; Mich. and westward.
C. acrostichoides (American Parsley Fern)

Cryptogramma stelleri
(*Slender Rock Brake*) is
rare in our area. (*Photo
by Don Lubin*)

SLENDER ROCK BRAKE
(FRAGILE ROCK BRAKE, STELLER'S ROCK BRAKE)

Cryptogramma stelleri (S. G. Gmel.) Prantl.

HABIT: Fragile, tiny fern with almost translucent fronds scattered along a long slender rhizome. Fronds ephemeral, dying back by midsummer. Sterile and fertile fronds differ in growth and form.

ECOLOGY: Sheltered, shaded, moist calcareous cliff crevices and rock ledges, typically in northern areas or cool coniferous forests. Rare.

RANGE: Nfld. to s. Ont., south to Pa., west to Minn. In w. U.S., Alaska to Wash. and disjunct populations in Rocky Mts. Also Europe and Asia.

FRONDS: 3–8 in. long. Sterile fronds lax and spreading; fertile fronds erect, taller, with distinctly narrower pinnules.

BLADE: Elongate triangular, widest near base; smooth, frail, membranous. Fertile blades narrower, more divided, with narrower pinnules than sterile blades.

PINNAE: 5–6 pairs. Alternate to opposite, broadest at base; lower pinnae cut into pinnules, upper pinnae mostly lobed. Sterile pinnae with broadly rounded outlines. Fertile pinnae narrower.

PINNULES: Very delicate, almost translucent; sterile pinnules rounded, oblong to fan-shaped; with toothed edges and very short stalks, sometimes overlapping; fertile pinnules narrow, pointed, lanceolate, not overlapping. Veins forked.

RACHIS: Green, smooth.

STIPE: Longer than blade, delicate, smooth, weak, straw-colored to dark brown below, often with a few hairs at base, pale green above.

RHIZOME: Slender, creeping, succulent, with colorless scales and sparse roots.

SORI: Borne beneath inrolled margins of fertile pinnae (margins occasionally unroll or open up with age). No true indusium.

NOTES: A fragile plant with creeping, slender rhizome; the portion of the rhizome with emerging fronds shrivels up two years after fronds emerge. Somewhat similar in appearance to a small *Pellaea* (Cliff Brake), but the fertile and sterile fronds are very different, and the rachises are greenish to straw-colored, not dark brown.

MARGINALIA: *A. Sterile pinna. B. Fertile upper pinna.*

DIAGNOSTIC ARROWS: *1. Long fertile stipe. 2. Lance-shaped fertile upper pinnae. 3. Rounded pinnules on sterile pinna.*

CRYPTOGRAMMA STELLERI
SLENDER ROCK BRAKE

AMERICAN PARSLEY FERN
Cryptogramma acrostichoides R. Brown
Synonym: *Cryptogramma crispa* (L.) R. Brown ex Hooker ssp. *acrosti-choides* (R. Brown) Hultén

A w. U.S. species that enters the western edge of our region in n. Mich. In contrast to *Cryptogramma stelleri* (Slender Rock Brake), this species grows in compact tufts in generally noncalcareous habitats and is a plant with larger, somewhat leathery fronds throughout the growing season.

Fertile fronds of Cryptogramma acrostichoides *are very different from the sterile fronds. (Photo by Cheryl Lowe)*

GENUS CYSTOPTERIS: BLADDER FERNS

(Greek: *kustis*, "bladder," + *pteris*, "fern"; referring to the inflated young indusium)

Cystopteris species are delicate ferns of cliffs, ledges, and rocky woodlands, often growing in clumps and tufts due to the short-creeping rhizomes. Stipes are light-colored and smooth, supporting finely dissected, deciduous fronds. Fertile and sterile fronds are similar, although the latter are often smaller and emerge first in the spring. The veins on *Cystopteris* species are simple or forked and reach the margins of the pinnae. The indusia, inspiration for the genus name, are roundish, thin, and attached to one side of the sori, arching over them when young like pockets or bladders, with the pocket openings facing the tip of the pinnules or lobes. The indusia wither as the sori mature, so they may not be visible when the sporangia are ripe. As with many ferns, some identifying characters such as minute glands can be seen only with a 10× hand lens.

All of the *Cystopteris* in our area send up new fronds throughout the season, so although they turn brown in summer drought conditions, they can unfurl fresh new fronds later in the summer if moisture returns. Young Bladder Ferns can be easily confused with young *Woodsia* species, but the indusium is distinctly different (pocketlike in Bladder Ferns; starlike or resembling an open hand "holding" the sori in *Woodsia* species), and the veins extend to the pinna margin in *Cystopteris* but not in *Woodsia*. Also, the stipes of *Woodsia* species are opaque and usually scaly, whereas the stipes of *Cystopteris* are translucent and smooth or with only a few scales at the base.

This genus contains approximately 20 species worldwide, mostly in temperate regions. Nine of these occur in North America; 4 in our region. *Cystopteris* is notorious for producing hybrids and polyploids ranging from the usual 2 (diploid) to 8 sets of chromosomes. *C. fragilis* (Fragile Fern) is a good example. It is highly variable in appearance from one geographic area or habitat to another, or even within the same area. It is a fertile hybrid (tetraploid, with 4 sets of chromosomes), probably derived from an unknown diploid parent and *C. reevesiana* (Southwestern Brittle Fern), although some studies suggest that, in the ne. U.S. at least, the second parent might be *C. protrusa* (Southern Bladder Fern). The expression of multiple chromosomes may account for its variability, but it also frequently hybridizes with other species and other hybrids. If you find a *Cystopteris* that seems to have characteristics of 2 or more species listed below, you may be looking at a *Cystopteris* hybrid.

1A. Rachis, costa, and indusia sparsely to densely covered with minute, gland-tipped hairs (best seen with 10× hand lens and more visible on younger fronds); bulblets on underside of blade. Go to 2.

> **2A.** Rachis and costa often with bulblets on underside. Blade long but triangular, widest at base and tapering gradually to tip. Rachis, costa, and indusia moderately covered with glandular hairs. **C. bulbifera (Bulblet Fern)**
>
> **2B.** Gland-tipped hairs sparse. Bulblets few and often misshapen. Blade tapering more abruptly at tip; widest at or above base. Go to 3.
>
> > **3A.** Blade ovate to lanceolate, widest just above base. **C. laurentiana (Laurentian Bladder Fern)**
> >
> > **3B.** Blade triangular, usually widest at base. Stipe scales tan to light brown. **C. tennesseensis (Tennessee Bladder Fern)**

1B. Rachis, costa, and indusia without gland-tipped hairs; no bulblets. Go to 4.

> **4A.** Fronds emerging 3/8–1 in. behind tip of rhizome; yellow hairs (felt or seen by gently removing leaf litter and soil near outermost fronds) on rhizome. Usually growing in soil. **C. protrusa (Southern Bladder Fern)**
>
> **4B.** Fronds emerging at tip of rhizome; no hairs on rhizome. Usually growing in rocks. Go to 5.
>
> > **5A.** Pinnae often angled toward tip and/or at acute angle to rachis (less than 90°), often curving toward blade tip; pinnae margins with rounded teeth. Stalked pinnules of lower pinnae taper to base. **C. tenuis (Mackay's Fragile Fern)**
> >
> > **5B.** Pinnae usually perpendicular to rachis, not curving toward tip of frond; if toothed, pinnae margins have sharp teeth. Pinnules of lower pinnae sessile and broad or rounded at base. **C. fragilis (Fragile Fern)**

Bulblets on underside of Cystopteris bulbifera (*Bulblet Fern*). (*Photo by Arthur Haines*)

Long, tapering fronds of Cystopteris bulbifera. (*Photo by Frank Bramley/NEWFS*)

Cystopteris laurentiana (*Laurentian Bladder Fern*). (*Photo by Arthur Haines*)

BULBLET FERN (Bulblet Bladder Fern)

Cystopteris bulbifera (L.) Bernh.

HABIT: Graceful, delicate, narrow-leaved fern usually in large masses with long streamerlike fronds hanging down over cliffs or covering moist rocks below limestone ledges. Small pealike bulblets on underside of blade are unique to this species and some of its hybrids.

ECOLOGY: Most often on ledges and in cracks of moist calcareous cliffs and slopes, but also on limestone rocks in woodlands, and occasionally on hummocks in calcareous swamps.

RANGE: Nfld. to s. Ont., south to Ga., west to Ark., north to Minn., disjunct in Tex. and Utah.

FRONDS: 12–32 in. long; 3 ± in. wide. Sterile fronds emerge early and are often shorter.

BLADE: Soft pale green to yellow-green; long and triangular, broadest at base and extended to a long, usually drooping tip. Cut into 20–30 pairs of pinnae, the lowest pair largest.

PINNAE: Mostly perpendicular to rachis, drooping at ends, and ranging from long and triangular to long and narrow. Mostly alternate, but lower pinnae opposite. Costa with scattered, short-stalked glands. Cut into lobed pinnules.

PINNULES: Most frequently long and narrow, but variable in shape; lobed; veins end in notches of lobes.

RACHIS: Shining yellow, densely covered with gland-tipped hairs.

STIPE: Shorter than blade; reddish to pink when young, later straw-colored to greenish throughout (sometimes with a darker base), mostly smooth, but base sparsely scaly.

RHIZOME: Short and creeping, slender, black, and scaly.

SORI: Between margin and midvein of pinnule. Indusium with minute, short-stalked glands. Spores mature in early summer.

NOTES: Bulblets (resembling small green peas) are produced at base of pinnae near rachis or along costa of pinnae; bulblets drop off and germinate into tiny new plants. 2–12 bulblets per frond. Similar to *Cystopteris fragilis* (Fragile Fern) but Bulblet Fern blade is much longer and more tapering; bulblets are usually present, and rachis, costa, and indusia have glandular hairs.

This species hybridizes with other *Cystopteris* species and hybrids are common when multiple taxa occur together.

MARGINALIA: *A. Pinna with bulblet. B. Fertile pinnule. C. Bulblet sprouting a young plant. D. Underside of fertile lobe.*

DIAGNOSTIC ARROWS: *1. Long, narrow, and thin blade. 2. Bulblet on pinna.*

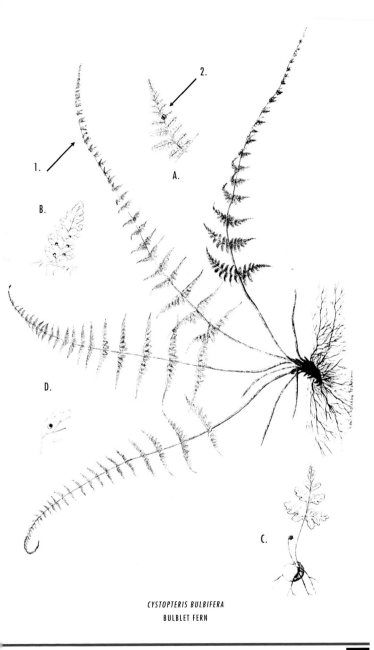

CYSTOPTERIS BULBIFERA
BULBLET FERN

FRAGILE FERN (BRITTLE FERN)

Cystopteris fragilis (L.) Bernh.

HABIT: Small, bright green fern grows in clusters, appearing early in spring in crevices of shaded ledges and among rocks, often disappearing during summer droughts. New fronds unfurl when moisture returns, or all summer if site stays moist.

ECOLOGY: Mostly shaded cliff faces and thin soil over rock (both acidic and basic). Frequently forming small mats among moist, shaded boulders below ledges.

RANGE: Greenland and across all of Canada, south to Va., west to Kans., n. N.M., and Calif. Also South America, Eurasia, Australia, Africa.

FRONDS: 4–1 o in. long; 1–3 in. wide. Varies a great deal in appearance, being erect, arched, or prostrate.

BLADE: Lanceolate with pointed tips, widest just below middle; variable color from light to dark green, and more or less dissected.

PINNAE: Usually about 1 2 pairs, at right angles to rachis, opposite or nearly so; lower pinnae widely spaced. Cutting of pinnae exceedingly variable, but usually into pinnules that are variably lobed with toothed to smooth margins. Veins ending at tip of toothed margin when present.

RACHIS: Smooth.

STIPE: A little shorter than blade; brittle, easily breaking off, especially near base. Deep reddish brown near rhizome, becoming straw-colored or green above; slender, smooth, with only a few scales near base.

RHIZOME: Slender, short-creeping; narrow brown scales; fronds emerging from tip of rhizome.

SORI: Few and scattered, on veins. Indusium without glandular hairs.

NOTES: Highly variable, but most often confused with *Cystopteris bulbifera* (Bulblet Fern) or *C. tenuis* (Mackay's Fragile Fern). Unlike the Bulblet Fern, Fragile Fern has no bulblets, the blade is shorter, and it has no glandular hairs on rachis or indusia. Mackay's Fragile Fern is similar to Fragile Fern, but the blade of Mackay's is larger, its pinnae are angled toward tip (perpendicular in Fragile Fern), and teeth on the margins are more rounded (sharp teeth if present in Fragile Fern).

MARGINALIA: *A. Pinnules at base of pinnae. B. Indusium. C. Fertile pinnae of* C. tenuis. *(See p. 1 1 2–1 3 for comparison.)*

DIAGNOSTIC ARROWS: *1 . Lower pinnae widely spaced. 2 . Smooth and brittle stipe dark at bottom. 3 . Pinnae perpendicular to stem, pinnules with toothed margins.*

A.

B.

C.

1.

2.

3.

CYSTOPTERIS FRAGILIS
FRAGILE FERN

Laura Louise Foster

SOUTHERN BLADDER FERN
(SOUTHERN FRAGILE FERN)

Cystopteris protrusa (Weatherby) Blasdell
Synonym: *Cystopteris fragilis* (L.) Bernh. var. *protrusa* Weatherby

HABIT: Scattered along creeping rhizome; rhizome projects forward beyond the current year's emerging fronds. Small, bright green fern appears early in spring on the forest floor. New fronds emerge all summer if site is moist, but disappear during summer droughts; new fronds unfurl when moisture returns.

ECOLOGY: Mostly in soil of moist woods, but also in crevices of shaded ledges and among rocks.

RANGE: S. Ont. to Conn., south to Ga., west to Okla., north to Minn., but primarily of Appalachian Mts.

FRONDS: 8–18 in. long; 1 1/2–4 in. wide. Earliest emerging fronds sterile and smaller than fertile ones. Fronds erect, arched, or prostrate.

BLADE: Lanceolate, pointed tips, widest just below middle; more or less dissected.

PINNAE: Lower pinnae closely spaced; all at right angles to rachis, opposite or nearly so. Usually cut into pinnules; margins toothed. Lower pinnules (near rachis) on lower pinnae have small stalks. Veins end at tip of tooth.

RACHIS: Smooth.

STIPE: Shorter or equal to blade, mostly straw-colored or green above; scattered scales near base.

RHIZOME: Long-creeping; rhizome tip extends ½–1 ½ in. forward beyond developing fronds (thus *protrusa*); with tan to golden hairs; scales mostly near rhizome tip.

SORI: Few and scattered, growing on veins. Indusium without glandular hairs.

NOTES: Distinguished from similar species by protruding, golden-haired rhizome and habit of growing in soil rather than on rocks. You can feel the protruding rhizome tip by gently exploring the soil just below outermost emergent fronds with your fingertips. Southern Bladder Fern hybridizes with many species and hybrids.

MARGINALIA: *A. Fertile lower pinna. B. Rootstock.*

DIAGNOSTIC ARROWS: *1. Rhizome tip extends beyond emergent fronds. 2. Pinnules on lower pinnae with distinct stems. 3. Grows in soil rather than on rocks. 4. Pinnae mostly perpendicular to rachis.*

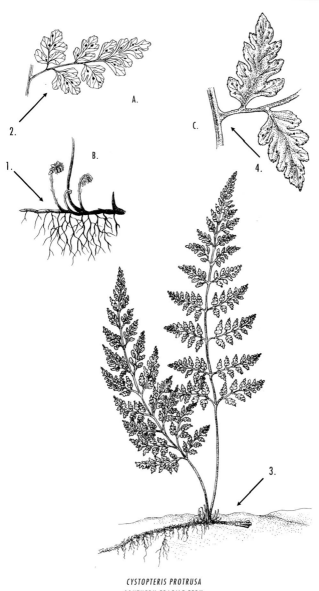

A.

C.

B.

2.

1.

4.

3.

CYSTOPTERIS PROTRUSA
SOUTHERN FRAGILE FERN

MACKAY'S FRAGILE FERN
(MACKAY'S BLADDER FERN)

Cystopteris tenuis (Michaux) Desvaux
Synonym: *Cystopteris fragilis* var. *mackayi* Lawson

HABIT: Asymmetrical clumps of small, bright green fronds; grows in soil and on rocks.

ECOLOGY: Mostly on shaded rock and cliff faces; also occasionally on forest floors.

RANGE: Common in e. U.S. From N.S. to s. Ont. south to Va. and in the Appalachian Mts. to N.C., west to Okla. and north to Minn., with disjunct populations in Utah, Ariz., and Nev.

FRONDS: 6–14 in. long; 1–3 in. wide. Fertile and sterile fronds similar; almost all fronds fertile; fronds erect, arching, or prostrate.

BLADE: Lanceolate, widest at or just below middle, with narrow tip. Dissected.

PINNAE: About 12 opposite or nearly opposite pairs, typically at acute angle to rachis, often curving toward the tip. Cutting of pinnae highly variable, but pinnules usually variably lobed with rounded margins. Pinnules of lowest pinnae sessile. Veins simple or forked, directed into teeth and notches.

RACHIS: Smooth.

STIPE: Shorter than or nearly same length as blade; brittle. Dark brown at base, mostly green to straw-colored above, with a few scales at base.

RHIZOME: Short-creeping, without hairs; narrow tan to light brown scales; fronds emerging at tip of rhizome.

SORI: Round, between midrib and margin; indusia without glandular hairs; disappear as sori mature.

NOTES: A hybrid (tetraploid) probably derived from a cross between *C. protrusa* (Southern Bladder Fern) and an unknown parent of *C. fragilis* (Fragile Fern). Difficult to distinguish from Fragile Fern and Southern Bladder Fern. Usually pinnae of Mackay's Fragile Fern are angled toward the tip (pinnae are perpendicular in the other two). Teeth on margin are rounded (teeth are sharp in Fragile Fern and mature Southern Bladder Fern). Also, Mackay's lacks protruding rhizome of Southern Bladder Fern.

MARGINALIA: *A. Lower pinnae with pinnules.*

DIAGNOSTIC ARROWS: *1. Pinnae at less than a 90° angle, often curving toward tip. 2. Rounded lobes or teeth on margin. 3. Fronds emerging from tip of rhizome.*

CYSTOPTERIS TENUIS
MACKAY'S FRAGILE FERN

LAURENTIAN BULBLET FERN

Cystopteris laurentiana (Weatherby) Blasdell

A fertile hybrid (hexaploid, with 6 sets of chromosomes) derived from *Cystopteris bulbifera* (Bulblet Fern) and *C. fragilis* (Fragile Fern). Primarily in the Great Lakes region and west into Iowa, Minn., and Wisc. but also in Vt., N.H., Pa., and Mass. on moist calcareous cliffs. Very similar to Fragile Fern, but it has sparse gland-tipped hairs, more ovate than lanceolate blades, and sometimes a few bulblets, which are often small, reddish, scaly, and misshapen.

TENNESSEE BULBLET FERN

Cystopteris tennesseensis Shaver

A fertile hybrid (tetraploid) derived from *Cystopteris bulbifera* (Bulblet Fern) and *C. protrusa* (Southern Bladder Fern) and is usually intermediate in character between those two parents. Usually on calcareous ledges, cliffs, or rock walls from Pa. south to Ga., west to Okla., and north to Wisc. This is the common Bulblet Fern of the Ozarks of Mo., Ark., and Okla. An unusual characteristic is that smaller blades are almost always fertile, whereas smaller fronds on other species are usually sterile.

GENUS *DENNSTAEDTIA*: HAY-SCENTED FERN

(Named for Augustus W. Dennstaedt, German botanist, 1776–1826)

This genus encompasses 70 species, mostly in the tropical and semitropical areas of South America and Asia. In our area, there is only the one species: *Dennstaedtia punctilobula*, the Hay-scented, or Boulder, Fern. Most botanists place this genus in its own family, the Dennstaedtiaceae; others place it in the Polypodiaceae.

The fronds of Dennstaedtia punctilobula *(Hay-scented Fern) have sharp-pointed tips. (Photo by Cheryl Lowe)*

Sometimes Hay-scented Fern dominates a large patch of forest understory and edge. (Photo by Cheryl Lowe)

Dennstaedtia punctilobula (Michx.) T. Moore

HABIT: Brittle yellowish green fern, becoming ragged and brownish in late summer. Usually occurs in large patches; whole fields or forest gaps filled with feathery fronds that, late in summer, give off a scent of crushed hay.

ECOLOGY: Dry, partially shaded woodlands and open pastures on open, sandy soils; sometimes excludes other plant species. Spreads rapidly by rhizomes and is difficult to eradicate.

RANGE: Common throughout our area from N.B. south to S.C. and W. Va., inland to Mo., Mich., and Que.

FRONDS: 16–30 in. long; 3 times as long as wide. Fronds arise mostly singly from the spreading rhizome. Sterile and fertile fronds similar, erect or somewhat arching.

BLADE: Yellowish green, not evergreen; usually lance-shaped (lanceolate) with a sharp pointed tip. Tapers only slightly near the bottom; covered with fine, glandular hairs. Cut into 20 ± pairs of pinnae.

PINNAE: Close together and subopposite, longer than wide; tapering tips with silvery, jointed, soft hairs on both surfaces.

PINNULES: Numerous, opposite, longer than wide, lobed.

RACHIS: Slender; light brown to straw-colored, darker at base; hairy.

STIPE: 7 in. ± long. Dark brown or almost black at the base, becoming light or reddish brown above, covered with white hairs of two types: long-jointed and short glandular.

RHIZOME: Horizontal and slender, rapidly growing; older parts dark brown and nearly smooth, younger parts green and covered with numerous reddish brown hairs.

SORI: Very small, at margins of pinnules. Surrounded by a unique, cup-shaped indusium.

NOTES: The blade of Hay-scented Fern does not taper gradually at the base like *Thelypteris noveboracensis* (New York Fern) and has numerous hairs on the stipe. *Athyrium filix-femina* (Lady Fern) grows in clumps and has dark brown scales rather than hairs on the stipe.

MARGINALIA: *A. Upper side of pinna. B. Underside of fertile pinnule. C. Cup-shaped indusium.*

DIAGNOSTIC ARROWS: *1. Narrow lance-shaped blades with narrowly pointed and relaxed tips. 2. Smooth or slightly hairy stipes. 3. Fronds growing singly along creeping rhizome.*

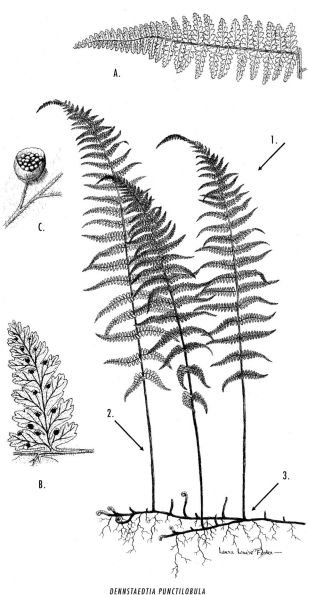

A.

C.

B.

1.

2.

3.

DENNSTAEDTIA PUNCTILOBULA
HAY-SCENTED FERN

GENUS *DEPARIA*: SILVERY GLADE FERN

(Greek: *depas*, "saucer"; for saucerlike indusium of *Deparia prolifera,* a Hawaiian species)

Deparia is primarily an Asian genus, with 50 mostly tropical species, 2 in North America and 1 in our region. Over the years, our species, *Deparia acrostichoides* (Silvery Glade Fern), has been placed in a number of genera, including *Athyrium, Diplazium,* and *Asplenium.* (The alternative common name, Silvery Spleenwort, comes from placement in this last genus.) The blades of this genus are divided into pinnae, each deeply cut into lobes but not quite separated into pinnules. *Deparia* is distinguished from other closely related genera by the hairs on the fronds and the separation of grooves on the costa from those on the rachis.

Sori of Deparia acrostichoides *(Silvery Glade Fern) form a herringbone pattern. (Photo by John A. Lynch)*

Deparia acrostichoides *grows in rich, moist woodlands. (Photo by William Cullina)*

Deparia acrostichoides (Sw.) M. Kato

Synonyms: *Athyrium thelypterioides* (Michx.) Desv.; *Diplazium acrostichoides* (Sw.) Butters; *Asplenium acrostichoides* Swartz

HABIT: Rather tall soft green fern with prominent silvery sori, and hairs that give a pale sheen to the fronds.

ECOLOGY: Rich, moist, well-drained woods or other semishaded moist areas.

RANGE: N.B. and N.S. south to Ga., west to Ark., north to Minn. Found throughout our area. Fairly common.

FRONDS: 12–30 in. ± long; 5–10 in. ± wide. Not evergreen; fertile fronds taller, more slender, more erect than sterile ones, appearing late summer.

BLADE: Tapering to both tip and base, broadest in the middle. Light green to bright green. Silvery hairs most common along costae and veins. Cut into 18 ± pairs of alternate pinnae.

PINNAE: 6 in. ± long. Narrow, pointed, sessile. Deeply cut into rounded, almost square-ended lobes. Margins serrate to entire. Lowest pair of pinnae often point downward. Veins not forked.

RACHIS: Pale green, slightly scaly, hairy. Grooves of costa not connected to groove on rachis.

STIPE: 4–18 in. long. Swollen at base with 2 rows of teeth. Stout, green to straw-colored above, slightly scaly and dark red-brown only at base. Usually much shorter than blade. Long white hairs at least until late summer; scales light brown and narrow.

RHIZOME: Black, creeping, sometimes semi-erect.

SORI: Narrow, long, straight, or slightly curved in a herringbone pattern; silvery at first, later blue-gray. Indusium elongate and attached on the vein side, silvery then light brown.

NOTES: Somewhat similar to *Athyrium filix-femina* (Lady Fern), but pinnae lobed (not cut into lobed pinnules) and margins not toothed. Might be confused with sterile fronds of *Osmunda cinnamomea* (Cinnamon Fern) or *O. claytoniana* (Interrupted Fern), but fronds of these are wider in proportion to length, with smooth stipes, and pinnae very close together.

MARGINALIA: *A. Section of underside of fertile pinna with sori. B. Pinna with blunt-tipped lobes.*

DIAGNOSTIC ARROWS: *1. Lowest pair of pinnae pointing downward. 2. Narrow double-tapering blade. 3. Short stipe. 4. Pinnae with deeply cut lobes.*

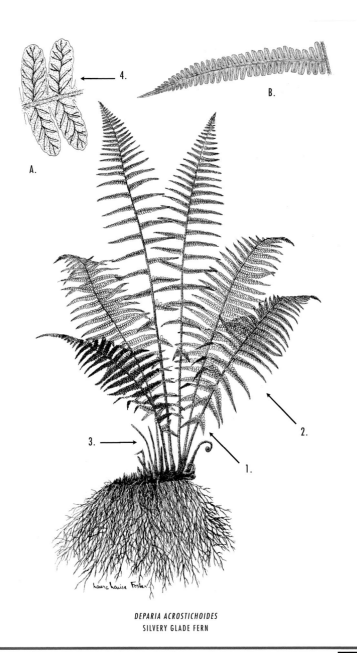

A.

B.

DEPARIA ACROSTICHOIDES
SILVERY GLADE FERN

GENUS *DIPLAZIUM*: GLADE FERN

(Greek: *diplazein*, "double," + *plasion*, "oblong"; for double sori)

Diplazium is mostly a tropical genus, with only three species in North America. Like *Deparia acrostichoides* (Silvery Glade Fern), *Diplazium pycnocarpon* (Narrow-leaved Glade Fern)—the one species in our area—was once included in *Athyrium* (Lady Ferns) and *Asplenium* (Spleenworts). Its alternative common name (Narrow-leaved Spleenwort) comes from its previous inclusion in *Asplenium*, but this is misleading because it is not a spleenwort. In our species, the sori are elongated but rarely double (back to back on the same vein), the latter a fairly common character in other species of this genus. The elongated indusium is often called "vaulted" because it is lifted up by the expanding sporangia.

The pinnae margins of Diplazium pycnocarpon *(Narrow-leaved Glade Fern) are slightly wavy but not toothed. (Photo by Dorothy Long/NEWFS)*

Slender, alternate, long-pointed pinnae of Diplazium pycnocarpon.
(Photo by William Cullina)

NARROW-LEAVED GLADE FERN
(NARROW-LEAVED SPLEENWORT)

Diplazium pycnocarpon (Spreng.) M. Brown

Synonyms: *Athyrium pycnocarpon* (Spreng.) Tidest.; *Asplenium pycno-carpon* Sprengel

HABIT: Distinguished by its tall, very narrow, bright green fronds, and almost circular clusters of 5–6 fronds from each rhizome.

ECOLOGY: Rich, moist woods, glades, and slopes in more neutral soils. Not common, but found throughout our area, usually in isolated colonies.

RANGE: Que. and Ont. south to n. Fla., west to La., and north to Minn.

FRONDS: 18–46 in. long; 5–10 in. wide. Deciduous. Fertile fronds appear later in the summer, are narrower, more erect, and with longer stipes than arching sterile ones.

BLADE: Narrow, lance-shaped, widest in the middle, with sharp pointed tip and slightly narrowed base. Cut into 20 ± pairs of slender, alternate pinnae.

PINNAE: 3 in. ± long; ½ in. ± wide. Narrow, long, with sharp pointed tips; base rounded or heart-shaped. Lowest pinnae with tiny stalks. Margins slightly wavy, not toothed or cut. Sterile pinnae not stiff and often slightly twisting; fertile ones stiff, straight, and very narrow. Smooth throughout. Veins once- or twice-forked.

RACHIS: Pale green; slightly hairy beneath.

STIPE: Shorter than blade; 6–16 in. Stout; reddish brown at base, green to straw-colored above, and slightly scaly, especially near base. Stipes of fertile fronds appreciably longer, stiffer, and more erect than sterile ones.

RHIZOME: Creeping, branching frequently; short, scaly, dark brown.

SORI: Long, slightly curved, in herringbone pattern; running from midvein almost to margin; dark brown when ripe. Indusium long, narrow, conspicuous.

NOTES: Somewhat similar to *Polystichum acrostichoides* (Christmas Fern), but Narrow-leaved Glade Fern has long, pointed pinnae without a basal lobe and long sori in a herringbone pattern. Possibly confused with *Asplenium platyneuron* (Ebony Spleenwort), but Narrow-leaved Glade Fern is much, much larger and the rachis is green, not dark brown.

MARGINALIA: *A. Underside of sterile pinna. B. Underside of fertile pinna. C. Section of fertile pinna showing shape and location of sori.*

DIAGNOSTIC ARROWS: *1. Growth form of fertile and sterile fronds. 2. Narrow pointed pinna with margin wavy, not toothed. 3. Rounded or heart-shaped base and tiny stalk of lowest pinna.*

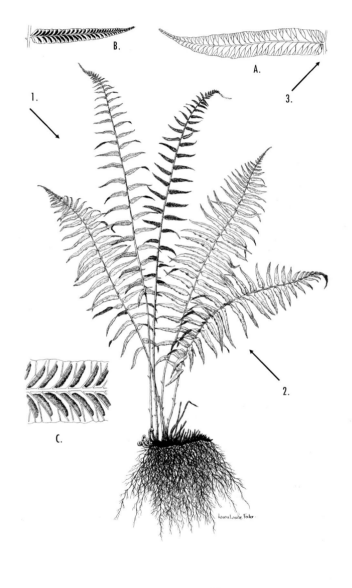

DIPLAZIUM PYCNOCARPON
NARROW-LEAVED GLADE FERN

GENUS *DRYOPTERIS*: WOOD FERNS

(Greek: *drys*, "tree," + *pteris*, "fern"; referring to forest habitat)

Dryopteris species are medium to large woodland ferns, often evergreen, with sterile and fertile fronds essentially the same shape and form. They are the epitome of ferns in appearance, many with finely cut, dark green fronds. Pinnae and pinnules are toothed or deeply cut. Sori are round and numerous. Indusia are clearly visible, kidney-shaped, and attached to the leafy tissue at the inner curve of the "kidney." The veins are forked, not netted, and do not extend fully to the margin of the pinnae or pinnule. Stipes are stout and scaly. Rhizomes are coarse, scaly, and erect, with fronds often emerging in basketlike clusters, or tufts.

There are approximately 250 *Dryopteris* species worldwide, with 14 in North America. The 11 species in our area occupy habitats ranging from low swampy areas to high, dry rocky cliffs. *Dryopteris cristata* (Crested Wood Fern) and *D. clintoniana* (Clinton's Fern) like moist feet, while the rare *D. fragrans* (Fragrant Cliff Fern) grows only in crevices of shaded, rocky cliffs in northern regions. *D. intermedia* (Evergreen Wood Fern) and *D. marginalis* (Marginal

The "fancy" fronds of Dryopteris carthusiana (*Spinulose Wood Fern*). (*Photo by John Lynch/ NEWFS*)

*Dryopteris fragrans (*Fragrant Wood Fern*), with its distinctive skirt of old fronds. (*Photo by Arthur Haines*)

Wood Fern) are often found in upland forests, but they live in a wide range of habitats. It is not uncommon to find many of the *Dryopteris* species—with the exception of *D. fragrans* (Fragrant Cliff Fern)—growing together, particularly in woodlands with both damp and dry areas.

The number of times the blade is divided (into pinnae, pinnules, and pinnule lobes) is an important clue in identifying the *Dryopteris* species. In our region, *Dryopteris* can be separated into two basic groups. One group has blades that are once-cut into pinnae (pinnate), which are sometimes partially but not completely divided into pinnules (pinnate-pinnatafid). In the other group, sometimes called the "fancy fronds" group, at least the lower portion of the blade is twice-cut (pinnae fully divided into pinnules, or bipinnate), and in some species, the pinnules are also partially divided again (bipinnate-pinnatafid).

The shape of the basal (lowest) pinnae on the blade and the relative length of that pinna's inner pinnules are other important characters that distinguish *Dryopteris* species.

Hybrids. Some of the species described below are actually derived hybrids, now recognized as stable, fertile species. Most of these have four sets of chromosomes (tetraploid). Although new *Dryopteris* hybrids (usually sterile) are not common, 27 Wood Fern hybrids have been reported in our area. They are most frequently found where several species are growing near one another, often in woodlands with juxtaposed rocky slopes and low swampy areas, although hybrids may be found in the absence of either parent. The 2 most common ones are described at the end of the *Dryopteris* section but are not included in the key.

Sterile hybrids are often identified by examining the spores and sporangia of a plant. Most of these have unopened, empty, or shrunken (aborted) sporangia (which can be seen with a 10× hand lens) and misshapen, whitish spores (which need greater magnification). Plants of fertile species have uniform, plump spores when sporangia are mature, and open, empty sporangia after spores have been released. Both recent and derived hybrids tend to exhibit physical characters of both parents. For example, *Dryopteris* × *boottii* has the glandular hairs of its *D. intermedia* (Evergreen Wood Fern) parent, and the narrower blades and triangular lowest pinnae of its *D. cristata* (Crested Wood Fern) parent.

DRYOPTERIS KEY

1A. Fronds with aromatic glands (fruity fragrance), dense scales on underside of blade tissue; fronds usually less than 10 in. Old fronds persist at base for 2–3 years. Rare fern of cliff habitats.
D. fragrans (Fragrant Cliff Fern)

1B. Fronds without fragrant glands, few to no scales on blade tissue; fronds usually more than 10 in. Old fronds at base do not persist more than 1 year. Ferns of swamps, woods, and rocky habitats. Go to 2.

2A. Lower part of blade more than bipinnate (bipinnate-pinnatifid to almost tripinnate, i.e., pinnae divided into pinnules that are lobed or deeply lobed); pinnae margins have bristle-tipped teeth. Go to 3.

3A. Innermost lower pinnule of basal pinnae usually shorter than or equal to adjacent pinnule on same side of costa; costae, midribs, and indusia with glandular hairs. Evergreen. **D. intermedia (Evergreen Wood Fern)**

3B. Innermost lower pinnule of basal pinnae longer than or equal to adjacent pinnule on same side of costa; no glandular hairs. Deciduous late in the season. Go to 4.

4A. Innermost pair of pinnules of basal pinnae not quite opposite each other, with the lower one of the pair not much wider and 2 times the length of the opposite pinnule; blade length approx. 2 times its width. **D. carthusiana (Spinulose Wood Fern)**

4B. Innermost pair of pinnules of basal pinnae clearly not opposite (offset from each other), with the lower one of the pair twice the width and 3–5 times the length of the upper one; blade length approx. 1 ½ times its width (blade wider than *D. carthusiana*). Go to 5.

5A. Scales on stipe tan, sometimes with darker base but without central dark stripe; Appalachian Mts. north to ne. Canada.
D. campyloptera (Mountain Wood Fern)

5B. Scales on stipe tan with a dark central stripe; mostly northern and western edges of our range.
D. expansa (Northern Wood Fern)

2B. Lower part of blade pinnate to pinnate-pinnatifid to bipinnate (pinnae with lobes, deeply cut lobes, or pinnules); pinnae margins with or without bristle-tipped teeth. Go to 6.

6A. Sori very near margin; margins without teeth.
D. marginalis (Marginal Wood Fern)

6B. Sori between midrib and margin; margins toothed. Go to 7.

7A. Many scales of 2 distinct shapes—broad and hairlike; scales abundant on stipe, rachis, and costa; stipe less than $^1/_4$ of blade length; 20–30 pairs of narrow, long-pointed pinnae.   **D. filix-mas (Male Fern)**

7B. Scales broad to narrow, but not hairlike or of 2 distinct shapes; scales abundant only on stipe; stipe $^1/_4$–$^1/_3$ length of blade; 10–25 pairs of pinnae. Go to 8.

8A. Shape of basal pinnae ovate (egglike, widest near but not at base); scales at base of stipe dark brown with pale border or tan-brown with dark center; teeth mostly not bristle-tipped; blade ovate or lanceolate. Go to 9.

9A. Sori close to midvein; blade large and ovate, tapers abruptly at tip; scales at base of stipe dark brown with pale border. Upland habitat at base of slopes and talus.
D. goldiana (Goldie's Fern)

9B. Sori midway between margin and midvein; blade lanceolate, tapers gradually to tip; scales tan or brown with dark central stripe. Swamp habitat.   **D. celsa (Log Fern)**

8B. Shape of basal pinnae triangular (widest at base); scales at base of stipe light brown (scales on *D. clintoniana* sometimes with dark center); teeth bristle-tipped; blade lanceolate or with parallel sides. Go to 10.

10A. Pinnae of fertile fronds twisted to horizontal, like venetian blinds. Basal pinnae broadly triangular (approaching blunted equilateral triangle).   **D. cristata (Crested Wood Fern)**

10B. Pinnae of fertile fronds somewhat twisted, but approx. halfway to horizontal. Basal pinnae elongated triangular.
D. clintoniana (Clinton's Wood Fern)

3A. *D. intermedia*
(Evergreen Wood Fern)

4A. *D. carthusiana*
(Spinulose Wood Fern)

4B. *D. campyloptera*
and *D. expansa*

MOUNTAIN WOOD FERN

Dryopteris campyloptera (Kuntze) Clarkson

Synonyms: *Dryopteris spinulosa* (Muell.) Watt var. *americana* (Fischer ex Kunze) Fern.; *Dryopteris austriaca* (Jacq.) Schinz & Thellung.

HABIT: Widely arching crown of large, lacy fronds in cool, moist woods.

ECOLOGY: Cool, moist woods in the North, and at higher elevations farther south, where it is usually limited to mountain summits.

RANGE: Nfld. to e. Que., south to N.Y. and n. Pa., disjunct farther south in the Appalachian Mts. at higher elevations Va. to N.C.

FRONDS: 10–36 in. long. Sterile and fertile fronds similar; not evergreen.

BLADE: Oval-triangular, wider than other Dryopteris species, with rapidly narrowing tip; light green. Cut into 15–20 pairs of pinnae.

PINNAE: Lanceolate, pinnae surface parallel to plane of blade. Basal pinnae asymmetrically triangular, but not shorter than pinnae above.

PINNULES: Innermost, lower pinnule nearest to rachis on basal pinnae is not only much longer (3–5 times as long) but also twice as wide and offset (not directly opposite) from innermost upper pinnule on same pinnae. Toothed margins, with bristles on teeth.

RACHIS: Scaly.

STIPE: Scaly at base; scattered, brown scales above. $1/3$–$1/2$ length of blade.

RHIZOME: Dark brown, stout, creeping or semi-erect, many brown scales.

SORI: Prominent, halfway between midvein and margin. Indusium sometimes has a few glands.

NOTES: Best distinguished by the much longer, wider, offset inner, lower pinnules of the basal pinnae and the broadly triangular frond silhouette (much wider than similar *Dryopteris*). Perhaps think of the longer, lower pinnules as stakes holding down a tent when camping (for *campyloptera*). This species is derived from a cross between *D. expansa* (Northern Wood Fern) and *D. intermedia* (Evergreen Wood Fern).

MARGINALIA: *A. Pinnule with sori.*

DIAGNOSTIC ARROWS: *1. Wide triangular fronds. 2. Innermost pinnule of basal pinnae is wider and longer than the others. 3. Bristles on prominent teeth along margin.*

1.

2.

3.

A.

DRYOPTERIS CAMPYLOPTERA
MOUNTAIN WOOD FERN

SPINULOSE WOOD FERN
(Toothed Wood Fern)

Dryopteris carthusiana (Vill.) H. P. Fuchs

Synonyms: *Dryopteris spinulosa* (O. F. Müll.) Watt; *Dryopteris austriaca* (Jacq.) Schinz & Thellung. var. *spinulosa* (O. F. Müll.) Fiori

HABIT: Another large, lacy-cut, "fancy" fern. Tends to form clumps, because of short-creeping rhizome.

ECOLOGY: Often swamps, but also moist to wet woods, stream banks, moist wooded slopes. In soils that are mostly subacid.

RANGE: Nfld. south to S.C., west to Ark., north to N.D., across s. Canada. Also south into Wash., Idaho, Mont.

FRONDS: 8–30 in. long; 4–12 in. wide. Fertile fronds deciduous; sterile fronds may stay green into winter.

BLADE: Narrowly oval to triangular; nearly same width at base as middle of blade; often light to yellow-green; no glandular hairs; cut into 10–15 pairs of pinnae.

PINNAE: Lanceolate, often angled upward; lower pinnae asymmetrical elongated triangles; basal pinnae narrows rapidly from broad base, often slightly shorter than adjacent pinna.

PINNULES: Pinnules closest to rachis usually longest; innermost lower pinnule (closest to rachis) in basal pinnae twice as long as opposing (subopposite) upper pinnule. Fine-toothed margins with bristle tips that often curve inward (toward tip of pinnule).

RACHIS: Scattered pale brown scales.

STIPE: 2–12 in. long; stout, shorter than blade, pale brown scales at base and scattered above, $^1/_4$–$^1/_3$ of frond.

RHIZOME: Thick, coarse, scaly, short-creeping.

SORI: Small, midway between midvein and margin. Indusium without glands.

NOTES: Spinulose Wood Fern is a fertile tetraploid (4 sets of chromosomes), derived from a cross between *Dryopteris intermedia* (Evergreen Wood Fern) and an unknown parent. Easily confused with the former, Spinulose Wood Fern is less lacy, without glands on fronds or indusia, and not evergreen.

Best identifying characters are the longer, innermost lower pinnule of the basal pinnae and the fine, spine-tipped, toothed margins whose tips curve slightly toward tip of pinnule.

MARGINALIA: *A. Lowest pinna. B. Pinnule.*

DIAGNOSTIC ARROWS: *1. Longest inner pinnule of basal pinnae. 2. Spine-tipped, toothed margin. 3. No glandular hairs on blade.*

DRYOPTERIS CARTHUSIANA
SPINULOSE WOOD FERN

CLINTON'S WOOD FERN

Dryopteris clintoniana (D. C. Eaton) Dowell
Synonyms: *Dryopteris cristata* (L.) Gray var. *clintoniana* (Eaton) Underwood

HABIT: Narrow, erect, fertile fronds with pinnae widely spaced and somewhat tilting toward horizontal. Fertile fronds deciduous; smaller sterile fronds green through winter.

ECOLOGY: Swamps and wet woods.

RANGE: N.B. south to N.J., west to Ind., north to Ont. and Que.

FRONDS: 18–40 in. long; 5–8 in. wide. Fertile fronds taller, erect, narrow, not evergreen. Sterile fronds smaller, spreading, evergreen.

BLADE: Green, lanceolate with nearly parallel sides.

PINNAE: 10–15 pairs. Fertile pinnae twisted out of plane of blade but not fully parallel to ground; narrowly triangular; basal pinnae more triangular and slightly shorter than other pinnae.

PINNULES: Innermost pinnules longer than or equal to adjacent pinnules; lower innermost pinnule and upper opposite pinnule equal. Pinnule margins with bristle-tipped teeth.

RACHIS: Green, with only a few scales.

STIPE: 1/4–1/3 length of blade, scaly at base and scattered above; scales tan, sometimes with dark center.

RHIZOME: Stout, short-creeping, scaly.

SORI: Midway between midvein and margin. Indusia without glands.

NOTES: A naturally occurring fertile hybrid of *Dryopteris cristata* (Crested Wood Fern) and *D. goldiana* (Goldie's Fern). Similar to Crested Wood Fern, but basal pinnae of Clinton's Wood Fern are more narrowly triangular, fertile pinnae do not turn completely horizontal, and Clinton's Wood Fern is larger. Uncommon except locally (i.e., not common throughout its range, but fairly common within certain local areas), it prefers the same wet habitats as its Crested Wood Fern parent and damp pockets on rocky hillsides, like its Goldie's Fern parent.

MARGINALIA: *A. Basal pinnae.*

DIAGNOSTIC ARROWS: *1. Broader, taller fronds than Crested Fern with partially tilting pinnae. 2. Narrow triangular basal pinnae.*

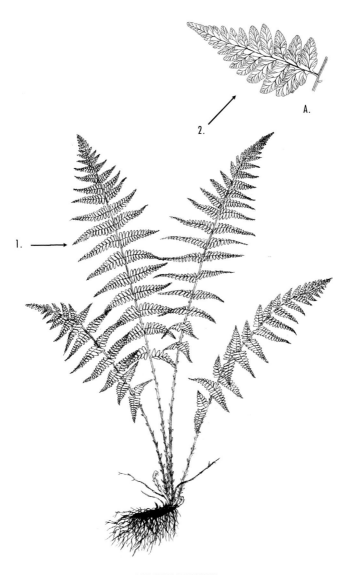

1.

2.

A.

DRYOPTERIS CLINTONIANA
CLINTON'S WOOD FERN

CRESTED WOOD FERN (CRESTED FERN)

Dryopteris cristata (L.) Gray

HABIT: Firm-textured, green to bluish green fern of damp woods. Narrow, erect fertile fronds with pinnae widely spaced and oriented horizontally.

ECOLOGY: Wet, swampy woods and shrubby open wetlands.

RANGE: Nfld. south to N.C. and Tenn., west to Iowa and Neb., and northwest into Sask., s. Alberta, s. B.C., with disjunct populations elsewhere. Also Europe.

FRONDS: 14–28 in. long; 3–5 in. wide. Fertile fronds taller, stiffly erect, narrow, not evergreen. Sterile fronds shorter ($^1/_2$–$^3/_4$ length of former), spreading, slightly broader than fertile fronds; evergreen.

BLADE: Narrow; sides almost parallel (middle to lower pinnae same length), tapering to blunt-pointed tip. No glandular hairs. Cut into 10–20 pairs of pinnae, basal ones slightly shorter.

PINNAE: Fertile pinnae distinctly oriented to a horizontal position (parallel to the ground). Lowest pair broadly triangular. Lower pinnae widely spaced. Pinnae toward tip of blade less triangular and closer together. Cut into 6 ± pairs of blunt-pointed lobes, some cut almost to costa. Serrated margins with bristle-tipped teeth only near lobe tip is distinctive and a clue for *D. cristata* hybrids.

RACHIS: Green, stout, slightly scaly on lower parts.

STIPE: 10 in. ± long. Many scattered, pale brown scales. $^1/_4$–$^1/_3$ length of blade.

RHIZOME: Dark brown, stout, creeping, many brown scales.

SORI: Prominent, halfway between midvein and margin on upper pinnae. Indusium not glandular.

NOTES: Readily identified by blunt, triangular basal pinnae; narrow, erect fertile fronds with pinnae like open venetian blinds (widely spaced and tilting toward horizontal); and smaller, glossy, spreading sterile fronds that remain green throughout winter. Crested Wood Fern is a fertile tetraploid species (4 sets of chromosomes) believed to have originated as a hybrid of *Dryopteris ludoviciana* (Southern Wood Fern) and an unknown diploid parent. Hybrid offspring of Crested Wood Fern tend to exhibit the narrow blades and triangular lowest pinnae of this species.

MARGINALIA: *A. Fertile pinna. B. Basal pinna. C. Sterile frond.*

DIAGNOSTIC ARROWS: *1. Narrow upright fertile frond with widely spaced and tilting pinnae. 2. Small triangular basal pinnae on fertile frond. 3. Smaller sterile fronds.*

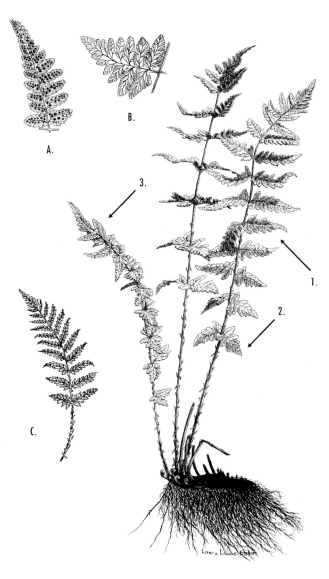

A.

B.

C.

3.

1.

2.

DRYOPTERIS CRISTATA
CRESTED WOOD FERN

MALE FERN

Dryopteris filix-mas (L.) Schott

HABIT: Upright, stately, dark green wood fern that forms a beautiful upright crown, often growing in clusters.

ECOLOGY: Cool, moist woods, talus slopes; mostly on limy soils in our area; in open rocky woods and granite talus in Rocky Mts.

RANGE: Greenland, Nfld. and N.S., south to mts. of Vt. and Me. Upper midwest, disjunct in Rocky Mts. from Tex. to Wash. and B.C. Rare in our area. Also Europe, Asia, and Africa, although these may actually be closely related but different species.

FRONDS: 10–40 in. long; 3–12 in. wide. Not evergreen.

BLADE: Ovate to narrowly lanceolate, semitapering to base, widest ⅓ up from base. Deep green when mature; firm to leathery texture. Cut into 20 ± pairs of pinnae.

PINNAE: Narrow, long-pointed; most are cut almost to midvein into 24 ± pairs of short, rounded lobes with slightly toothed margins.

RACHIS: Green, scaly beneath.

STIPE: 4 in. ± long; short (<¼ length of frond), stout; grooved, densely covered with 2 kinds of light brown scales—one broad and one hairlike.

RHIZOME: Thick, short, erect, very scaly.

SORI: Large, prominent, between midvein and margin, usually only on upper half of blade, near costa. Indusium often with small hairs on edges but no glands.

NOTES: Looks a bit like *Dryopteris marginalis* (Marginal Wood Fern), but stipe is shorter and stouter, and sori are not near the margin. Distinguishing characters of Male Fern are the two distinct types of scales on the short stipe and the leathery, long, narrow, pointed pinnae.

MARGINALIA: *A. Pinna. B. Sterile lobe.*

DIAGNOSTIC ARROWS: *1. Short stipe with 2 kinds of scale. 2. Slightly toothed pinna lobes. 3. Long, narrow, pointed pinnae.*

DRYOPTERIS FILIX-MAS
MALE FERN

FRAGRANT CLIFF FERN
(FRAGRANT WOOD FERN)

Dryopteris fragrans (L.) Schott

HABIT: Smallest wood fern, evergreen, with upright green fronds surrounded by gray-brown clump of old fronds persisting 2–3 years at base of plant. Usually small isolated plants.

ECOLOGY: Cool, shaded, often north-facing cliffs, rocky banks, and talus slopes, often in limestone. Rare, local, in northern areas of our range.

RANGE: Greenland to Me., west through N.Y. to Mich. to Minn., northwest into n. Alta. to Alaska. Also n. Europe, Asia.

FRONDS: 3–16 in. long. Evergreen.

BLADE: Narrowly lanceolate, with same width for most of blade, but narrowed at both base and apex; leathery texture; covered with glands on upper and lower surface that give off a sweet, fruity fragrance.

PINNAE: 1 in. ± long. 15–25 pairs, alternate to almost opposite; crowded to overlapping; margins often rolled under; lower surface usually covered by sori.

PINNULES: 6–10 pairs of pinnules. Innermost pinnules (closest to rachis) longer than adjacent ones, but upper and lower pinnules on pinnae equal. Margins with rounded teeth and no bristles.

RACHIS: With few to many scales; glandular.

STIPE: Short, up to ¹/₃ length of frond; covered with shining brown to reddish scales.

RHIZOME: Short and thick, nearly vertical; covered with brown scales and withered fronds of previous years.

SORI: Midway between midvein and margin. Very large, soon crowded and chocolate-brown, cover most of lower surface. Indusium glandular on margins.

NOTES: Easily identified by sweet, fruity fragrance; skirt of old brown fronds at base of clump; and being limited to cool, northern locations. Not closely related to any other *Dryopteris* species.

MARGINALIA: *A. Underside of fertile pinna. B. Sterile pinna.*

DIAGNOSTIC ARROWS: *1. Fruity fragrance. 2. Withered fronds of previous years.*

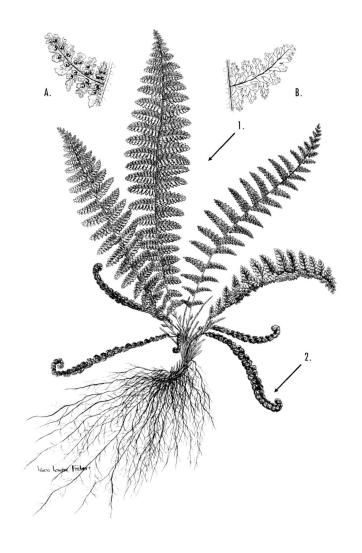

A.

B.

1.

2.

DRYOPTERIS FRAGRANS
FRAGRANT CLIFF FERN

GOLDIE'S FERN

Dryopteris goldiana (Hook.) Gray

HABIT: The giant of our wood ferns. Bright green fronds often have pale green tips, and the large, broad, arching fronds form dense clusters.

ECOLOGY: Rich soils of cool, moist woods throughout our area, especially ravines, talus slopes, limey seeps, and swamp edges.

RANGE: N.B. south to Va. and in Appalachian Mts. south to Ga., west to Mo., and north to Minn.

FRONDS: 14–47 in. long; 6–16 in. wide. Deciduous.

BLADE: Mostly oval with parallel sides and abruptly pointed tip. Green, often pale green toward blade tip. Cut into 12 ± alternate pairs of pinnae.

PINNAE: Lanceolate, broadest in middle with abruptly pointed tip and semitapered to rachis; short stalk. Basal pinnae 8 in. ± long.

PINNULES: 18 ± pairs; mostly opposite, with rounded and forward-pointed tips, margins slightly toothed at ends of veins.

RACHIS: Green, pale scales.

STIPE: Up to 16 in. long; thick, $^1/_3$ length of frond, grooved. Very scaly at base and scattered scales throughout. Scales long and pointed, glossy dark brown to black, with pale edges.

RHIZOME: Short, stout, semi-erect, very scaly.

SORI: Evenly spaced, near midvein. Indusium without glands.

NOTES: Distinguished by the large blade with abruptly pointed tip and glossy, distinctive scales with dark to rich brown center and pale to amber edge. Fiddleheads emerge wearing the same shaggy, glossy scales. Hybrids between Goldie's Fern and other species carry the dark color of the scales and the abruptly pointed blade tip.

MARGINALIA: *A. Pinna. B. Fertile pinnule showing veins and sori.*

DIAGNOSTIC ARROWS: *1. Blades tipping backward from stipe. 2. Long scaly stipes. 3. Large, broad blade with abruptly narrowing tip. 4. Sori near midveins. 5. Scales with brown center and pale edge.*

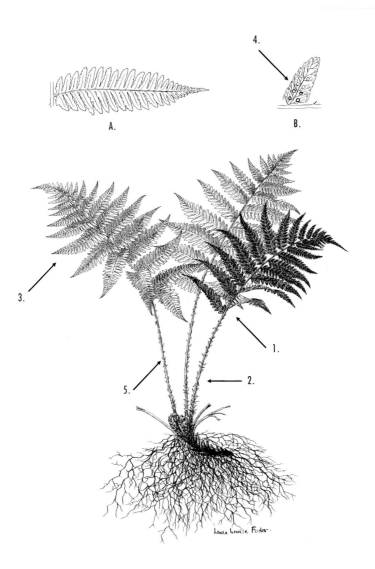

DRYOPTERIS GOLDIANA
GOLDIE'S FERN

EVERGREEN WOOD FERN (Fancy Fern)

Dryopteris intermedia (Muhl. ex Willd.) Gray

Synonyms: *Dryopteris spinulosa* (Mueller) Watt. var. *intermedia* (Muhl.) Underw.; *Dryopteris austriaca* (Jacq.) Woynar var. *intermedia* (Muhl.) Morton

HABIT: Evergreen, semi-arching, lacy-cut fern; its delicate green fronds rise in upright circular clusters from a central rhizome.

ECOLOGY: Moist or dry rocky woods, especially hemlock-hardwood forests; ravines, rock ledges, and edges of swamps. In soils rich in humus and subacid to almost neutral pH. Common.

RANGE: Nfld. south to N.C. and Tenn., southwest to n. Ala. at higher elevations, west to Mo., north to Minn. and s. Ont.

FRONDS: 13–35 in. long; 4–10 in. wide. Evergreen.

BLADE: Oval to narrowly triangular, middle to lower pinnae nearly same length; with glandular hairs mostly on rachis, costa, and indusia. Cut into 10–20 pairs of pinnae, primarily opposite.

PINNAE: Oblong, parallel sides for more than half of length, short stalks; extends out at right angles to rachis, but in same plane. Basal pinnae somewhat asymmetrically triangular, but same length as other pinnae. Costae have glandular hairs.

PINNULES: Innermost pinnules (closest to rachis) of basal pinnae slightly shorter or same length as adjacent pinnules on same side of costa; lower innermost pinnules in basal pinnae longer, but less than twice as long as upper innermost pinnules. Margins toothed, bristle-tipped. Pinnules on lower pinnae sometimes cut almost to center; the most dissected of the *Dryopteris* species.

RACHIS: With glandular hairs.

STIPE: ¼–⅓ of frond length, light brown scales at base of stipe, scattered above.

RHIZOME: Thick, coarse, scaly, erect.

SORI: Small, between midvein and margin. Indusia with glandular hairs most visible early in season, obscure later.

NOTES: The only lacy-cut fern that is fully evergreen. Its hybrids have distinctive glandular hairs on indusia and usually on costa. It is a progenitor of *Dryopteris carthusiana* (Spinulose Wood Fern) and *D. campyloptera* (Mountain Wood Fern).

MARGINALIA: *A. Basal pinnae. B. Pinnule and costa segment.*

DIAGNOSTIC ARROWS: *1. Glandular hairs on costa and rachis. 2. Shorter length of inner lower pinnule on basal pinnae. 3. Lacy, evergreen habit.*

A.

2.

3.

B.

1.

DRYOPTERIS INTERMEDIA
EVERGREEN WOOD FERN

MARGINAL WOOD FERN

Dryopteris marginalis (L.) Gray

HABIT: Leathery, evergreen, woodland fern growing in scattered individual clumps among roots and rocks. Upright fronds emerge from a base of withered, persistent fronds.

ECOLOGY: Abundant in rocky wooded slopes and ravines, edges of woods, and semishaded pockets of well-drained soil (acid, alkaline, or neutral).

RANGE: Greenland and Nfld. south to Ga. and Miss., west to Okla., north to Wisc. and Ont.

FRONDS: 12–39 in. long; 4–10 in. wide. Evergreen.

BLADE: Oblong; ascending and arching; leathery and evergreen; blue-green above, light green beneath. Cut into 15–20 pairs of pinnae.

PINNAE: Lance-shaped, widest at base, rapidly tapering to a point at tip; alternate to almost opposite; more widely spaced in lower portion of blade; wide-spreading with tips curving upward; with short stalk. Cut into 20 ± pairs of deeply cut lobes (pinnatifid) or pinnules on lower pinnae; blunt-tipped; margins entire or slightly lobed, not toothed; inner pinnule (next to rachis) usually longer than adjacent ones on same side of costa; inner, lower pinnule longer than opposing upper pinnule.

RACHIS: Pale, slightly chaffy underneath with smaller scales.

STIPE: $^1/_4$–$^1/_3$ length of frond. Swollen at base; stout, brittle, grooved in front; many long, bright golden-brown scales, particularly at base; some scales slender and in dense tufts like fur.

RHIZOME: Stout; ascending; shaggy with large golden-brown scales.

SORI: Near the margins; prominent; single or in well-spaced rows; dark brown when ripe in July or Aug. Indusium without glands.

NOTES: Easily identified by untoothed margin of pinnae lobes or pinnules, marginal sori, and its evergreen habit. Sometimes confused with *Dryopteris filix-mas* (Male Fern), but unlike Marginal Wood Fern, Male Fern sori are not marginal, and the lowest pinnae are much shorter than the middle pinnae.

MARGINALIA: *A. Sterile pinnule. B. Fuiting pinna.*

DIAGNOSTIC ARROWS: *1. Marginal sori. 2. Blunt pinnules. 3. Pinna rapidly tapering to point. 4. Chaffy stipe. 5. Withered old fronds.*

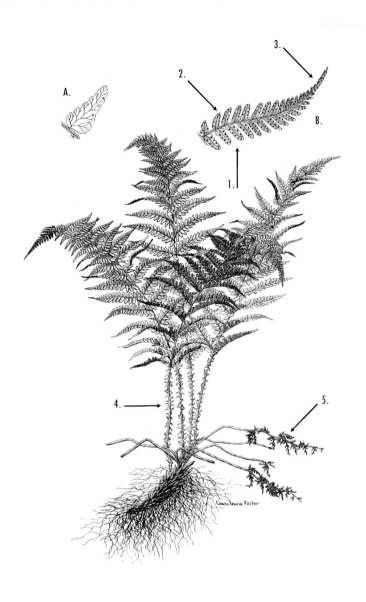

DRYOPTERIS MARGINALIS
MARGINAL WOOD FERN

BOOTT'S WOOD FERN

Dryopteris × boottii (Tuckerm.) Underw.

Common hybrid of *Dryopteris cristata* (Crested Wood Fern) and *D. intermedia* (Evergreen Wood Fern); similar to Crested Wood Fern with its triangular lowest pinnae and the pinnae of the fertile leaves somewhat twisted and parallel to the ground, like venetian blinds. Unlike Crested Wood Fern, it has glandular hairs on rachis, costa, and indusia, and its pinnae are more lacy-cut, like its Evergreen Wood Fern parent's. It is, however, variable in form between the two, sometimes being "lacier." Found in moist to wet habitats, often near Crested Wood Fern; may occur as a single plant or a larger group of plants.

LOG FERN

Dryopteris celsa (Palmer) Knowlton

A fertile tetraploid (4 sets of chromosomes) hybrid of *Dryopteris goldiana* (Goldie's Fern) and *D. ludoviciana* (Southern Wood Fern). Log Fern is somewhat similar to Goldie's Fern but has narrower, uniformly dark green blades that taper gradually to the tip and dark brown or tan scales with a dark central stripe. Occurs mostly in the Piedmont and coastal plain, from N.Y. to Ga., west to Ark. and Mo.

NORTHERN WOOD FERN

(SPREADING WOOD FERN)

Dryopteris expansa (C. Presl) Fraser-Jenkins & Jermy

Very lacy-cut, deciduous fern found in cool, moist woods and rocky slopes, mostly in ne. Canada and the Pacific Northwest. A progenitor of *Dryopteris campyloptera* (Mountain Wood Fern), which is much more common in our area. Very similar to Mountain Wood Fern but more erect, the scales have a dark stripe, and the basal pinnae are slightly smaller than Mountain Wood Fern's. Northern Wood Fern, however, grows only in the northern edges of our area.

TRIPLOID WOOD FERN

Dryopteris × triploidea Wherry

This hybrid of *Dryopteris carthusiana* (Spinulose Wood Fern) and *D. intermedia* (Evergreen Wood Fern) is quite common but difficult to identify because it is intermediate in form between its rather similar parents. Look for aborted sporangia and spores. Lower innermost pinnules on basal pinnae are nearly the same length as adjacent lower pinnules. Glandular hairs on rachis, costa, and indusia are less dense than on Evergreen Wood Fern. Plants may grow in the absence of either parent and may occur as individual plants or groups of plants.

Dryopteris filix-mas *(Male Fern) forms a beautiful upright crown. (Photo by William Cullina)*

The evergreen fronds of Dryopteris marginalis *(Marginal Wood Fern) are often found in well-drained soils of rocky woodlands. (Photo by Cheryl Lowe)*

Dryopteris × bootii

Dryopteris celsa *frond and basal pinnae.*

GENUS *GYMNOCARPIUM*: OAK FERNS

(Greek: *gymnos*, "naked," + *karpos*, "fruit"; referring to lack of indusia)

All oak ferns are small, delicate, triangular-leaved ferns of cool, shady habitats. Fronds arise from slender, widely creeping rootstocks, creating patches of cheerful spring greenery on the forest floor. The stipes are longer than the blade, and are fine, wiry, brittle, and smooth. Blades are deciduous, thin in texture, and appear to be divided into three triangular sections with prominent stems. Sori are round and have no indusia. Veins are simple or seldom forked and reach all the way to the margin.

There are 8 species of *Gymnocarpium*, 5 of them in North America. *Gymnocarpium dryopteris* (Common Oak Fern) is the only widespread species in our area. Three other species of *Gymnocarpium*, rare in our area, are only briefly described here.

GYMNOCARPIUM KEY

1A. Rachis and both surfaces of blade with few or no glandular hairs; two lowest (basal) pairs of pinnae nearly as long as terminal pinnae. Go to 2.

> **2A.** Second pair of pinnae (just above basal pinnae) usually sessile, their innermost basal pinnules equal to or longer than adjacent pinnules. Wide-ranging.
> **G. dryopteris (Oak Fern)**

> **2B.** Second pair of pinnae (just above basal pinnae) usually stalked, or if sessile, innermost basal pinnules shorter than adjacent pinnules. Very rare; restricted to central Appalachian Mts. **G. appalachianum (Appalachian Oak Fern)**

1B. Rachis and underside of blade surface with glandular hairs; two lowest (basal) pinnae not nearly as long as terminal pinnae. Go to 3.

> **3A.** Upper surface of blade with glandular hairs but many more on lower surface and rachis; basal pinnae ± perpendicular to rachis; restricted to cool northern limestone areas. **G. robertianum (Limestone Oak Fern)**

3B. Glandular hairs only on blade's undersurface; basal pinnae curve strongly toward blade tip; occasional on acid or neutral granite or shale in cool northern areas.

G. jessoense ssp. parvulum (Nahanni Oak Fern)

(Above) Gymnocarpium dryopteris *(Oak Fern) has delicate fronds on wiry stems. (Photo by Jean Baxter/NEWFS)* (Below) *Oak fern blades have three distinct sections. (Photo by Cheryl Lowe)*

Gymnocarpium dryopteris (L.) Newm.

HABIT: Small, delicate, bright lime green, triangular blades tilting almost to the horizontal. Emerge individually from a spreading rhizome; looks like a wavy carpet over the woodland floor. Produces new fronds all summer, maintaining a fresh, spring-green look.

ECOLOGY: Moist, subacid, shaded, rocky soil. Cool, coniferous, mixed woods, and at base of shale talus slopes.

RANGE: Across s. Canada and from Greenland south to Pa., west through W. Va. to Minn., disjunct populations in Rocky Mts. and Mont. west to Wash., north to Alaska. Also Europe, Asia.

FRONDS: 5–18 in. long; 4–10 in. wide. Deciduous.

BLADE: Broadly triangular, appearing 3-parted, each section with distinct stalks and each deeply divided.

PINNAE: Two lowest pinnae are opposite each other and only slightly shorter than apical section. Lower pinnae slightly asymmetrical, borne at right angles to stipe and lie almost parallel to ground; 6–12 pairs of opposite pinnules. Apical section is symmetrical and arches to horizontal, with 6–12 pairs of tapering, blunt-pointed pinnae cut into pinnules.

PINNULES: Pinnules of lowest pinnae cut almost or completely to midvein. Upper surface without glandular hairs; lower surface with few or no glandular hairs. Innermost pinnules of second pinnae pair (those just above large basal pinnae) are same length as adjacent pinnules.

RACHIS: Green, delicate; without glands or nearly so.

STIPE: 4–11 in. long. Longer than blade; sparse glandular hairs and scattered scales; slender, brittle, yellow-green, dark at base.

RHIZOME: Slender, black, scaly, long-creeping. Roots: Black, tiny, wiry, sparse.

SORI: Small, round, few, near margin; no indusium.

NOTES: Fiddleheads are a trio of small, green, delicate crosiers— one for each of the 3 sections of the blade. Produced all summer, they look like little green fists among fronds. Oak Fern is a fertile hybrid (tetraploid, with 4 sets of chromosomes) derived from *Gymnocarpium appalachianum* (Appalachian Oak Fern) and *G. disjunctum* (Western Oak Fern). It hybridizes with both parents, as well as with *G. jessoense* (Nahanni Oak Fern) and *G. robertianum* (Limestone Oak Fern).

MARGINALIA: *A. Underside of fertile pinnule.*

DIAGNOSTIC ARROWS: *1. Horizontal growth. 2. Triangular 3-part blade. 3. Fiddleheads of developing 3-part blade.*

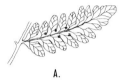

A.

GYMNOCARPIUM DRYOPTERIS
OAK FERN

APPALACHIAN OAK FERN
Gymnocarpium appalachianum Pryer & Haffler

pinnule

Very rare, limited to maple-birch-hemlock woods on mountain slopes and summits, on moist sandstone or talus slopes with cold air seepage in the central Appalachian Mts. (Md., Ohio, Pa., Va., W. Va., and N.C.). *Gymnocarpium appalachianum* (Appalachian Oak Fern) differs from *G. dryopteris* (Oak Fern) in having the basal pinnules of the second pair of pinnae (those just above the basal pinnae) distinctly shorter than the adjacent pinnules. As with Oak Fern, the stipe and blade of Appalachian Oak Fern are without glandular hairs.

NAHANNI OAK FERN
Gymnocarpium jessoense Koidzumi ssp. *parvulum* Sarvela

Rare in our area; grows on cool, granitic or shale talus slopes, from central to w. Canada south to n. Iowa and Mich., with disjunct populations in New England. Resembles *Gymnocarpium robertianum* (Limestone Oak Fern) but lacks glandular hairs on the upper surface of the blade, and the two basal pinnae are curved toward the tip of the blade (these pinnae are ± perpendicular to rachis in Limestone Oak Fern).

LIMESTONE OAK FERN
Gymnocarpium robertianum (Hoffmann) Newman

silhouette

Similar to *Gymnocarpium dryopteris* (Oak Fern) but rare in our area; found only in cool, northern limestone areas from Newfoundland to s. Ont., south to n. Iowa, Wisc., and Mich. Lower two triangular pinnae are noticeably shorter than apical section, so the fronds appear less like an equilateral triangle. Rachis is densely glandular, as are the upper and lower surfaces of blade.

Greek: *lugodes,* "flexible")

There are 39 species in this genus (in the family Schizaceae), most of which are tropical and subtropical. In our area, there is only 1 species in the genus, *Lygodium palmatum* (Hartford Fern). South of our area, *L. japonicum* escaped from cultivation many years ago and has spread to S.C. and westward to Tex.

Note the hand-shaped pinnules of Hartford
Fern, which is quite unlike any other "vine" in
our region. (Photo by Cheryl Lowe)

HARTFORD FERN (CLIMBING FERN)

Lygodium palmatum (Bernh.) Sw.

HABIT: More like a climbing vine than a fern. Long and slender twining rachis carries many pairs of little ivylike, palmate (hand-shaped) pinnules, deeply cleft into 3–7 blunt-tipped, wide-spreading lobes or "fingers."

ECOLOGY: In moist or wet acid soil rich in humus; in low thickets, open swamps, bog margins, and along banks of streams, and in ravines—often where mountain laurel grows. Likes a certain amount of sunlight, but must have wet feet.

RANGE: S. N.H. to e. N.Y., Ohio, south to Miss. Generally rare and local, except in Cumberland Plateau of Ky. and Tenn.

STERILE PINNULES: 2 in. ± long; 1½ in. ± wide. Hand-shaped, with 3–7 deep lobes round to pointed at tip; margins not toothed. Thin texture, lightly hairy on the upper surface, light green; evergreen until next year's growth. On separate wiry stalks 1 in. ± long.

FERTILE PINNULES: Borne only at tips of vine, which is several times branched. Also 5- to 7-fingered; hand-shaped. Smaller and more dissected, and more deeply or irregularly cut than sterile pinnules, and greatly constricted when in full fruit. Fertile pinnules not evergreen.

RACHIS: 48 in. or more long. Sinuous and branching. Grows individually from rhizome and branches aboveground, unlike most other ferns. Round, dark, shining black and slightly hairy at base, upper parts brownish or green and slightly flattened, sometimes with edges ridged. Wiry, brittle, and smooth throughout.

RHIZOME: Slender, cordlike, black, creeping below surface. Younger parts covered with bristly red hairs.

SORI: Each lobe of the fertile pinnule holds 2 rows of 6 ± egglike sporangia covered by indusium-like flaps of leaf tissue.

MARGINALIA: *A. Enlarged section of fertile pinna. B. Sterile pinnae. C. Fertile pinnae.*

DIAGNOSTIC ARROWS: *1. Vinelike growth form. 2. Fertile pinnae at top of "vine." 3. Five-fingered ivylike sterile pinnule.*

A.

B.

C.

1.

2.

3.

laura louise Foster

LYGODIUM PALMATUM
HARTFORD FERN

GENUS *MARSILEA*: WATER SHAMROCK

(Italian: named for Count Luigi Marsigli, a fungus specialist in Bologna)

There are more than 50 species of *Marsilea* throughout the world, but only 1 species, the aquatic *Marsilea quadrifolia* (Water Shamrock), is established in our area. This species was first introduced to this country from Europe into Bantam Lake, Litchfield Cty., Conn., in 1862. It has since multiplied profusely and spread to other New England and middle-western states. Though a native of Mediterranean climates, Water Shamrock grows as far north as Me., N.H., and Vt., where it tolerates thick ice and frigid water temperatures.

Water Shamrock grows in still, quiet, fresh waters. Its roots and often its rhizomes are anchored in the muddy bottom. Its blades, divided into 4 pinnae like a shamrock, are borne on single slender green stipes of lengths dependent on the mean depth of the water. The pinnae usually float at or just above the surface of the water, like small pond lilies. The aerial pinnae are broad and entire, while the submerged pinnae are narrower. The aerial pinnae of Water Shamrock also frequently fold up at night.

Like the other aquatic fern of our area, *Azolla caroliniana* (Mosquito Fern), Water Shamrock produces spores of two kinds: egg-bearing megaspores and sperm-bearing microspores. Unlike Mosquito Fern, the spores are held together in one or two hard-shelled, brown or purplish bean-shaped capsules (sporocarps) consisting of several compartments. When the spores are ripe and swollen, the capsule bursts open and expels the microspores. Each compartment is surrounded by a gelatinous ring, which holds the megaspore long enough for its egg to be fertilized by one of the many sperm newly released from the microspores.

Water Shamrock is an apt common name for Marsilea quadrifolia, *a unique cloverlike aquatic fern. (Photo by Cheryl Lowe)*

Marsilea quadrifolia *can spread rapidly to form dense masses on the surface of lakes and ponds. (Photo courtesy of NEWFS)*

WATER SHAMROCK
(WATER CLOVER; PEPPERWORT)

Marsilea quadrifolia L.

HABIT: Aquatic fern grows from roots embedded in bottoms of ponds and forms spreading colonies with pinnae floating above or just below surface of water. Fronds consist of a whorl of 4 (rarely 6) pinnae, resembling a shamrock.

ECOLOGY: Still bodies of fresh waters, usually lakes or ponds. Hardy and persistent once established.

RANGE: Me. south to Del., inland to Ky., Mo., Mich., Ont.

PINNAE: $1/2$–1 in. in diameter. Wedge-shaped with rounded outer edges, arranged in whorl like a four-leaf clover, smooth or sparsely hairy. Veins forked.

STIPE: Thin, green, 2–6 inches long depending on water depth. Very slender and often entwined with other water plants.

RHIZOME: Creeping along bottoms of ponds, lakes, or slow-moving streams.

SPOROCARPS: Borne singly or in pairs near roots, hard-shelled, beanlike in shape, $1/8$–$3/16$ in. long, covered with yellowish hairs when first forming.

MARGINALIA: *A. Top view. B. Sporocarps.*

DIAGNOSTIC ARROWS: *1. Shamrocklike cluster of 4 pinnae.*

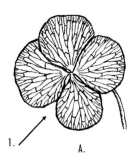

1.

A.

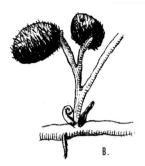

B.

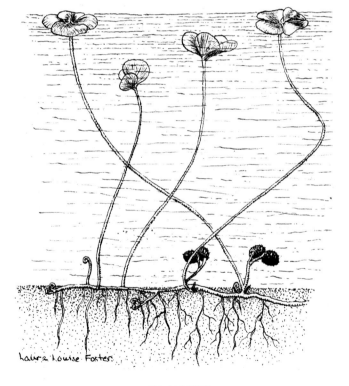

MARSILEA QUADRIFOLIA
WATER SHAMROCK

GENUS *MATTEUCCIA*: OSTRICH FERN

(Named in honor of Carlo Matteucci, an Italian physicist, 1811–1868)

A circumboreal genus with only 3 species, *Matteuccia* are large ferns and closely related to *Onoclea*. Plants in Europe and North America are considered different varieties of the same species. Ours is *Matteuccia struthiopteris* var. *pensylvanica* (Ostrich Fern). Fertile and sterile fronds are very different; the large sterile ones resemble ostrich feathers (the species name *struthiopteris* from Greek *struthos*, "ostrich," and Latin *pteris*, "fern," describes the shape of the frond). The fertile fronds persist through the winter, and sporangia release green spores early the following spring before new leaves emerge (when the wind can disperse spores easily).

Large, gracefully arching fronds of Matteuccia struthiopteris *(Ostrich Fern) in a garden. (Photo by Hal Horwitz/NEWFS)*

Unfurling fiddleheads of Ostrich Fern. (Photo by John A. Lynch/NEWFS)

Matteuccia struthiopteris (L.) Todaro var. *pensylvanica* (Willd.) C. V. Morton

HABIT: One of our largest ferns, a tall, erect, and gracefully arching fern growing in basketlike tufts of rich green, ostrich-plume fronds. Sterile fronds wither with first frost, but stiff, dark brown, compact fertile fronds remain through the winter.

ECOLOGY: Rich woods, stream banks, floodplains, swamps, and places with wet or damp soils.

RANGE: Nfld. south to Va., west to Mo., north through N.D., all across s. Canada.

STERILE FROND: 20–50 + in. long; 5–10 in. wide. Not evergreen.

STERILE BLADE: Oblong, widest near top, with rapidly pointed tip, gradually tapering toward base. Cut into 20–60 pairs of pinnae.

FERTILE FROND: 12–28 in. long. Emerges mid- to late summer.

FERTILE BLADE: Narrow, stiff, green at first, dark brown later. Shaped like a canoe paddle, cut into pinnae.

STERILE PINNAE: Long, narrow, pointed, alternate, slightly ascending in upper portion. Deeply cut into 20–40 pairs of lobes; veins not forked, extending to margin. Lower pinnae much smaller, and sometimes clasping the rachis.

FERTILE PINNAE: Contracted, curling around the sori, forming hard "peapods" 2 in. ± long, $^1/_3$ in. ± thick.

RACHIS: Green, stout. Sterile rachis with whitish hairs.

STIPE: 3–16 in. long. Much shorter than blade; rigid, stout, dark brown, deeply grooved at base with rounded back. Stipe of fertile frond is dark, stiff, erect, about same length as fertile blade.

RHIZOME: Stout, with erect, emerging symmetrical crown. Spreads by numerous underground long, slender runners.

SORI: On margins, hidden in rolled edge of peapodlike pinnae.

NOTES: Fiddleheads of this species are edible and often harvested for commercial sale. Ostrich Fern might be confused with the sterile fronds of *Osmunda cinnamomea* or *O. claytonia* (Cinnamon or Interrupted Fern), but very small pinnae at the base of the blade and ostrich-feather shape are distinctive.

MARGINALIA: *A. Sterile pinna with deeply cut lobes. B. Pinna of sterile frond. C. Podlike fertile pinnae. D. Detail of fertile pinna tip.*

DIAGNOSTIC ARROWS: *1. Arching basketlike growth form. 2. Runners.*

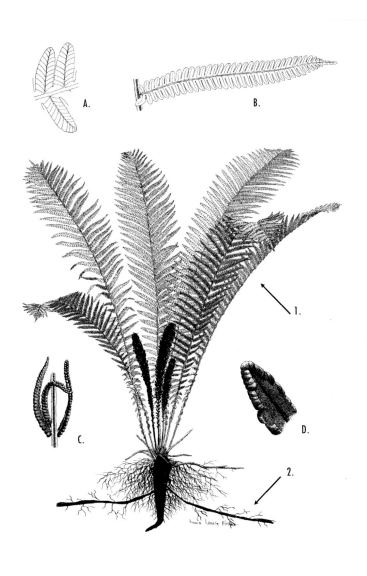

A.

B.

1.

C.

D.

2.

MATTEUCCIA STRUTHIOPTERIS
OSTRICH FERN

GENUS *ONOCLEA*: SENSITIVE FERN

(Greek: *onos*, "vessel," + *kleien*, "to close"; in reference to sori enclosed in rolled margins)

This genus, with only one species, is found in temperate regions of the Northern Hemisphere and Asia and is common in eastern North America. Description of the genus, therefore, is the same as for the species.

Onoclea sensibilis (Sensitive Fern) often forms large colonies; fronds emerge individually from a spreading rhizome. Sterile fronds have prominent netted veins. These fronds turn brown and die back with the first frost (thus, *sensibilis*, or sensitive), leaving only the erect, beadlike, fertile spikes. Like the related *Matteuccia* (Ostrich Fern), the fertile fronds of *Onoclea* persist through winter; sporangia release green spores early the following spring before new fronds emerge (when the wind can easily disperse spores). Fossils of this fern dating back more than 60 million years look remarkably similar to the plants of today, indicating they have survived quite unchanged since the Paleocene Epoch.

Sterile fronds of Onoclea sensibilis *(Sensitive Fern). (Photo by Cheryl Lowe)*

Note the prominent netted veins and wavy margins of Sensitive Fern. (Photo by David M. Stone/NEWFS)

SENSITIVE FERN

Onoclea sensibilis L.

HABIT: Sturdy, coarse fern with broad, almost triangular, fronds, forms colonies. Fronds emerge at irregular intervals, tilting toward the horizontal.

ECOLOGY: Open swamps, wet areas, marshes, or low woods, in sun or shade.

RANGE: Common. Nfld. west to s. Man., south to Fla., west to e. Tex., north to N.D.

STERILE FROND: 8–40 in. long. Not evergreen.

STERILE BLADE: Triangular, light grass green, scattered white hairs on undersurfaces. Cut into 12 ± nearly opposite pairs of pinnae.

FERTILE FROND: 10–20 in. long. Upright, compact. Produced midsummer to Oct., persistent through winter.

FERTILE BLADE: Numerous steeply ascending, very narrow pinnae. Sori in small, hard, beadlike divisions of fertile pinnae, at first green, dark brown when mature.

STERILE PINNAE: Opposite. Lower pairs widely spaced and tapering to rachis, lowest or next-to-lowest pair the longest. Upper pinnae often connected by wings of leafy tissue to rachis; little or no tapering toward rachis. Margins wavy, not toothed. Larger plants sometimes with strong indentations on pinnae margins. Veins depressed, prominent, and conspicuously netted.

RACHIS: Smooth, winged, glistening; pale tan or yellow.

STIPE: Usually longer than blade; yellowish, with thick brown base and a few scales.

RHIZOME: Stout, extensively creeping, forking near surface.

SORI: Completely enclosed by rolled edge of pinnae.

NOTES: Fiddleheads are a lovely pale red. Similar to *Woodwardia areolata* (Netted Chain Fern) with which it grows, but Sensitive Fern has opposite lower pinnae on the sterile fronds, and pinnae margins are not toothed. When plants have been mowed over or otherwise injured, emerging fronds are sometimes intermediate in form between fertile and sterile fronds.

MARGINALIA: *A. Netted veins. B. Beadlike fertile pinna.*

DIAGNOSTIC ARROWS: *1. Beaded fertile pinna. 2. Lower pairs of pinnae widely spaced. 3. Margins of sterile pinnae indented and wavy.*

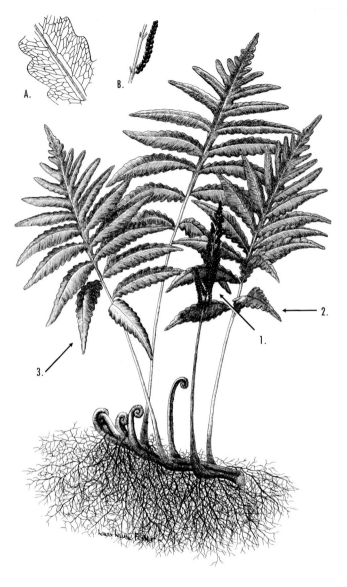

A.

B.

2.

1.

3.

ONOCLEA SENSIBILIS
SENSITIVE FERN

GENUS *OSMUNDA*: FLOWERING FERNS

(possibly from *os + mund,* Saxon for "god" and "protector," or from Latin *os + mundane* for "bone" and "to cleanse," in reference to medicinal uses)

The *Osmundas*, some of the largest of our native ferns, form beautiful circular clumps with the sterile fronds surrounding the more erect, fertile ones. They are extremely common and widespread, found most often in moist or wet places such as swamps, marshes, and moist forests. They are also among the first ferns to emerge in the spring, the crosiers covered with woolly white or reddish brown hairs. Fertile fronds emerge first.

The sporangia are one of the primary distinguishing characters of this ancient family and genus. Unlike most ferns, sporangia are not aggregated in distinct sori; instead they are individually attached and clustered on modified pinnae on the fertile fronds. Sporangia are large, spherical, thin-walled, with a poorly developed annulus, and are mounted on a short, stout stalk. When they are present, you can see them clearly with a good 10× hand lens. The sporangium opens through a long slit on the top, looking like Pac-Man on the attack. The empty sporangia turn a rich brown before disintegrating. Spores are green and short-lived, so they must be sown within a week or so after they ripen. The gametophytes are green and semi-heart-shaped, but longer and narrower than those of most other ferns.

Osmunda roots are numerous, black, very wiry, and tightly matted together. In older plants, the dense rhizomes may rise a foot or more above the ground, like the trunks of tree ferns. These matted masses of roots and rhizome are widely used in the culture of orchids. The fiddleheads, once considered edible, are now known to be carcinogenic.

Osmunda is a cosmopolitan genus, found in temperate and semitropical areas of the Americas, Europe, Asia, Africa, and New Zealand. In fact, *Osmunda regalis* (Royal Fern) may be the only vascular plant reported to grow on all seven continents. There are 3 species in our area, plus one unusual hybrid, named *Osmunda × ruggii*, which is the progeny of *O. claytoniana* (Interrupted Fern) and *O. regalis* (Royal Fern).

OSMUNDA KEY

1A. Sterile pinnae divided completely into widely spaced oblong stalked pinnules. Fertile pinnae at tip of blade.

O. regalis var. spectabilis (Royal Fern)

1B. Sterile pinnae lobed (divided almost to costa). Fertile pinnae either on separate fronds or limited to blade midsection. Go to 2.

2A. Sterile blade and pinna apices pointed (angle <40°); tufts of white to light brown hairs at base of pinna. Fertile frond completely different from sterile frond, very narrow and covered with sporangia.   ***O. cinnamomea* (Cinnamon Fern)**

2B. Blade and pinna apices blunt (angle >50°); few or no hairs at base of pinnae; fertile pinnae produced in midsection of leafy, fertile blade.   ***O. claytoniana* (Interrupted Fern)**

(Above) *Cinnamon wands, the fertile fronds of* Osmunda cinnamomea *(Photo by Cheryl Lowe) and* (top right) *the dark green fertile pinnae of* Osmunda claytoniana *(Photo by Arieh Tal) are gone by summer.* (Bottom right) Os-*munda* regalis *(Royal Fern) is found on all seven continents. (Photo by Cheryl Lowe)*

CINNAMON FERN

Osmunda cinnamomea L.

HABIT: Large, vigorous, clump-forming fern, arching in growth, with distinctive cinnamon-colored wands of fertile fronds in late spring.

ECOLOGY: Widespread in swamps, wet woods, wet meadows.

RANGE: Common from Nfld. south to Fla., west to e. Tex., north to Minn. and Ont. Also South America, Asia. Among most common and prominent ferns in our area.

STERILE FRONDS: 20–60 in. long or more in ideal growing conditions; mostly erect or arching.

FERTILE FRONDS: First to appear, and first to wither; 7–16 in. long, bright green at first, soon turning cinnamon-brown.

STERILE BLADE: Large, broadly lanceolate; cut into 20 or more pairs of pinnae, narrowing gradually to tip. Mostly smooth, but in spring covered with scattered tufts of wool.

FERTILE BLADE: Stiff, erect, narrow, pointed; all pairs of pinnae short (1–5 in.), narrow, steeply ascending (hugging close to main rachis).

PINNAE: Slender and oblong; narrowing gradually to tip; cut deeply into nonoverlapping lobes; opposite to alternate. Pale cinnamon wool tufts on underside at base near rachis. Veins forked 1–3 times.

RACHIS: Smooth, green; semigrooved in front; with scattered tan to pale cinnamon-colored wool during early part of the season.

STIPE: Smooth, green; covered with cinnamon wool at first, only a little remaining when mature. Slightly shorter than blade. Fertile fronds die back early summer; often found as withered entwining stalks covered with light cinnamon-tan wool, still holding rusty empty sporangia at the ends.

RHIZOME: Very stout; stubbly.

SORI: None. Naked sporangia large, short-stalked, in clusters; deep green when mature, turning golden-brown after dehiscing.

NOTES: Fiddleheads large and densely covered with silvery white hairs, which turn cinnamon-brown as fronds expand. Although this species might be confused with *Osmunda claytoniana* (Interrupted Fern), *Woodwardia virginica* (Virginia Chain Fern), or *Matteuccia struthiopteris* (Ostrich Fern), all of which occur in similar habitats, only Cinnamon Fern has the pale tan tufts of wool at the base of the pinnae (sometimes referred to as its "hairy armpits").

MARGINALIA: *A. Underside of sterile pinna. B. Fertile pinnae. C. Sporangia.*

DIAGNOSTIC ARROWS: *1. Woolly tuft at base of pinna. 2. Very narrow fertile frond. 3. Pointed tips of pinnae and frond.*

A.

B.

C.

1.

3.

2.

3.

OSMUNDA CINNAMOMEA
CINNAMON FERN

INTERRUPTED FERN

Osmunda claytoniana L.

HABIT: Large, coarse fern, arching in growth, with distinct interruptions in center of many fronds, caused by fertile pinnae.

ECOLOGY: Moist woods, ditches, swamp edges, wet or dry meadows. Often in fairly well-drained soils as well as wet areas.

RANGE: Nfld. south to Ga., west to Ark., north to Minn. and Ont. Also Asia.

FRONDS: 1–5 ft. long. Grows in arching form from a central crown; fertile fronds more erect; sterile fronds more arching and spreading.

STERILE BLADE: Large, coarse, elliptic; broadest in middle, blunt at blade apex (angle >50°). Covered in thick, white wool when first expanding, later smooth throughout. Cut into 10–20 pairs of pinnae.

FERTILE BLADE: More erect, taller, and often more numerous. Interrupted by 2–5 pairs of fertile pinnae in midsection of blade.

STERILE PINNAE: Narrow, lanceolate, broadest near rachis, tapering gradually to blunted tips. Lower pinnae below interruption are ascending, opposite, widely spaced, often much smaller than upper pinnae. Deeply cut into oval, blunt-tipped or rounded, semi-overlapping lobes. Young pinnae have light tan wool, soon lost. Veins forked once.

FERTILE PINNAE: 2–5 pairs of small pinnae in lower half of fertile blade. Dark green, densely covered with mature sporangia, later turning deep dark brown. Ripens and withers rapidly, leaving interrupted space in blade from early summer onward.

RACHIS: Smooth, green; semigrooved in front.

STIPE: With light brown hairs early, then becoming smooth; green; quite stout. Stipes of fertile fronds longer.

RHIZOME: Very stout; creeping; stubbly, with remnants of stipe bases.

SORI: None. Naked sporangia short-stalked, clustered; green at first, then dark brown.

NOTES: Fiddleheads are stout; very woolly, white to light tan; among earliest to appear in spring, and difficult to distinguish at this point from *Osmunda cinnamomea* (Cinnamon Fern). Once fertile fronds of the two species emerge, species are easily distinguished; but if fertile fronds are not present, only Cinnamon Fern has residual tufts of tan wool at base of sterile pinnae, and silhouette of both pinnae and blade tips taper to a narrower tip than those of Interrupted Fern. Named in honor of John Clayton, an early American botanist.

MARGINALIA: *A. Fertile pinna below sterile pinna. B. Deeply cut lobes of sterile pinnae showing veining and forward-pointing tips. C. Sporangia.*

DIAGNOSTIC ARROWS: *1. Interruptions. 2. Tall erect fertile fronds with widely spaced lower pinnae. 3. Smaller, arching sterile fronds.*

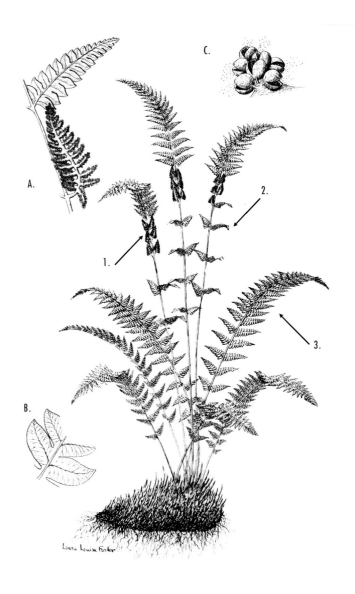

A.

B.

C.

1.

2.

3.

OSMUNDA CLAYTONIANA
INTERRUPTED FERN

ROYAL FERN (Flowering Fern)

Osmunda regalis L. var. *spectabilis* (Willd.) A. Gray

HABIT: At a distance, this large species is fernlike in appearance, but close up, it looks more like a locust tree or member of the pea family. Grows erect in a cluster. Foliage is a translucent pale green in sunlight, bright green with reddish stalks in less intense light.

ECOLOGY: Swamps, low woods, wet meadows, stream banks, marshes, bogs, usually in acid soils.

RANGE: Nfld. south to Fla., west to e. Tex., north to Minn. and Ont. and all seven continents.

FRONDS: 3 ft. ± long. Large, semicoarse, arching.

STERILE BLADE: Oblong, highly variable in size and silhouette; blade cut into 6 or more pairs of pinnae, which are cut into pinnules. Widely separated pinnae and pinnules give it pealike appearance.

FERTILE BLADE: Similar to sterile blade but with a very distinctive cluster of branched, light brown, sporangia-bearing pinnules at blade tips; these pinnules densely clustered and contracted.

PINNAE: 2–11 in. long. Oblong, ascending (angled toward tip of blade); subopposite and widely spaced. Cut into 8 or more pairs of widely spaced pinnules.

PINNULES: Narrow, oblong, ends blunt-tipped or rounded; bases rounded; small distinct stalks; mostly alternate. Pinnules near pinna tip are longer, often semi-eared; very variable. Veins forked; main vein distinct.

RACHIS: Slender, round; pale pinkish straw color to greenish.

STIPE: 8–20 in. long. Smooth, pinkish, reddish at base.

RHIZOME: Often 6 in. aboveground; semi-erect, covered with old stipe bases, typically forming a tussocklike base, deeply embedded in ground.

SORI: None. Naked sporangia, short-stalked, in clusters, bright green when ripe, becoming rusty then dark brown after opening.

NOTES: Fiddleheads are smooth, wine-colored, fairly stout; prominent in early spring. When in water "up to its knees" will reach heights of over 6 ft. "Royal Fern" easily remembered by "crown" of fertile pinnae at top of fertile fronds. Alternate common name is "Flowering Fern," referring to the "flowers" at the end of the fertile frond. The closely related *Osmunda regalis* var. *regalis* is found throughout Europe and Asia.

MARGINALIA: *A. Sterile pinna. B. Fertile pinna. C. Sporangia.*
DIAGNOSTIC ARROWS: *1. Fertile pinnae at top of frond. 2. Pinnae widely spaced and opposite. 3. Pinnules narrow, oblong, widely spaced, not opposite.*

3.

A.

B.

C.

1.

2.

OSMUNDA REGALIS
ROYAL FERN

GENUS *PELLAEA*: CLIFFBRAKES

(Greek: *pellos*, "dark"; referring to dark stalks)

The Cliffbrakes are small to medium-sized, rock-loving, often evergreen ferns. Many species have a stiff, dark or purple rachis that contrasts beautifully with the blue-green to gray-green foliage. Their rhizomes are usually embedded in cracks and crevices of dry, rock outcrops (mostly calcareous rocks in our area). Differences between sterile and fertile fronds are not pronounced, although sterile and fertile pinnae are somewhat different in growth and form. The margins of the fertile pinnules often roll over the sori, acting as false indusia; this curling under makes these pinnules appear narrower than the sterile ones.

In our area we have only 2 of the 40 or so species listed worldwide for the genus *Pellaea*. *Pellaea atropurpurea* (Purple-stemmed Cliffbrake) is one of the few northeastern ferns that has expanded its range northward and eastward into our area from its center of distribution in the southwestern U.S. Both *Pellaea* species in our area reproduce by apogamy (see Glossary); the sporophyte grows from an unfertilized gametophyte.

PELLAEA KEY

1A. Stipe and rachis without short, curly hairs; lower surface of pinnules with few or no hairlike scales.
P. glabella ssp. *glabella* (Smooth Cliffbrake)

1B. Stipe and rachis with short curly hairs on upper surfaces; lower surface of pinnules with scattered hairlike scales.
P. atrop urp urea (Purple-stemmed Cliffbrake)

(Above) *The wiry, reddish purple stipe and rachis of* Pellaea atropurpurea *have short, curly hairs.* (Below) *those of* Pellaea glabra *are smooth and without hairs.* (*Photos by Arthur Haines*)

PURPLE-STEMMED CLIFFBRAKE

Pellaea atropurpurea (L.) Link

HABIT: Stiff, wiry fern growing in clumps, widely arching fronds with lustrous purple stipe and rachis, and narrow bluish gray-green blades. Evergreen in many areas.

ECOLOGY: Crevices of dry and exposed limestone cliffs and rocky slopes; also on mortared walls in some regions. Rare in our area.

RANGE: S. Que. and Ont. south to n. Fla., west to Nev., north through Wyo., and east to Minn. Also Central America.

FRONDS: 2–18 in. long; 1½–7 in. wide. Clustered; sterile fronds shorter and less divided.

BLADE: Elongated-triangular to lanceolate; variable, with 5–11 mostly opposite pinnae; leathery, dull blue-green.

PINNAE: Lance-shaped to long and narrow; upper ones undivided, lower ones divided into 3–15 pinnules; perpendicular to rachis or angled toward tip of blade; margin inrolled on fertile pinnae; veins forked.

PINNULES: Oval to lanceolate, sometimes with 1 or 2 basal lobes.

RACHIS: Reddish purple throughout; short, curly appressed hairs on upper surface.

STIPE: About half as long as blade; wiry, dark reddish purple to nearly black; curly, appressed hairs like those on the rachis (these sometimes disappear with age).

RHIZOME: Very short, erect or ascending, densely covered by tangle of narrow brown scales.

SORI: Borne beneath margins of fertile pinnae or pinnules; pale brown. No true indusium. Spores mature mid-summer.

NOTES: This species, unlike *Pellaea glabella* ssp. *glabella* (Smooth Cliffbrake), has an abundance of short, curly hairs on stipe and rachis and scattered hairlike scales on underside of blade. Although sometimes mistaken for *Cryptogramma stelleri* (Slender Cliffbrake), Purple-stemmed Cliffbrake is easily distinguished from that species by the larger, closely spaced fronds; leathery pinnules (rather than fragile and somewhat translucent ones); and hairy stipes and rachis. It also occupies drier habitats than *C. stelleri.*

MARGINALIA: *A. Fertile pinna showing rolled-in edges covering sori.*

DIAGNOSTIC ARROWS: *1. Stiff, wiry purple stipe and rachis. 2. Lanceolate pinnules. 3. Short curly hairs on stipe and rachis.*

PELLAEA ATROPURPUREA
PURPLE-STEMMED CLIFFBRAKE

SMOOTH CLIFFBRAKE

Pellaea glabella Mettenius ex Kuhn ssp. *glabella*
Synonyms: *Pellaea atropurpurea* (L.) Link var. *bushii*

HABIT: Tufts of stiff, wiry, bluish gray-green fronds with smooth, reddish brown stipes and rachises emerge from rocks and ledges. (*Glabella* means "smooth.") Evergreen in many areas.

ECOLOGY: Shady cliffs, ledges, and rocky slopes, mostly limestone but also sandstone and shale.

RANGE: S. Que. and Ont. south to Va. and Tenn., west to Ark., e. Kans., and north to Minn.

FRONDS: 4–16 in. long; 1–3 in. wide. Clustered; sterile and fertile fronds similar in shape, but sterile ones shorter and less divided.

BLADE: Narrowly oblong; cut into 5–10 mostly opposite pinnae; leathery, blue-green.

PINNAE: Lanceolate to long and narrow; upper ones not divided, lower ones divided into 1–5 pinnules; somewhat angled toward tip of blade; margin inrolled on fertile pinnae; veins forked.

PINNULES: Oval to lanceolate, sometimes with 1 or 2 basal lobes; underside of some pinnules have 1–2 hairlike scales along midrib.

RACHIS: Brown throughout, smooth or with only a few hairs or scales.

STIPE: Wiry, shiny, dark reddish brown; about half as long as blade; smooth or with only a few hairs or scales.

RHIZOME: Short, ascending, with narrow reddish brown scales.

SORI: Borne beneath inrolled margins of fertile pinnae or pinnules; no true indusium.

NOTES: Usually smaller than *Pellaea atropurpurea* (Purple-stemmed Cliffbrake), with few hairs or hairlike scales. Smooth Cliffbrake includes four geographically isolated and genetically different subspecies; only the one described here grows in our range.

MARGINALIA: *A. Fertile pinna showing rolled-in edges covering sori.*
DIAGNOSTIC ARROWS: *1. Stipe and rachis smooth, shiny, reddish brown.*
2. Lower pinnae nearly same length as upper pinnae.

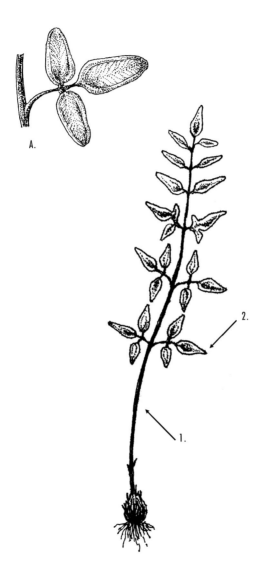

A.

PELLAEA GLABELLA
SMOOTH CLIFFBRAKE

GENUS *PHEGOPTERIS*: BEECH FERNS

(Greek: *phegos*, "beech," + *pteris*, "fern")

Closely related to the genus *Thelypteris*, this genus contains only 3 species worldwide, 2 of which occur in more northern parts of our region; the other occurs in Asia. Until recently the species of *Phegopteris* were placed in *Thelypteris*, but they differ from *Thelypteris* species in having wings along the rachis and not having indusia. Although the fronds of these species emerge late in spring, they do produce fronds all summer.

PHEGOPTERIS KEY

1A. No winged tissue on rachis between lowest 2 pairs of pinnae although upper pinnae may be somewhat winged or fused; lowest pinnae are distinctly angled downward.
P. connectilis (Narrow Beech Fern)

1B. Rachis with winged tissue between pinnae; lowest pinnae are longest; the lowest pair of pinnae are not angled downward or only slightly downward. **P. hexagonoptera (Broad Beech Fern)**

Phegopteris connectilis (*Narrow Beech Fern*) has narrow, tapered fronds. (*Photo by Cheryl Lowe*)

Narrow Beech Fern

Broad Beech Fern

Phegopteris hexagonoptera (*Broad Beech Fern*) *has robust lower pin-nae.* (*Photo by Cheryl Lowe*)

NARROW BEECH FERN
(NORTHERN BEECH FERN)

Phegopteris connectilis (Michaux) Watt
Synonyms: *Thelypteris phegopteris* (L.) Slosson

HABIT: A spreading, light green fern with narrow triangular fronds. Where it grows on cliffs, the fronds grow "drippingly" downward. *Connectilis* refers to the fact that the upper pinnae essentially fuse toward the long-tapering frond tip.

ECOLOGY: Wet, rocky pockets near cool, running water; often under small waterfalls. Also in acid soils on cliffs, in ravines, on shaded banks along streams and brooks, or in colonies in the semishade of rich, moist woodlands.

RANGE: Greenland west to Alaska and Wash., south to Tenn., west to Ind., Iowa, and Mich. Also n. Europe, Asia. A much wider, more northern range than Southern Beech Fern (*P. hexagonoptera*). Common in northern regions, less common along the mid-Atlantic coastal areas.

FRONDS: 6–14 in. long. Sterile and fertile fronds the same shape and size.

BLADE: 4–8 in. wide. Sometimes tilts backward; yellow-green, narrowly triangular with rapidly tapering tip; often hairy above and beneath. Cut into 12 ± pairs of nearly opposite, sessile pinnae.

PINNAE: Quite narrow, with long, pointed tips. All but lowest pair semitapered to rachis. Lowest pair of pinnae characteristically angled downward and distinctly spaced from next upper pair; lowest pinnae tapered at both ends; not significantly longer than other pinnae. Cut almost to costa into 18 ± rounded lobes with hairy margins. Costa and veins hairy, with tan to brown scales. Veins forked.

RACHIS: Green, scaly, hairy above and beneath; not winged adjacent to lowest pinnae.

STIPE: 6–14 in. long. Straw-colored; slender, scaly, hairy; variable in length, but usually about ⅓ longer than the blade.

RHIZOME: Slender, black, scaly, branching, creeping.

SORI: Small, round, near margins at ends of veins. No indusium.

MARGINALIA: *A. Double-tapering basal pinna. B. Fertile pinnule with sori.*

DIAGNOSTIC ARROWS: *1. Rapidly tapered pointed tips. 2. Downward-pointing lowest pinnae. 3. Free space on rachis between lowest pinnae and next upper pinnae.*

A.

B.

1.

2.

3.

PHEGOPTERIS CONNECTILIS
NARROW BEECH FERN

BROAD BEECH FERN (Southern Beech Fern)

Phegopteris hexagonoptera (Michx.) Fée
Synonym: *Thelypteris hexagonoptera* (Michx.) Nieuwland

HABIT: Larger and more erect of the two Beech Ferns. *Hexagonoptera* refers to the angular appearance of its winged rachis.

ECOLOGY: Prefers moist, rich, moderately acid to more alkaline woodland soils.

RANGE: Throughout our area, but more southerly of the two Beech Ferns, extending from N.B. and Que. to Fla. and Tex., inland to Mich.

FRONDS: 7–17 in. long. Sterile and fertile fronds the same shape and size.

BLADE: 6–13 in. Usually as broad or broader than long, distinctly triangular with the longest pinnae near the base. Tilts backward; slightly hairy, dull green. Cut into 12 ± almost opposite pairs of pinnae.

PINNAE: Double-tapered, widest at about middle. Deeply cut almost to the rachis, but pinnae are connected along the rachis by winged tissue. Two lowest pairs largest, broadest-spreading, and usually more distantly spaced from the next set of pinnae, with the rachis between broadly winged. Cut almost to costa into 20 ± blunt-pointed lobes often with distinctly lobed margins. Veins often forked. Straight hairs on costa, some veins, and margins.

RACHIS: Green, winged throughout, with whitish scales.

STIPE: 6–16 in. long. Slightly longer than blade; slender, straw-colored, smooth above, darker and slightly scaly (with tan scales) and hairy at base.

RHIZOME: Slender, very scaly, black, widely creeping, branching.

SORI: Small, round, scattered in a single row near margins just before the end of the vein. No indusium.

NOTES: The closely related *Phegopteris connectilis* (Narrow Beech Fern) does not have a winged rachis between lowest 2 pairs of pinnae.

MARGINALIA: *A. Upperside of lowest pinna, showing double-tapering and winged rachis. B. Lobe of fertile pinna and scattered sori.*

DIAGNOSTIC ARROWS: *1. Tilting frond growth. 2. Lowest pinna winged at rachis. 3. Pinna lobes have distinctly lobed margins.*

A.

3.

B.

2.

1.

PHEGOPTERIS HEXAGONOPTERA
BROAD BEECH FERN

GENUS *PLEOPELTIS*: SHIELD-SORUS FERNS

(Greek: *pleos,* "many," + *pelte,* "shield"; referring to the shieldlike scales that cover sori)

This genus contains some 50 species, the majority confined to the New World tropics. Some species, known as the scaly polypodies, have been recently moved from the genus *Polypodium* into the genus *Pleopeltis.* This group includes the Resurrection Fern, which is common along the southern boundary of our area.

RESURRECTION FERN (Gray's Polypody)

Pleopeltis polypodioides (L.) E. G. Andrews & Windham var. *michauxiana* (Weatherby) E. G. Andrews & Windham
Synonym: *Polypodium polypodioides* (L.) Watt var. *michauxianum* Weatherby

HABIT: Forms large, matlike colonies. Curls up, appearing dead, in drought.

ECOLOGY: Stumps, fence posts, old wooden buildings, branches of live oaks, magnolias, and elms, with Spanish Moss (*Tillandsia* spp.).

RANGE: Common throughout se. quarter of U.S., from Md. west to Kans. and south to Tex. and Fla. Also through Central America.

FRONDS: To 10 in. ± long. Taller leaves are erect or spreading, smaller leaves often prostrate.

BLADE: Narrowly triangular to oblong, longer than wide, leathery, densely scaly below, deeply dissected into 6–12 pairs of straight, oblong pinnae.

PINNAE: Narrow, rounded tips, wavy edges, undersurfaces pale grayish green; pointed gray scales with dark reddish brown centers; veins obscure, forked; sometimes netted. Fertile pinnae with prominently raised bumps from the embedded sori.

RACHIS: Upper surface green and smooth; undersurface pale grayish green, some scales.

STIPE: About $^1/_3$ ± length of blade, slender, round; upper surface grooved, densely scaly; swollen at base where it joins rhizome.

RHIZOME: Slender, cordlike, horizontally creeping, scaly.

SORI: Small but prominent, round, usually in one row on either side of the pinna midrib, often obscured by grayish scales. More numerous on upper pinnae; outlines appear as raised bumps on upper side of pinnae. Indusium absent.

MARGINALIA: *A. Dry blade curled. B. Underside of scaly pinna. C. Upperside of pinna showing sunken midrib and raised dots from sori.*
DIAGNOSTIC ARROWS: *1. Chaffy stipes. 2. Dark-centered, pointed scales below.*

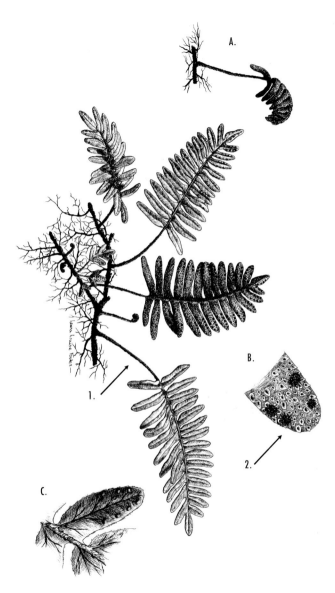

A.

B.

C.

1.

2.

PLEOPELTIS POLYPODIOIDES
RESURRECTION FERN

GENUS *POLYPODIUM*: POLYPODIES

(Greek: *polys*, "many," + *pous*, "foot"; referring to the many knoblike appendages remaining on the rhizome after the leaves are shed)

This genus has undergone taxonomic revision due to recent genetic studies. Formerly thought to include over 1,000 species, the genus now encompasses about 100 species worldwide. With the transfer of *Polypodium polypodioides* to the genus *Pleopeltis*, there are just two species indigenous to the northeastern United States: *Polypodium virginianum* (Rock or Common Polypody), and *P. appalachianum* (Appalachian Polypody). Appalachian Polypody is a recently described, diploid species (with 2 chromosome sets), whereas Common Polypody is a tetraploid species (4 sets). Common Polypody arose from hybridization between Appalachian Polypody and a species from northwestern Canada, *P. sibiricum* (Siberian Polypody). Common Polypody and Appalachian Polypody can hybridize, creating a sterile, triploid hybrid (3 chromosome sets) known as *Polypodium × incognitum,* the characteristics of which are intermediate between its parents; it often has misshapen sori.

The Polypodies are evergreen and grow in dense colonies that scramble around rocks. Though they may wither in a drought, they promptly become green again after exposure to moisture. Their leathery blades are cut into narrow, blunt-tipped lobes. Fertile and sterile fronds do not differ in form. The sori are round, naked, and prominent. The rhizome is horizontally creeping and scaly.

POLYPODIUM KEY

1A. Blades widest just above base; lobes with narrowed tips; scales on rhizome uniformly golden brown.
>>> ***P. appalachianum* (Appalachian Polypody)**

1B. Blades widest near the middle; lobes with blunt tips; scales on rhizome of two shades of brown.
>>> ***P. virginianum* (Common Polypody)**

Polypodium virginianum *(Common Polypody) tucked into a rock crevice.*
(Photo by Cheryl Lowe)

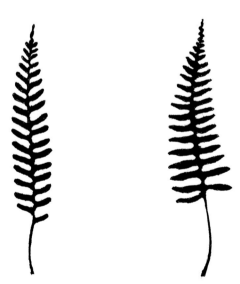

Silhouette of Common Polypody   Silhouette of Appalachian Polypody

COMMON POLYPODY

Polypodium virginianum L.

Synonym: *Polypodium vulgare* L. var. *virginianum* (L.) D. C. Eaton

HABIT: Thoreau refers to the "fresh and cheerful communities" of the Polypody in early spring that form a lustrous mantle over rocky surfaces. This common, evergreen, and vigorous fern greens up the rugged contours of rocky woods, even in winter.

ECOLOGY: Abundant throughout the area at all altitudes where rocks and cliffs provide semishaded surfaces with rich, often very shallow, subacid soil. Most luxuriant in cool damp shade on (often north-facing) rocks along watercourses. Also grows on stumps or old logs or in tiny cracks in cliffs.

RANGE: Greenland and Nfld. south to Ga., Tenn., and Ark., north through Ky. and Minn. to Alta. and N.W.T.

FRONDS: To 16 in. ± long (often shorter). Variable in form; taller fronds erect and spreading, lower fronds spreading, small young fronds often prostrate.

BLADE: Leathery; deep green on both sides, often lustrous above; to 3 in. wide, oblong to lanceolate, widest near the middle; cut almost to rachis into 10–20 pairs of lobes, which are smooth, mostly alternate, and entire or with tiny, rounded teeth. Lowest pair of lobes usually smaller than middle pairs. Upper lobes blunter, diminishing evenly and rapidly in size to a prominent tip at end of blade. Veins obscure, forked.

RACHIS: Smooth, green, slender, sparsely scaly. Appears sunken below plane of blade's upper surface, slightly raised on undersurface.

STIPE: Up to ⅓ length of blade. Slender, round, smooth, light dull green, sometimes with sparse, narrow, brownish scales. Swollen at base where attached to rhizome.

RHIZOME: Horizontal, widely spreading and creeping, often with a whitish bloom; produces linear rows of fronds. Slender; densely covered with scales in two shades of brown. Often scarred from broken-off, withered remnants of stipes; sometimes exposed at the surface of shallow soils.

SORI: Large, round, pale brown; in rows on either side of the midvein or scattered; more numerous on upper pinnae. Often merge into one another at maturity, releasing spores in autumn, but often obvious all year. Indusium absent.

MARGINALIA: *A. Undersurface of lobe.*

DIAGNOSTIC ARROWS: *1. Slender, smooth green stipe. 2. Blunt-tipped leathery lobes; green and smooth on both sides. 3. Lobes winged at rachis.*

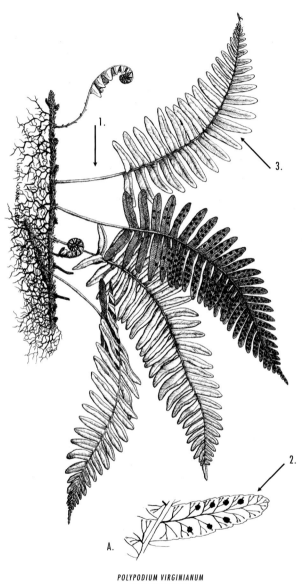

1.

3.

2.

A.

POLYPODIUM VIRGINIANUM
COMMON POLYPODY

APPALACHIAN POLYPODY
Polypodium appalachianum Haufler & Windham

Often called the "rock cap fern" because it densely festoons rock surfaces, this polypody resembles *Polypodium virginianum* (Common Polypody) in most features, forming dense, creeping, evergreen colonies. It differs from Common Polypody in having blades (to 14 in. long) widest near the base, lobes with narrowed tips, and uniformly colored, golden-brown rhizome scales. It usually grows on cliffs or rocky slopes on diverse types of bedrock, although it has been seen growing high in the canopy of a tulip tree. It ranges from N.B. to Nfld. through New England and N.Y. south to Ga., Tenn., and Ala., north through Ky. and Ohio to Que.; a narrower, more easterly range than Common Polypody. Misshapen spores may indicate a hybrid of Appalachian Polypody and Common Polypody.

(Left) *The frond of* Polypodium virginianum *is evenly wide.*
(Above) *The frond of* Polypodium appalachianum *(Appalachian Polypody) is widest at the base.*
(*Photos by Arthur Haines*)

GENUS *POLYSTICHUM*: HOLLY FERNS

(Greek: *polys*, "many," + *stichos*, "rows"; referring to rows of sori common in this genus)

Polystichum species are sturdy, mostly evergreen ferns. It is a large genus of approximately 260 species, with at least half of the species in tropical zones; 15 species grow in North America, 3 of them in our area. Two species, *Polystichum acrostichoides* (Christmas Fern) and *P. braunii* (Braun's Holly Fern), are well established in our area. The more common is Christmas Fern, which is quite tolerant of a range of soil pH. Plants of this species may also be highly variable in form, with unusual extra lobes or twisted pinnae. These forms are often seen in the horticulture trade. Braun's Holly Fern, on the other hand, is limited in our area to more calcareous soils with a pH near neutral and is fairly stable in growth form. *P. lonchitis* (Northern Holly Fern) grows mostly north and west of our region.

The narrow fronds of *Polystichum* emerge in bouquetlike clusters, with short, stout, and scaly stipes. Pinnae and pinnules are shiny, lustrous green, with bristle-toothed edges. Rhizomes are short, stout, and very scaly. The indusium is round, with its center attached to the pinna like a shield. As the sori grow, the indusium becomes funnel-shaped, then tubular, and finally disappears in certain species as the underside of the pinna becomes completely covered by sori. Fertile pinnae of *Polystichum* species are usually the same shape as the sterile pinnae. The most common species in our area, Christmas Fern, is unusual—in this species, the fertile pinnae are usually narrower, especially when heavy with maturing sori.

POLYSTICHUM KEY

1A. Pinnae divided into pinnules in lower part of blade; fertile pinnae similar to sterile ones; sori do not completely cover lower surface of fertile pinnae when mature.

P. braunii (Braun's Holly Fern)

1B. Pinnae not divided into pinnules. Go to 2.

2A. Upper, fertile pinnae similar to sterile ones; sori often distinct when mature; lowest pinnae triangular; in our region, only in n. Mich.

P. lonchitis (Northern Holly Fern)

2B. Upper, fertile pinnae noticeably narrower and smaller than lower, sterile pinnae; sori completely cover lower surface of fertile pinnae when mature.

P. acrostichoides (Christmas Fern)

Polystichum acrostichoides (Michx.) Schott

HABIT: Lustrous, dark green fronds in circular, arching clumps from central rhizome. Upper portions of fertile fronds distinctly smaller and narrower. In winter, sterile fronds and nonfertile portions of fertile fronds stay evergreen, though often somewhat flattened by snows, a welcome sight in winter woods.

ECOLOGY: Woodlands and shady, rocky slopes, moist to moderately dry sites. Common.

RANGE: N.S. to s. Ont., south to Fla., west to e. Tex., north to Minn.

FRONDS: 12–32 in. long; 1½–5 in. wide. Fertile fronds taller, more rigid, more erect; only upper portion bears spores.

BLADE: Leathery; lance-shaped and rapidly tapering upward from middle. Surface smooth on upper side, with linear scales (some hairlike) on underside. Cut into 20–40 pairs of pinnae.

PINNAE: Lance-shaped with 1 distinctive basal lobe, or "ear," on upper side of pinna (resembling the "toe" on a Christmas stocking); edges bristle-tipped with teeth curving upward. Two lowest pinnae almost opposite and sometimes angled downward; middle and upper pinnae alternate; fertile pinnae smaller. Veins forked, reaching the margin.

RACHIS: Green, very scaly.

STIPE: ¼–⅓ length of blade; brown at base, green above; scales dense, light brown, and smaller farther up the stipe.

RHIZOME: Short, creeping to erect; very scaly.

SORI: Numerous, oblong (not typical for the genus), in 2 or more rows along midvein; crowded and often covering back of pinnae completely when ripe; tan-colored; indusium circular, attached at center, disappears with age.

NOTES: Fiddleheads are scaly and stout, with silvery white scales, very prominent in early spring especially when surrounded by last year's prone but still evergreen leaves. It is possible to confuse this species with *Diplazium pycnocarpon* (Narrow-leaved Glade Fern), but pinnae of Christmas Fern are leathery and dark green, and have the distinctive "ear." Christmas Fern hybridizes with *Polystichum braunii* (Braun's Holly Fern) and, much more rarely, with *P. lonchitis* (Northern Holly Fern).

MARGINALIA: *A. Typical sterile pinna. B. Typical fertile pinna.*
DIAGNOSTIC ARROWS: *1. Fertile pinnae much smaller than sterile pinnae. 2. Two lowest pinnae often down-pointed. 3. Scaly stipe. 4. Eared pinnae.*

B.

A..

POLYSTICHUM ACROSTICHOIDES
CHRISTMAS FERN

BRAUN'S HOLLY FERN

Polystichum braunii (Spenner) Fée

HABIT: Shiny, spiny fern. Large, lustrous dark green fronds, with dense, pale to reddish brown scales on stipe and rachis; fronds arch up and out from central rhizome.

ECOLOGY: In soils with neutral pH; moist places in northern forests and other cool deep woods, particularly moist talus slopes.

RANGE: Nfld. to Ont. south to Conn., west to n. Wis. W. U.S. from n. Pacific Coast and B.C. to Alaska. Also Eurasia.

FRONDS: 12–36 in. long.

BLADE: Lanceolate, thick, rigid, often arching, widest above the middle, tapering from center downward to base and upward to tip. Semi-evergreen. Cut into 20–40 pairs of pinnae.

PINNAE: Middle and upper pinnae lance-shaped to slightly crescent-shaped and pointed; lowest pinnae short and blunt. Pinnae spaced fairly close but not overlapping. Upper pinnae lobed, lower pinnae cut to costa, forming 6–18 pairs of pinnules. Upper surface slightly leathery, shiny texture with a few narrow scales; underside with fine hairlike scales.

PINNULES: Oblong or ovate, spaced very close, often overlapping; margins with bristly, forward-pointing teeth.

RACHIS: So scaly that rachis appears very thick. Scales diminish upward toward the top.

STIPE: Very short; thickly covered with long, large scales and fine hairlike scales. Scales silvery at first, becoming light to medium brown.

RHIZOME: Very scaly; stout; medium brown.

SORI: Small, round; in 2 rows nearer midvein than margin. Indusium circular, fixed at center, with wavy margin.

NOTES: Braun's Holly Fern is a tetraploid hybrid (4 sets of chromosomes). Tight fiddleheads visible through winter and decorated with dense cinnamon-brown scales.

MARGINALIA: *A. Underside of sterile pinna. B. Sterile pinnule. C. Fertile pinnule showing sporangia after indusium has withered.*

DIAGNOSTIC ARROWS: *1. Short, very scaly stipe. 2. Small sori in 2 rows near center vein. 3. Pinnules close together. 4. Bristly forward-pointing teeth.*

POLYSTICHUM BRAUNII
BRAUN'S HOLLY FERN

NORTHERN HOLLY FERN
Polystichum lonchitis (L.) Roth

Extremely local in most northerly and northwesterly portions of our area. In rock crevices in boreal, subalpine, and alpine areas, mostly in the w. and nw. U.S. and Canada but also in isolated pockets in the e. end of the Gaspé Peninsula, in the Great Lakes region, Mich., Minn., and Wisc. Similar to *Polystichum acrostichoides* (Christmas Fern) in form, but its sterile and fertile blades are of similar shape, blades are narrower, and lowest pinnae are small and triangular rather than lanceolate. Also, margins of pinnae have small spines. This species definitely prefers limy soils.

(Top left) Polystichum acrostichoides (*Christmas Fern*). (Bottom left) Polystichum braunii (*Braun's Holly Fern*) *has dense scales on stipe and rachis.* (Above) *Underside of* Polystichum lonchitis (*Northern Holly Fern*) *showing sori.* (*Photos by David Longland/NEWFS, Hal Horwitz/NEWFS, and William Cullina*)

(Greek: **pteris,** "fern")

The genus *Pteridium* has only 1 species, *Pteridium aquilinum,* which is variable enough to consist of several varieties, 2 of which occur in our area. *P. aquilinum* is perhaps the world's most cosmopolitan fern, common throughout the globe. Its large, starchy rhizomes creep over large areas, and its profuse fronds can suppress the growth of other plants. The rhizomes and roots are often deep in the ground, so they are impervious to wet, cold, drought, herbicides, heat, and fire, and they are difficult to remove once they colonize an area. As such, Bracken is generally considered the preeminent weed of the fern family, along with its only other close relative in our region, *Dennstaedtia punctilobula* (Hay-scented Fern), which similarly forms tenacious colonies. Bracken is easy to recognize, because it is the only large fern (to 3 ft.) with a blade appearing to be coarsely divided into three parts with two basal pinnae very large relative to the others. The blade is often held horizontally (parallel to the ground) atop the long, tough, grooved stipe.

Bracken Fern frequently gains dominance after a fire, logging, grazing, or other landscape disturbance because its deep rhizome is so resilient. It tolerates sun and shade, dry and moist (not wet) conditions, and low-nutrient soils. Although it can transport itself to new sites via its spores, these seldom form and young sporophytes are rarely found; it mainly proliferates by spreading vegetatively. Some Bracken clones are estimated to be over 1,000 years old.

Humans have used Bracken for centuries as thatch, livestock bedding, potash, and food. Native Americans pounded the rhizomes for flour, and young fiddleheads of Asian varieties are still peeled and eaten. However, the plant does contain several poisonous and carcinogenic chemical compounds, including hydrogen cyanide and thiaminase (an enzyme that breaks down vitamin B); livestock graze mainly on tiny crosiers and become sick if fed older plants. Although harmful to many insects, Bracken secretes a sweet nectarlike substance at the base of the pinnae that attracts ants.

Two varieties of Bracken Fern are found in our area: *P. aquilinum* var. *latiusculum* and *P. aquilinum* var. *pseudocaudatum.* They are distinguished by the length and shape of the pinnules (very long and tapering in var. *pseudocaudatum,* short-tapering in var. *latiusculum*) and hairs on the margins of these pinnules (only in var. *latiusculum*). Var. *latiusculum* extends to a more northerly range than var. *pseudocaudatum,* and is the more common of the two in our area.

BRACKEN

Pteridium aquilinum (L.) Kuhn

HABIT: Common; strong, coarse. Produces new fronds all season. Often grows taller than knee-high in large colonies. Wavy, yellow-green to dark green, almost horizontal fronds.

ECOLOGY: At home in many places; often indicates poor and barren soil. In full sun, woods, old pastures, burned-over areas; sandy semishaded areas, and thickets.

RANGE: Widespread throughout the area. *Pteridium aquilinum* var. *latiusculum:* Nfld. and Que. south to Fla., west to La., north to Man.; scattered populations in B.C. *P. aquilinum* var. *pseudocaudatum:* from Mass. and Conn. south to Fla., west to e. Tex., north to Ind. and s. Ill.

FRONDS: 3 ft. ± tall. Sterile and fertile fronds the same.

BLADE: 2 ft. ± wide. Broadly triangular, divided into 3 nearly equal parts; reflexed almost to the horizontal (parallel to ground); coarse, leathery or papery texture.

PINNAE: Longer than wide. Lowest pinnae form 2 parts of triangular blade, are large relative to upper pinnae, almost opposite, distinctly stalked, and cut into pinnules. Upper pinnae less divided, with uppermost barely lobed. In var. *latiusculum,* the ends of the pinnules are 2–4 times longer than wide, giving a short-tapering tip to the pinnule. The margins, lower surface, and costa have shaggy hairs. In var. *pseudocaudatum,* the ends of the pinnules are 6–15 times longer than wide, giving the appearance of a very long-tapering tip. The margins, lower surface, and costa have a few, sparse hairs or are hairless.

PINNULES: Narrow, close together, variable; usually with narrowed tips, more elongate in var. *pseudocaudatum.*

STIPE: Long, about same length as blade, smooth, rigid; green, dark brown later in growing season; grooved with square corners.

RHIZOME: To 1 in. thick. Dark, scaleless, sometimes hairy. 15 ft. or more long, and sometimes 10 ft. deep in ground.

SORI: Form infrequently in narrow lines near margins of pinnules, covered or partially covered by their reflexed edges; silvery at first, dark brown later. Indusium formed by overlapping pinnule margin.

NOTES: In crosier form, the 3 sections of the frond uncoil like opening of an eagle's claw (which may give the species its Latin epithet, *aquilinum,* for "eagle").

MARGINALIA: A. *Underside of pinnule.* B. *Pinnules of basal pinna of var.* pseudocaudatum. C. *Pinnules of basal pinna of var.* latiusculum.

DIAGNOSTIC ARROWS: 1. *Narrow-tipped pinna.* 2. *Pinna with variable pinnules.* 3. *Smooth and grooved stipe.*

A.

B.

1.

2.

C.

3.

PTERIDIUM AQUILINUM
BRACKEN

GENUS *SCHIZAEA*: CURLY GRASS FERN

(Greek: *schizein,* "to split")

This genus contains 10 species, most tropical or subtropical. One species, however, is found along the mid-Atlantic Coast and in N.S. and Nfld. The same or a very similar species is also recorded from Peru. *Schizaea* is grasslike in growth and form (hence its common name), and only a few inches tall, truly unique among the ferns of our area.

CURLY GRASS FERN

Schizaea pusilla Pursh

HABIT: Minute plant that looks like its name, "curly grass." Because it is small and cryptic, it is almost impossible to find without lying flat on ground, except in winter when its evergreen, sterile, curling leaves may be distinguishable from surrounding dead grasses. Fronds emerge in tufts directly from the rhizome and have no stipe.

ECOLOGY: Wet, very acid soils, sphagnum and cranberry bogs, ledge crevices along shores, cedar swamps and under cedar trees, wet sandy soil, dense swamps.

RANGE: Highly disjunct distribution. Abundant in s. Nfld.; also in N.B. and N.S. Also in the coastal plain of N.Y., N.J., and Del.

STERILE FRONDS: $^1/_2$–2 in. long; less than $^1/_{32}$ in. wide. Numerous, threadlike, wiry, slightly flattened, coiled and twisted like a pig's tail, evergreen. Plants from the Canadian part of the range are often shorter and grow more densely than those farther south.

FERTILE FRONDS: 1–5 in. long. Quite erect, topped by fertile pinnae that are folded or fistlike.

RHIZOME: Slender.

SORI: In tiny segments on tips of fertile leaves; sporangia in 2 rows.

NOTES: Gametophyte is a thin, green, branching filament resembling algae, often mixed with mosses. Often found in association with *Lycopodiella inundata* (Bog Clubmoss), *Pseudolycopodiella caroliniana* (Slender Bog Clubmoss), and *Drosera filiformis* (Thread-leaf Sundew).

MARGINALIA: *A. Back of fertile frond. B. Front of fertile frond and sporangia.*

DIAGNOSTIC ARROWS: *1. Fingerlike pinnae holding sporangia. 2. Curling, hairlike sterile fronds. 3. Upright fertile fronds topped by triangular fistlike segments.*

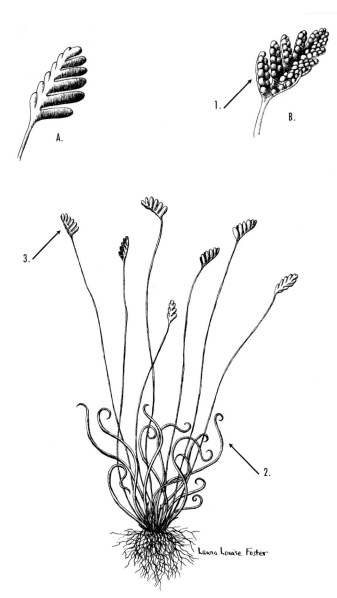

A.

B.

1.

3.

2.

Laura Louise Foster

SCHIZAEA PUSILLA
CURLY GRASS FERN

GENUS *THELYPTERIS*: MARSH FERNS

(Greek: *thelus*, "female," + *pteris*, "fern")

The genus *Thelypteris* contains about 875 species distributed worldwide. In our area, *Thelypteris* includes 3 species of small to medium-sized delicate ferns. The fronds are cut into pinnae and again into lobes (e.g., they are pinnate-pinnatifid); margins are not toothed. Rhizomes are slender and creeping, stipes are straw-colored, slender, and slightly scaly—not chaffy. The sori are round (sometimes with kidney-shaped indusia) and attached to the veins on the undersides of the pinnules about halfway between the midvein and the margin.

Our 3 *Thelypteris* species have been moved variously from one genus to another in the past. They were once classified in the genus *Dryopteris,* but are now regarded as separate species by virtue of several distinctive characters including transparent, needlelike hairs on the frond; the presence of only a few blade scales; veins that extend to the margins of the pinnae; and lower numbers of chromosomes than *Dryopteris* species. *Thelypteris noveboracensis* (New York Fern) and *T. simulata* (Massachusetts Fern) are classified in the subgenus *Parathelypteris*, while *T. palustris* var. *pubescens* (Marsh Fern) is assigned membership in the subgenus *Thelypteris*. In some treatments, the subgenera are elevated to genera (and the 2 former species become *Parathelypteris noveboracensis* and *P. simulata*); however, the majority of recent naming schemes retain the 3 species under *Thelypteris,* as we shall do here.

THELYPTERIS KEY

1A. Pinnae gradually taper in length both toward the base and the tip of the blade, with the lowest pinnae often shorter than 1 in. long; length of stipe shorter than the length of the blade.
T. noveboracensis (New York Fern)

1B. Length of basal pinnae similar to or slightly shorter than the length of middle pinnae on blade; stipe as long or longer than the blade. Go to 2.

New York Fern   Massachusetts Fern   Marsh Fern

2A. Fertile fronds appear more constricted than sterile fronds; veins of pinnae forked; frond can appear twisted along the vertical from base to tip; lower pinnae do not taper at the juncture with the rachis; indusium with no or extremely reduced orange glands. ***T. palustris* var. *pubescens* (Marsh Fern)**

2B. Sterile and fertile fronds similar in shape; veins of pinnae not forked; frond not twisting; lower pinnae taper at the juncture with the rachis; indusium with orange glands visible with a hand lens. ***T. simulata* (Massachusetts Fern)**

(Left) *The frond of* Thelypteris noveboracensis *(New York Fern) tapers at both ends. (Photo by Cheryl Lowe)* (Above) *Note the unforked veins and unrolled margin of* Thelypteris simulata *(Massachusetts Fern). (Photo by Janet E. Novak)* (Below, left) *Slightly twisting fronds of* Thelypteris palustris *(Marsh Fern). (Photo by Cheryl Lowe)* (Below, right) *Closeup of fertile frond of* Thelypteris palustris. *(Photo by Cheryl Lowe)*

Thelypteris noveboracensis (L.) Nieuwland

HABIT: Common, yellow-green, delicate, medium-sized fern grows in colonies, and spreads through areas in our woodlands where sunlit canopy gaps occur. Blade tapers sharply at both tip and base; this feature reminds one that "New Yorkers burn the candle at both ends"—a popular way of remembering this fern.

ECOLOGY: Common in sunny spots of mixed woodlands and drier edges of swamps, vernal seeps in ravines, and near streams.

RANGE: Nfld. south along coast to N.C., inland to Ga. and Miss., north through Tenn., Ky., Ill., to Mich. and Que.

FROND: 8–25 in. long. Grows in tufts of 3 or more fronds along rhizome. Not evergreen. Fertile fronds larger, narrower, and more upright than sterile fronds.

BLADE: Tapers from middle up to pointed tip and down to where it joins the rhizome. Widest at middle. Delicate, thin, yellow-green. Finely hairy underneath. Cut into 20 ± pairs of alternate, sessile pinnae.

PINNAE: Long, pointed, narrow, lance-shaped; cut nearly to midvein into narrow, rounded lobes. Lowest pinnae often minute in size, borne almost to ground level on the rachis. Veins rarely forked.

RACHIS: Green, pale, smooth or slightly hairy.

STIPE: 2–10 in. long. Straw-colored or light green, smooth or slightly hairy above, brown and with a few golden to reddish brown scales at base.

RHIZOME: Dark brown, slender, slightly scaly, widely creeping and branching, but produces fronds in tufts.

SORI: Few, round, small, near margins. Indusium kidney-shaped; pale tan, slightly hairy.

NOTES: In woodland habitats, New York Fern could be confused with *Dennstaedtia punctilobula* (Hay-scented Fern), but it is generally smaller and only slightly hairy along the rachis, grows in clumps rather than lines, and lowest pinnae are very small and borne low on frond. Since *Thelypteris palustris* var. *pubescens* (Marsh Fern) prefers wetter areas, it and New York Fern are seldom found close together.

MARGINALIA: *A. Sterile lobe of pinna, showing simple veins. B. Long, tapering pinna. C. Fertile pinna lobes and sori.*

DIAGNOSTIC ARROWS: *1. Double-tapering fronds. 2. Tiny bottom pinnae close to rhizome. 3. Semitufts of 3 fronds from branching rhizome.*

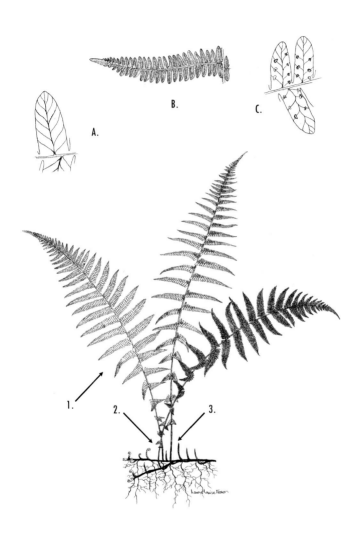

A.

B.

C.

1.

2.

3.

THELYPTERIS NOVEBORACENSIS
NEW YORK FERN

MARSH FERN

Thelypteris palustris Schott var. *pubescens* (Lawson) Fernald

HABIT: This thin, green, delicate, medium-sized, common fern produces fronds throughout summer.

ECOLOGY: Moist, sunny areas in full sun and partial shade; rich, muddy soil of swamps, bogs, marshes, open woodlands, wet meadows, and along ditches and streams; usually on higher ground in wetlands and less often in standing water.

RANGE: Entire e. U.S. to Neb. and N.D. and ne. and cent. Canadian provinces.

FRONDS: 7–36 in. long. Fertile fronds erect, with longer stipes than sterile fronds and constricted pinnae margins rolled over the sori. Fronds may appear to twist on their vertical axes because lower pinnae are oriented in a different plane from the upper pinnae.

BLADE: 2–8 in. wide. Lance-shaped with a pointed tip and widest above the base, tapering only slightly at the base. Thin, delicate, green or yellow-green; not evergreen. Cut into 1 2 ± pairs of nearly opposite, sessile pinnae.

PINNAE: Lance-shaped, cut nearly to midvein into 1 2 ± rounded or blunt-tipped lobes, margins not toothed. Widest where they join the rachis. Pinnae held perpendicular to ground level. Fertile pinnae appear narrow and constricted because the margins curve over the sori. Veins of sterile pinnae mostly forked.

RACHIS: Green, slender, smooth or with sparse small hairs.

STIPE: 5–28 in. long. Longer than blade; smooth, slender, pale green or straw-colored above, dark brown to black at base; very few or no tan scales. Stipes of fertile fronds longer than those of sterile ones.

RHIZOME: Slender, black, few scales; widely creeping, branching.

SORI: Numerous, round, mostly on upper pinnae in close rows near midvein. Indusium pale, narrow, kidney-shaped, often hairy, but not glandular.

NOTES: This fern can sometimes be confused with *Dennstaedtia punctilobula* (Hay-scented Fern), though Hay-scented Fern has hairy stipes that are shorter than the blade. *Athyrium felix-femina* (Lady Fern) is also similar, but Lady Fern has true pinnules with toothed margins and a stipe much shorter than the blade; it also grows in distinct clumps.

MARGINALIA: *A. Sterile pinna lobes showing forked veins. B. Basal pinna not tapered to rachis. C. Fertile pinnules and partially covered sori.*

DIAGNOSTIC ARROWS: *1. Twisting growth form. 2. Tall, slender, smooth stipe. 3. Fertile pinnules curving over sori.*

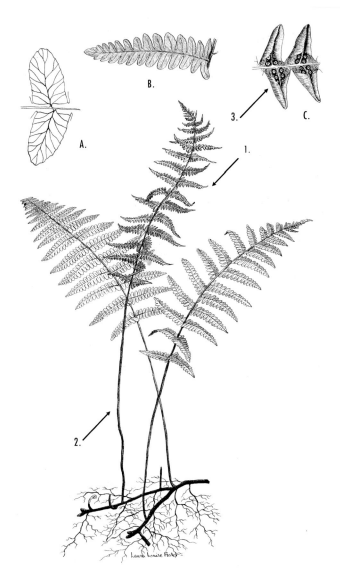

A.

B.

C.

3.

1.

2.

Laura Louise Foster

THEYLYPTERIS PALUSTRIS
MARSH FERN

Thelypteris simulata (Davenport) Nieuwland

HABIT: Feathery fern of wet, acidic places, with narrow pinnae.

ECOLOGY: Cedar, spruce, larch, and sphagnum swamps and bogs, often with *Sphagnum* moss; also moist, acid, shady woods. Its habitat preference is intermediate between the open and wet habitats of *Thelypteris palustris* var. *pubescens* (Marsh Fern) and the dry, semi-shaded habitats of *T. noveboracensis* (New York Fern).

RANGE: The narrowest distribution of the *Thelypteris* species. Occasional from the coastal areas of N.B. south to Va. and in some inland areas of W. Va. Disjunct populations in the unglaciated southern region of Wisc.

FRONDS: 8–28 in. long; erect. Fertile fronds slightly more erect, with relatively longer stipes than sterile fronds, but otherwise similar in form to sterile fronds.

BLADE: Lance-shaped with pointed tip and slightly narrowed at base, widest (3–6 in.) near middle. Thin, yellow-green; not evergreen. Cut into 18 nearly opposite, sessile pinnae.

PINNAE: Narrowed near the rachis (particularly the lower pinnae) as well as tip, cut almost to midvein into 15 ± pairs of blunt lobes, margins not toothed. Lower pairs of pinnae often held in a horizontal plane, parallel to ground level. Veins not forked.

RACHIS: Green, slightly hairy above, smooth beneath.

STIPE: 3–16 in. long. Shorter than blade; slender, yellow-green and a little hairy above, light brown and few scales at base.

RHIZOME: Slender, black, few pale brown scales, creeping.

SORI: Small, round, distinct. Indusium pale tan, with minute orange glands best seen with a hand lens, narrowly kidney-shaped.

NOTES: The species name *simulata* is from of its "similarity" to *Thelypteris palustris* var. *pubescens* and *T. noveboracensis* (Marsh and New York Ferns, respectively) and to *Athyrium felix-femina* (Lady Fern). However, basal pinnae taper at both the tip and at the juncture with the rachis. The indusium also has yellowish orange glands, which are much reduced in other species of *Thelypteris* and absent in *Athyrium*.

MARGINALIA: *A. Sterile lower pinna. B. Section of fertile pinna and sori. C. Section of pinnae showing veins.*

DIAGNOSTIC ARROWS: *1. Double-tapering lowest pair of pinnae. 2. Slender, slightly scaly stipe. 3. Simple, unforked veins.*

A.

B.

C.

1.

2.

3.

THELYPTERIS SIMULATA
MASSACHUSETTS FERN

GENUS *TRICHOMANES*: FILMY FERNS

(Greek: *trichomanes*, "hair"; referring to the bristly, sporangium-bearing structure projecting out of the indusium)

This genus (in the family Hymenophyllaceae) contains about 300 mostly tropical species. Two are found in our area but are rarely seen. Filmy Ferns have tiny, thin, delicate, and translucent pinnae. An entire colony of one species can be covered by a twenty-five-cent piece. In most species, the fronds are made of only 1 layer of cells with no stomata (pores that transport air into the leaf). They require abundant moisture and, in our area, grow exclusively on rocks. Their rhizomes are slender and creeping, with a reduced root system (absent in some species). The sporangia are short-stalked, thin-walled, and round or disclike, surrounded by an annulus, or ring, which opens the sporangium to release the spores. The sori are borne at the ends of veins, inside a conelike, sunken structure on the margins of the fertile pinnae. In the genus *Trichomanes*, the indusium is shaped like a vase or cone with 2 lips. The sporangia are borne on a distinct projecting stalk which, after the spores are shed, persists as a long, thin bristle. The gametophyte is a thin, long, and profusely branched filament. Asexual gemmae can bud off the filaments and propagate the gametophyte vegetatively.

Only *Trichomanes boschianum* (Filmy Fern) and *T. intricatum* (Weft Fern) are known in our region. Filmy Fern forms sporophytes with genuine, albeit miniscule, pinnae. Weft Fern has been observed only in the gametophyte phase, and it resembles a filamentous alga more than a fern, except that it produces rhizomelike structures and gemmae.

Rich growth of Trichomanes boschianum *(Filmy Fern) covers a bedrock ceiling. (Photo by Donald Farrar)*

A verdant clump of Trichomanes boschianum *(Filmy Fern) in Alabama.*
(Photo by Donald Farrar)

Trichomanes intricatum *(Weft Fern) is known only from gametophytes.*
(Photo by Donald Farrar)

FILMY FERN (Bristle Fern)

Trichomanes boschianum Stürm

HABIT: Probably the daintiest and most delicate of our ferns. Translucent fragile fronds only 1 cell thick, adapted to use light more efficiently in its dimly lit, cavernous habitat. Fronds often dense and overlapping.

ECOLOGY: On rocks in damp acid grottoes of sandstone cliffs, or in wet, acid, rocky pockets in shallow caves well away from direct light.

RANGE: S. Ohio, Ill., Ind., Ky., Va., W. Va., Ala., Ark., N.C., S.C., Tenn. Also Mexico. Very rare in our area.

FRONDS: 2–8 in. long; ½–1 ½ in. wide. Translucent, light green, evergreen; oval and lance-shaped, 1 cell thick. Lacy-cut into 6 ± pairs of pinnae and often cut again into 2 ± pairs of pinnules (which, when dried, have the texture of parchment).

PINNAE: Irregularly cut or lobed, blunt-tipped.

STIPE: 1 ½ in. ± long. Translucent, green; prominently winged almost to junction with rhizome. Fragile.

RACHIS: Broadly winged; green.

RHIZOME: ⅛ in. ± thick. Black, wiry, branching and creeping.

SORI: Surrounded by a cone-shaped structure appearing at the ends of lateral veins at base of 3 or 4 interior lobes of fertile pinnae; lips on cones not flaring or dark-edged. Contain tiny green cylindrical sporangia that surround and extend halfway up the bristle.

MARGINALIA: *A. Fertile pinna. B. Indusium, sorus, and projecting hairlike bristle. C. Section of rhizome and lower portion of a sterile frond.*

DIAGNOSTIC ARROWS: *1. Blunt, squared tips of pinnules. 2. Delicate growth form. 3. Hairy rhizome. 4. Cuplike indusium on interior lobe of fertile pinnule with bristle.*

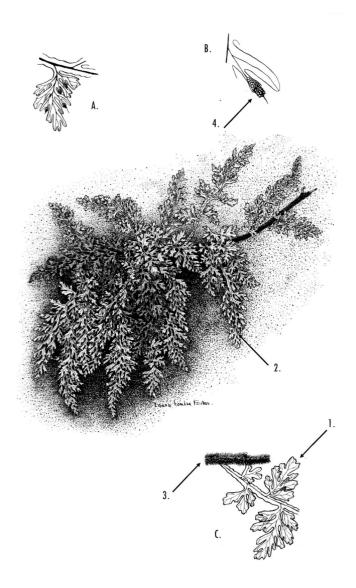

A.

B.

4.

2.

1.

3.

C.

TRICHOMANES BOSCHIANUM
FILMY FERN

WEFT FERN

Trichomanes intricatum Farrar

Occurring only in the gametophyte phase of the fern life cycle, this species has been overlooked because of its threadlike habit, which resembles algae more than a typical fern. However, the presence of short roots, distinctive gemmifers (special flask-shaped cells), and tiny, filament-shaped gemmae (asexual propagules, 4–10 cells long) produced by the gemmifers distinguish it from algae. These features can be seen with a strong hand lens. Plants intertwine to produce feltlike mats that hang in wefts from the ceilings of deeply shaded, noncalcareous grottoes and crevices—hence the common name. The species occurs throughout the Appalachian Mts. and Plateau east of the Mississippi River, north in the mountains to Vt. and N.H. Spore-producing phases have not been found in nature or produced in culture; these ferns appear to reproduce entirely by means of asexual gemmae. The gametophyte populations may be all that remain from an earlier time when the species still produced sporophytes; a related European species, *T. speciosum*, similarly has gametophytes that are now much more widespread than sporophytes.

GENUS *VITTARIA*: SHOESTRING FERN

(Latin: *vitta*, "ribbon" or "stripe"; referring to shape of the plant)

The genus *Vittaria* (family Vittariaceae) contains about 50 species worldwide, with 3 recorded in North America. One species, *Vittaria lineata,* is a common epiphyte on palm trees in Florida, and another, *V. graminifolia,* is known only in Louisiana. Only *V. appalachiana* (Appalachian Shoestring Fern) inhabits our area, and it does so almost exclusively in the gametophyte stage; rare, abortive sporophytes have been found in Ohio as well as produced in culture. This species has long been known as common in the Appalachian Mountains and Plateau, but it was not always recognized as the gametophyte of a fern. Genetic studies have confirmed it is a species of *Vittaria* and distinct from all other species of this genus in the New World.

(Right) Vittaria appalachiana *(Appalachian Shoestring Fern) produces gemmae (asexual plantlets) on the ends of the gametophytes and* (below) *forms mosslike mats. (Photos by Donald Farrar)*

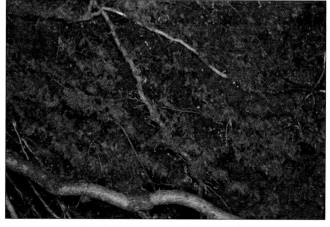

APPALACHIAN VITTARIA
(Appalachian Shoestring Fern)

Vittaria appalachiana Farrar & Mickel

HABIT: Individual plants are branching ribbons $1/4$–1 in. long, with aerial branches bearing gemmae (asexual plantlets) at the tips composed of 2–12 cells that are easily shed and dispersed to start new plants. Plants grow in dense colonies, much like mosses, and can form mats up to several square yards in area.

ECOLOGY: Found coating deeply shaded rock outcrops of acidic bedrock, especially sandstones. Frequently in dark pockets and crevices and in the deep recesses of cavernous jumbles of larger boulders known as "rockhouses." Not easily seen without the aid of a flashlight.

RANGE: Locally abundant south of the southern boundary of Pleistocene glaciation in Ind., Ohio, Penn., and southward in the Appalachian Mts. and Plateau. Rare in sw. N.Y.

SPOROPHYTES: Spore-bearing plants have been found only at one site (in Ohio); these are very small (less than $1/2$ in. tall), and do not produce viable spores. Sporophytes of other *Vittaria* species are highly susceptible to damage from freezing.

NOTES: *Vittaria appalachiana* may have become established in North America during a past period of warmer climate; it is now restricted to the small (but highly successful) gametophyte stage of its life cycle. Can be locally abundant in the heart of its range. However, it is vulnerable to degradation of its specialized habitat as a result of rock-climbing, quarrying, and other human activities.

MARGINALIA: *A. Closeup (microscopic view) of gemmae forming on a plant. B. Cluster of individual plants. C. Rocks with small plants colonizing them.*

DIAGNOSTIC ARROWS: *1. Mosslike growth form on rock ledge. 2. Gemmae.*

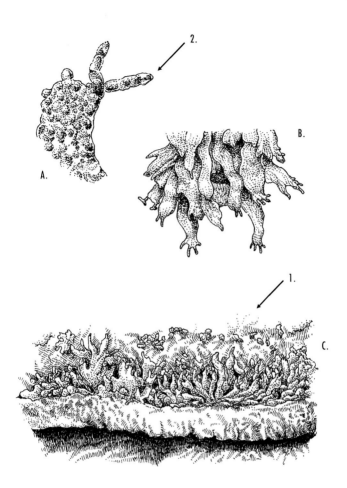

2.

B.

A.

1.

C.

VITTARIA APPALACHIANA
APPALACHIAN VITTARIA

GENUS *WOODSIA*: CLIFF FERNS

(In honor of English botanist Joseph Woods)

The *Woodsias* are small, compact plants that grow on cliffs, ledges, and in rocky woodlands, usually emerging early in the spring. They are often confused with *Cystopteris* species (Bladder Ferns), but the veins of *Woodsia* do not extend to the margin and often have an enlarged or swollen vein tip. Also, *Woodsia* species all have a distinctive, multilobed indusium that envelops the sorus from underneath, rather than arching over it from one side. The *Woodsia* indusium enfolds immature sori with its elongated segments like a fist, later opening and framing the sori like an open hand before (usually) disappearing under the fully mature sori. The shape and length of the indusium lobes (some species with broad segments and others with hairlike or straplike lobes) are important characters for distinguishing between species. The sori are round and in some plants so numerous as to completely cover the backs of the pinnae. Fertile and sterile fronds are similar and grow in upright clusters from an erect and scaly rhizome. Hairs, scales, or glands cover the stipes, blade, and rachis. A tuft of old broken stipes, all the same height, surrounds the fronds of several species. These particular species all have a distinctive node or joint on the stipe, and in the autumn the stipes all break off at that node or joint.

There are approximately 30 species in this genus, primarily from north-temperate and high-elevation tropical regions; 10 species grow in North America, 6 of them in our area. Four of these are described in detail. Two rare and local species are briefly described here but not included in the key.

WOODSIA KEY

1A. Plants smooth, with a few stalkless glands; lower pinnae wider than long; stipes green to light brown.

W. glabella **(Smooth Woodsia)**

1B. Plants with hairs, scales, and/or stalked glands; lower pinnae usually longer than wide; stipes brown to dark brown at base (green to straw-colored in *W. obtusa*). Go to 2.

2A. Stipe green to straw-colored, not jointed; the persistent bases of old fronds of unequal length; pinnae with tiny, glandular hairs but no scales or long hairs.

W. obtusa **(Blunt-lobed Woodsia)**

2B. Stipe brown to reddish brown, jointed; the persistent bases of old fronds mostly of equal length; pinnae with scales and/or long hairs. Go to 3.

3A. Scales absent or rare on underside of blade (scales and hairs scattered on rachis); larger pinnae usually have only 2–3 pairs of pinnules; indusia with few ribbonlike (filamentous) segments.

W. alpina **(Alpine Woodsia)**

3B. Scales common on underside of blade and on rachis; larger pinnae with 9 pairs of pinnules; indusia with many filamentous segments.

W. ilvensis **(Rusty Woodsia)**

Woodsia glabella (*Smooth Woodsia*). (*Photo by Arthur Haines*)

Woodsia ilvensis (*Rusty Woodsia*). (*Photo by Lawrence Newcomb/NEWFS*)

Woodsia alpina (Bolton) S. F. Gray

HABIT: Very small, rare fern grows in erect, semirigid dense tufts. Slightly scaly, hairy. The old, broken stipes form persistent clusters of nearly equal length that you can see or feel at base of fronds.

ECOLOGY: High altitudes and moist northerly areas, primarily cool crevices and cliffs of limestone and slate.

RANGE: Greenland and all of n. Canada, south into Me., N.H., Vt., N.Y., Mich., Minn.

FRONDS: 1–8 in. long; $^1/_2$–1 in. ± wide.

BLADE: Narrow lance-shaped, slightly narrower at base, usually blunt-tipped; delicate to brittle; no glands. Cut into 4–14 pairs of stemless, subopposite pinnae. A few linear scales and hairs on underside, smooth above.

PINNAE: Ovate to slightly triangular; deeply cut, usually into 4–7 lobes, each with smooth or slightly lobed margins. Veins forked, not reaching margin; vein tips often enlarged.

RACHIS: Widely scattered scales and hairs; green to straw-colored.

STIPE: Short; reddish brown to dark purple at base, shading up to yellowish green; shiny, slightly scaly, with a swollen joint below the middle; scales lanceolate and brown.

RHIZOME: Fairly stout, upright with numerous, hairlike roots.

SORI: Small, distinct, near margin. Indusium is a tiny disc with many long hairlike segments radiating outward and surrounding sori from underside, visible only before sporangia mature.

NOTES: Fertile tetraploid hybrid (4 sets of chromosomes) derived from a cross between *Woodsia glabella* (Smooth Woodsia) and *W. ilvensis* (Rusty Woodsia). Alpine Woodsia may hybridize with Rusty Woodsia to form a rare triploid known as *Woodsia × gracilis,* which is intermediate in appearance between its parents. Dark, hairy stipes help distinguish Alpine Woodsia from *Asplenium viride* (Green Spleenwort) and *W. glabella* (Smooth Woodsia), with which it often grows.

MARGINALIA: *A. Veins with enlarged ends and sori. B. Underside of fertile pinnae.*

DIAGNOSTIC ARROWS: *1. Deeply cut pinnae. 2. Indusium with long radiating hairs. 3. Stipe dark at base.*

WOODSIA ALPINA
ALPINE WOODSIA

SMOOTH WOODSIA (Smooth Cliff Fern)

Woodsia glabella R. Br ex Richards.

Synonyms: *Woodsia alpina* (Bolton) S. F. Gray var. *glabella* (R. Br. ex Richards.) D. C. Eaton

HABIT: Tiny rare northern fern growing in erect, densely clustered tufts. Pale green and smooth throughout. The species epithet *glabella* means "smooth." Fronds are the narrowest of all *Woodsia* species. Old, broken stipes form persistent clusters of nearly equal height.

ECOLOGY: High altitudes in shaded, moist, limestone crevices.

RANGE: Greenland and across much of Canada and Alaska, south into Me., Minn., N.H., N.Y., Vt. Also n. Eurasia.

FRONDS: 1–6 in. long; $^1/_4$–$^1/_2$ in. wide.

BLADE: Narrow; pale green, delicate; smooth surfaces. Cut into 4–10 pairs of pinnae.

PINNAE: Oval to slightly triangular; usually cut into 3 lobes; both surfaces smooth. Lower pairs widely spaced, wider than long, almost fan-shaped, and smaller than upper pinnae. Upper pinnae usually longer than wide, with rounded tip, and more deeply cut. Veins forked, not reaching the margin; vein tips slightly (if at all) enlarged.

RACHIS: Smooth, green.

STIPE: Shorter than blade; greenish to straw-colored; smooth above, jointed below middle, scaly below joint, scales brown and lanceolate.

RHIZOME: Tiny, slender, upright; brown scales; sparse, fine roots.

SORI: Small, distinct, near margin. Indusium a tiny disc on underside of sori with few, short, hairlike segments surrounding the sori and visible only before sporangia mature.

NOTES: Sometimes mistaken for *Woodsia alpina* (Alpine Woodsia) or *W. ilvensis* (Rusty Woodsia), but stipes of these two species are reddish brown or dark purple near base. *Asplenium viride* (Green Spleenwort) is also sometimes confused with this species, but in Green Spleenwort, sori are elongate and indusium is attached to the side of the sorus, not underneath it.

MARGINALIA: *A. Veins and sori. B. Underside of fertile pinnae.*

DIAGNOSTIC ARROWS: *1. Slightly triangular pinnae. 2. Indusium with short, hairlike segments. 3. Stipe and rachis green to straw-colored throughout.*

2.

A.

1.

B.

3.

WOODSIA GLABELLA
SMOOTH WOODSIA

RUSTY WOODSIA (Rusty Cliff Fern)

Woodsia ilvensis (L.) R. Br.

HABIT: Small fern producing tufts of fronds with silvery white undersides that turn rusty brown in fall and during dry seasons. Whole plant turns brown in extended drought but sends up new green fronds when rains return.

ECOLOGY: Cliffs and dry, rocky slopes, often in full sun. Acid to neutral soils.

RANGE: Greenland and throughout cent. and e. Canada, south to N.C., west to Iowa and Minn. In w. North America, from Alaska south into Alta. Also n. Eurasia.

FRONDS: 2–10 in. long; ½–1½ in. wide.

BLADE: Stiff, erect, narrowly lanceolate with pointed tips; upper surface deep green, undersides with dense white wool (dense scales and hairs) that later turns rusty brown. Cut into 4–12 pairs of nearly opposite, stemless pinnae; lower pinnae slightly shorter than those above.

PINNAE: Oval and slightly pointed; largest ones cut into 4–7 pairs of variable, rounded lobes, some cut almost to costa. Margin edge with scattered hairs. Veins forked, not reaching margins; vein tips enlarged.

RACHIS: Abundant hairs and scales; green to straw-colored.

STIPE: Shiny brown below to green above; stout, brittle, hairy, and scaly; jointed (with a swollen node) about 1 in. above rhizome, forming a bristly stubble of more or less uniform length after stipes have broken off at the joints.

RHIZOME: Compact, dark brown, erect, with abundant narrow brown scales and tiny, lacy rootlets.

SORI: Small, near margin, often hidden by scales and hairs. Outer edges of indusia fringed with many long, hairlike segments radiating out from under sori.

NOTES: Fiddleheads covered with silvery white hairs and visible spring through fall. Highly variable in form—plants in shade may have fewer hairs. An abundance of scales on blades and rachises distinguishes this species from all other *Woodsia* species in our area. May hybridize with *Woodsia alpina* (Alpine Woodsia) to form the rare, sterile triploid *Woodsia × gracilis*, which is intermediate in appearance between its parents.

MARGINALIA: *A. Underside of fertile pinnae lobed or cut to costa. B. Upper side of sterile pinna. C. Underside of fertile pinna. D. Veins and sori.*
DIAGNOSTIC ARROWS: *1. Stubblelike broken-off stipes. 2. Erect, pointed narrow blade. 3. Indusia with long radiating hairs.*

A.

B.

C.

1.

2.

3.

D.

WOODSIA ILVENSIS
RUSTY WOODSIA

BLUNT-LOBED WOODSIA
(Blunt-lobed Cliff Fern)

Woodsia obtusa (Spreng.) Torr.

HABIT: Our most common and largest *Woodsia,* with erect fronds of green to yellow-green. Produces new leaves throughout the growing season.

ECOLOGY: Shady moist ledges and rocky slopes. Common in limestone areas, but also on a variety of substrates, including granite.

RANGE: Throughout our area, Que. and Ont. south to Fla., west to Tex., north to Neb. and Wisc.

FRONDS: 3–24 in. long; 1–5 in. wide.

BLADE: Lanceolate; cut into 6–20 + pairs of widely spaced, subopposite, short-stemmed pinnae at right angles to rachis.

PINNAE: Longer than wide, narrowing to an acute angle, but with rounded tips. Two lowest pairs of pinnae shorter than others and more triangular. Fertile pinnae often narrow and pointed when exposed to full sun. Glandular hairs on both surfaces, and along costae. Cut into 5–9 pairs of blunt-lobed pinnules.

PINNULES: Subopposite, oblong, lobed. Veins forked, not reaching margin; vein tips enlarged.

RACHIS: Covered with glandular hairs and scattered, often hairlike scales; yellow-green.

STIPE: Yellowish green above, sometimes pale brown at base. Prominent, narrow brown scales near base, some bicolored with dark central stripe and pale brown edges. Stipe not jointed, the previous year's old, broken-off stipes of variable lengths.

RHIZOME: Short, stout, nearly erect; with mostly bicolored scales.

SORI: Pale brown, more or less centered between margin and midvein. Indusium starlike, with 5 or 6 broad, irregular, glandular segments, visible only before sporangia mature.

NOTES: Superficially similar to *Cystopteris fragilis* (Fragile Fern), distinguished by starlike indusium under sori, yellow-green stipes (no dark brown base), and pinnae with glandular hairs, not smooth. Blunt-lobed Woodsia has been separated into 2 subspecies. *W. obtusa* ssp. *obtusa* is a tetraploid (4 sets of chromosomes) in the range just described. The diploid form, *W. obtusa* ssp. *occidentalis,* is found on sandstone and granite in Ark., Kans., Mo., Okla., and Tex.

MARGINALIA: *A. Section of fertile pinna. B. Upperside of fertile pinna (more typical in sun). C. Sterile pinna. D. and E. Indusium expanded and indusium half open.*

DIAGNOSTIC ARROWS: *1. Hairy rachis and scaly stipe. 2. Blunt-tipped pinnules. 3. Widely spaced pinnae. 4. Star-shaped open indusium.*

WOODSIA OBTUSA
BLUNT-LOBED WOODSIA

MOUNTAIN WOODSIA

Woodsia scopulina ssp. *appalachiana* (T. M. C. Taylor) Windham
> Primarily in the southern Appalachian Mts. and comes into our area in se. Ky., sw. Va., and W. Va. It has distinctly toothed pinna margins and is distinguished by its many flat, whitish hairs.

OREGON WOODSIA

Woodsia oregana ssp. *cathcartiana* (B. L. Robinson) Windham
> Primarily a species of the w. U.S., entering our range in Mich., Wisc., and N.Y. Although it has the reddish brown stipes of several species in our area, it does not have long hairs or jointed stipes; the indusia have narrow, filamentous segments (often concealed by maturing sporangia); and pinna margins often appear ragged.

(Left) Woodsia obtusa (*Blunt-lobed Woodsia*) *has widely spaced pinnae and* (above) *sori midway between margin and midvein. Note indusium cupped around developing sporangia. (Photos by Janet E. Novak)*

GENUS *WOODWARDIA*: CHAIN FERNS

(Named for Thomas Jenkinson Woodward, an English botanist, 1745–1820)

Fourteen species of this genus are recorded for the northern temperate zones and Central America, 2 in our area: *Woodwardia areolata* (Netted Chain Fern) and *W. virginica* (Virginia Chain Fern). The fronds, which are glossy green, emerge individually, scattered along the rhizome. Stipes are usually longer than the blades. Veins are netted, at least near the midrib. The sori are long and narrow and run along both sides of and parallel to the midveins, abutting each other end-to-end, thus forming a "chain." The indusia open toward the midvein. Both our species are ferns of acid swamps or other shaded, acid, wet places.

WOODWARDIA KEY

1A. Sterile and fertile fronds similar in shape and size, with more than 12 pairs of pinnae; veins of pinnae forming a netted pattern only near the midrib.
W. virginica (Virginia Chain Fern)

1B. Fertile frond with much narrower pinnae than sterile frond, 7–10 pairs of pinnae; veins of pinnae netted throughout.　　**_W. areolata_ (Netted Chain Fern)**

(Left) *The narrow pinnae of a fertile frond of* Woodwardia areolata *(Netted Chain Fern). (Photo by John A. Lynch)* (Above) *Chainlike rows of sori on fertile pinnae of* Woodwardia virginica *(Virginia Chain Fern). (Photo by David M. Stone/NEWFS)*

NETTED CHAIN FERN

Woodwardia areolata (L.) T. Moore

HABIT: Glossy green fern of continuously moist places, often forms extensive dense colonies.

ECOLOGY: Shaded areas of swamps, acidic bogs, wet woods, and moist sandstone cliffs. Most common along coastal plain areas, sometimes in semibrackish waters.

RANGE: N.S. to Fla., west to Tex., north along Ozark and Cumberland Plateaus of Okla., north to Mo., Ohio, Ind., Ill. Range limited by cold temperatures; not found in the high elevations of the Appalachians or interior limestone regions.

STERILE FROND: 24 in. ± long, 6 in. ± wide. Oval, acutely pointed tip; glossy green.

FERTILE FROND: Narrower than sterile frond, persisting upright through the winter for one year.

STERILE BLADE: Cut into 10 ± pairs of pinnae.

STERILE PINNAE: Sharp-pointed; narrow; wavy, fine-toothed margins; winged where they join the rachis except lower pairs, which may have a small stalk. Third lowest pair of pinnae is usually the longest. Veins raised, prominent, forming a conspicuous net.

FERTILE PINNAE: Constricted when mature, widely spaced, with shallow lobes frequently recurved over the sori.

RACHIS: Prominent, olive-colored, slightly scaly on underside.

STIPE: Usually longer than blade, stout, yellow-green above, shining chestnut-brown at base, flattened and slightly grooved, with few, scattered, brown scales.

RHIZOME: Deep brown; covered at apex with glistening, pale brown scales. Creeping and forking; grows about 3 in. per year and produces 4–5 fronds along new growth.

SORI: Longer than wide, deeply embedded, lined up end-to-end halfway between midvein and margin. Indusium membranous or slightly leathery, wrapped over sori, disintegrating with age, but not opening to expose sporangia as in most ferns.

NOTES: Resembles a small *Onoclea sensibilis* (Sensitive Fern), but the pinnae margins of Netted Chain Fern are wavy and fine-toothed, not entire, and the sori of Sensitive Fern are clustered on separate beadlike pinnules.

MARGINALIA: *A. Fertile pinna in contracted mature form. B. Section of pinna showing netted veins.*

DIAGNOSTIC ARROWS: *1. Lowest pair of pinnae not winged at rachis. 2. Fertile frond with long, thin, contracted pinnae. 3. Wavy margin of pinna with fine-toothed edges.*

WOODWARDIA AREOLATA
NETTED CHAIN FERN

VIRGINIA CHAIN FERN

Woodwardia virginica (L.) Smith

HABIT: Upright fern of wet places with very long, dark purple-brown stipe and rachis; one of the taller ferns in our area.

ECOLOGY: *Sphagnum* bogs, swamps, roadside ditches, muddy wet spots in woods. Rooted mostly in water that is often a foot or more deep. Acidic and shady locations.

RANGE: Concentrated mainly along the coastal plain from N.B., south to Fla., west to Tex. Species extends inland along the northern part of its range to Mich.

FRONDS: Up to 48 in. long, 10 in. ± wide. Broadest in middle, deciduous. Unlike *Woodwardia areolata* (Netted Chain Fern), the sterile and fertile fronds are the same shape and size.

BLADE: Leathery texture, glossy; with 15 ± pairs of closely spaced pinnae.

PINNAE: Narrow, tapering to both ends, cut 3/4 way to midrib, forming lobes with a narrow wing along the costa; lobes are round or blunt-pointed at the tip, and angled slightly upward toward pinna tip. Veins netted only near midrib, becoming free and forked between sori and margin.

RACHIS: Lower portion dark purple-brown, upper portion green, smooth and shiny; several grooves, slightly ridged at bases of pinnae.

STIPE: Twice or more the length of the blade, distinctly dark, shining purple-brown. Lower part of stipe swollen, almost tuberous where it joins the rhizome, spongy, slightly scaly, and deeply grooved.

RHIZOME: 1/2 in. ± thick; coarse; widely creeping in mud and ooze. Glistening brown scales cover the growing tip and are scattered along rhizome.

SORI: Chainlike, elongate, in double rows along midvein and at tip of pinnae lobes, often occupy nearly all lower surface of pinnae. Indusium leathery, inconspicuous, dark brown often hidden as spores are released.

NOTES: Can be mistaken for *Osmunda cinnamomea* (Cinnamon Fern), which grows in clusters from individual crowns; however, fronds of Virginia Chain Fern tend to grow in a line rather than circular clumps; the fertile and sterile fronds are similar (whereas those of Cinnamon Fern are different); stipe is dark purple-brown rather than green; and pinnae have partially netted—rather than forked—veins.

MARGINALIA: *A. Pinna. B. Pinna lobes. C. Fertile pinna lobes.*

DIAGNOSTIC ARROWS: *1. Swollen bases of stipes. 2. Tall dark stipe.*
3. Upward-pointing pinnae. 4. Chainlike rows of sori.

WOODWARDIA VIRGINICA
VIRGINIA CHAIN FERN

GENERA *BOTRYCHIUM* AND *OPHIOGLOSSUM:* SUCCULENT FERNS

The Ophioglossaceae (Succulent Fern family) is represented in our area by two genera: *Botrychium* (the Moonworts, Rattlesnake Ferns, and Grape Ferns) and *Ophioglossum* (the Adder's-tongue Ferns). The Succulent Ferns are among the oldest taxa in the long evolutionary history of ferns, and though true ferns, they are not closely related to other extant fern families. Unlike the majority of true ferns (the large "leptosporangiate" group), these genera belong to a "eusporangiate" group, producing large thick-walled sporangia. The plants are smooth, without scales of any kind, and they have soft, fleshy stems and roots with no hardened tissues.

Botrychium and *Ophioglossum* plants do not generally emerge as fiddleheads. The young plant emerges through the soil in an uncoiled form— smooth and straight for the Adder's-tongues and most of the Moonworts, and in a bent form for the Rattlesnake and Grape Ferns. This unique growth form is called "erect vernation" ("straight up in the spring"). Each year, a new frond (usually only one), formed the year before, grows from the subterranean rhizome.

The gametophytes are subterranean and contain no chlorophyll. They sometimes associate with a fungus for their nourishment. Gametophytes are strong and persistent and it is not rare to find the remains of one of them at the base of a mature sporophyte. Gametophytes can exist underground for 5 or more years before a sporophyte emerges. Fertilization appears to happen most often through union of sperm and eggs on the same gametophyte; that is, inbreeding is the predominant mode of reproduction, giving rise to low levels of genetic variation within populations. Despite the prevalence of inbreeding, however, hybrids between species do occur occasionally where two or more closely related species grow together.

The sporophyte, or spore-producing plant, usually grows very slowly and takes several years to produce its first frond. The single fleshy shoot divides to produce a sterile, photosynthetic blade called the trophophore, and one fertile blade, or sporophore, which bears the sporangia. Sporangia are formed on branches of the sporophore. They are spherical, lack an indusium, and have no ring (annulus). When mature, the sporangia open by a transverse slit to release spores.

Sporangia releasing spores

Although *Botrychium virginianum* (Rattlesnake Fern) may grow a foot or more in height and is a conspicuous plant in woodlands, many of the species described here are tiny and difficult to find, since they may be well hidden among other plants. This is especially true of *Ophioglossum vulgatum* (Southern Adder's-tongue), which is often surrounded by dense grasses. The diminutive *B. matricariifolium* (Daisyleaf Grape Fern) is likewise often difficult to see in shadow-specked woodlands. *B. simplex* (Dwarf Grape Fern) is not only scarcer than the others, but most frequently is a tiny plant. However, be alert to these species and don't be discouraged. The initial challenge lies in finding one's first example in the field and gaining a search image; after that, others are usually readily spotted.

Succulent ferns inhabit a very diverse array of environments but seem to have a general affinity for slightly disturbed soils without an especially deep litter layer. Their apparent lack of habitat specialization, plus difficulties in definitively identifying them, makes it hard to accurately assess how rare or common these ferns are in our area. The botanist who chooses to delve into this group will be richly rewarded by discovering and observing these fascinating plants and can provide new and valuable information needed to understand and protect these species.

GENUS *BOTRYCHIUM*

(Greek: *botrys,* "bunch"; referring to the grapelike bunch of sporangia on the sporophore)

The genus *Botrychium* includes nearly 60 species worldwide, with centers of highest diversity in northern regions and at high elevations. *Botrychium* species differ from *Ophioglossum* in having lobed or compound sterile blades (trophophores) rather than simple ones. Likewise, the sporophore (fertile spike) of *Botrychium* is often branched, with sporangia on the surface, in contrast to *Ophioglossum* species' linear, compact sporophores with embedded sporangia.

The distribution and relationships of *Botrychium* species are only now beginning to come to light. Several new species have been discovered recently, and detailed genetic studies have clarified the origins of species with multiple sets of chromosomes (polyploids) and hybrids. Individual plants within populations of *Botrychium* are notoriously variable, making definitive identification a challenge. Often, many stems must be carefully studied in order to gain a reliable "gestalt" of the species. Moreover, different *Botrychium* species often co-occur, but because of individual variability, observing different species side by side both highlights and obscures dissimilarities among taxa.

Twenty or so species of *Botrychium* have been documented in the northeastern United States, although this number is likely to change with further study. These species fall into three groups, called subgenera: *Osmundopteris* (with 1 species, the Rattlesnake Fern), *Botrychium* (the Moonworts), and *Sceptridium* (the Grape Ferns). We have organized our key and descriptions by these subgenera. Certain authors have elected to elevate these subgenera to generic level, but this designation is not yet widely used. Thus, in keeping with the *Flora of North America* (1993) and the majority of current treatments, we retain the species under the single genus *Botrychium*, while supplying the corresponding synonym. Fourteen of the species have very limited ranges or occur on the outskirts of our region. Although they receive less detailed mention here, it is worthwhile looking for them; they may be more common than we think!

You will notice in the following key that a few species of the subgenus *Botrychium* pop up twice. This is because the characteristics of single plants vary widely within a species or over the course of development, and a one-size-fits-all approach does not work for all characters.

BOTRYCHIUM KEY

1A. Sterile blade (trophophore) of mature plants usually wider than 2 in. and longer than 4 in. from base to apex; distinctly triangular in overall shape; diverges from sporophore below-ground at base of plant, or aboveground. Go to 2.

> **2A.** Sporophore and sterile blade diverge well above the base of the plant; fertile plants 6–20 in. tall; sterile blade sessile, highly dissected, not leathery, deciduous.
> **B. virginianum (Rattlesnake Fern), p. 248**

2B. Sporophore and sterile blade separate near or below ground level; sterile blade is long-stalked, fleshy or leathery, and held more or less parallel to ground level. Go to 3.
(subgenus *Sceptridium*, the Grape Ferns, p. 265)

3A. On sterile blade, pinnules toward the tip of the pinnae longer than wide. Go to 4.

4A. Sterile blade dark green; pinnule tips entire and pointed, the terminal pinnules elongated. Plants of low or brushy woods.
B. biternatum (Sparse-lobed Grape Fern), p. 270

4B. Blade bright green or blue-green; pinnule margins toothy; terminal pinnules not elongated. Go to 5.

5A. Tips of terminal pinnules come to a point; pinnule margins toothed and deeply lobed; plants turn purple or bronze in winter or when growing in full sun.
B. dissectum (Cut-leaved Grape Fern), p. 266

5B. Tips of pinnules blunt or rounded, margins with small teeth; plants remain bright green when exposed to sun.
B. oneidense (Blunt-lobed Grape Fern), p. 270

3B. Pinnules on sterile blade toward the tip of the pinnae rounded or diamond-shaped, not elongate. Go to 6.

6A. Sterile blade thick, fleshy, and leathery; pinnae and pinnules slightly concave on the upper surface (margins point upward), margins entire or with small rounded teeth; wide-ranging species throughout North America.
B. multifidum (Leathery Grape Fern), p. 268

6B. Sterile blade with a thin, somewhat crinkly texture; pinnae and pinnules convex on the upper surface (margins point downward), with toothed or lobed margins; restricted to St. Lawrence Valley to Vt.
B. rugulosum (St. Lawrence Grape Fern), p. 270

1B. Sterile blade narrower than 2 in. and generally shorter than 4 in. from basal pinnae to tip, trowel-shaped to slightly triangular (i.e., basal pinnae usually not substantially longer than pinnae toward the tip), always diverges from sporophore slightly to much aboveground. Go to 7.
(subgenus *Botrychium*, the Moonworts), p. 250

7A. Sterile blade pinnate-pinnatifid (pinnae are lobed) to bipinnate (pinnae divided into separate pinnules), pinnae elongated. Go to 8.

8A. Sterile blade appears to be divided into 3 nearly equal parts due to large size of basal pinnae. Go to 9.

    9A. Outline of sterile blade 3-lobed to narrowly triangular; long-stalked because it diverges from sporophore near ground level; middle pinnae fan-shaped, dull yellow-green (note that these can sometimes appear to clasp the stalk; see below). ***B. simplex*** **(Least Moonwort), p. 258**

    9B. Outline of sterile blade triangular to pentagonal, stalkless or nearly so; middle pinnae longer than wide, wavy-margined to lobed; lustrous. Go to 10.

        10A. Lower pinnae straight, lowest lobes of pinnae approximately the same size as the next lowest lobes, margins of lobes concave, plant entirely green.
        B. lanceolatum* ssp. *angustisegmentum **(Little Triangle Moonwort), p. 250**

        10B. Lower pinnae upwardly curved, lowest lobes of pinnae longer than next lowest lobes, margins of lobes convex with respect to the midrib, stipe reddish. ***B. lanceolatum* ssp. *lanceolatum*** **(Lance-leaved Moonwort), p. 250**

8B. Sterile blade with lower pinnae not significantly larger than the pinnae near the tip; more trowel-shaped, oblong, or linear than triangular. Go to 11.

    11A. Sterile blade with 3–4 pairs of narrow, serrated to coarsely toothed pinnae; surface lustrous. (Note: some larger plants can have more triangular trophophores; see above.)
    B. lanceolatum* ssp. *angustisegmentum **(Little Triangle Moonwort), p. 250**

    11B. Sterile blade outline oblong to oval-shaped; 4–6 pairs of broad, lobed pinnae. Go to 12.

        12A. Sporophore divided evenly into similar-sized pinnae, even in large specimens; sterile blade lustrous deep green. (Note: can strongly resemble *B. matricariifolium*; see below.) ***B. pseudopinnatum*** **(False Northwestern Moonwort), p. 263**

        12B. Sporophore with lower pinnae larger than upper pinnae in robust specimens; sterile blade dull pea green. Go to 13.

            13A. Sterile blade stalkless or nearly so; second pinna pair distinctly less lobed or divided relative to lowest pinnae, often nearly entire.
            B. michiganense **(Michigan Moonwort), p. 263**

13B. Sterile blade distinctly stalked, second pinna pair with the same degree of lobing or division as the basal pinnae. *B. matricariifolium* (Daisyleaf Moonwort), p. 254

7B. Sterile blade pinnate, with wedge or fan-shaped pinnae (no pinnules). Go to 14.

14A. Union of sporophore and sterile blade near ground level; stalk of sterile blade nearly as long as the blade itself; basal pinnae often disproportionately enlarged, often clasping sporophore stalk; pinna margins rounded. (Note: larger specimens of this species can have lobed or divided pinnae; see above.)
B. simplex (Least Moonwort), p. 258

14B. Union of sporophore and sterile blade well above ground, stalk of sterile blade much shorter than the blade itself, lowest pinnae seldom disproportionately enlarged. Go to 15.

15A. Middle (and sometimes basal) pinnae of sterile blade wider than long, often diamond-shaped (rhombic), broadly attached to rachis; pinna base sometimes extending down the rachis below the point of attachment. Go to 16.

16A. Plants slender; pinnae of sterile blade delicate, yellow-green, outer margins rounded.
B. tenebrosum (Shade-loving Moonwort), p. 260

16B. Plants stout; pinnae fleshy, white to pale yellow, with more or less straight outer margins.
B. mormo (Little Goblin), p. 263

15B. Middle pinnae of sterile blade longer than wide, not rhombic, narrowly attached at their bases (appearing stalked). Go to 17.

17A. Lowest pinnae of sterile blade narrow, with a span (degrees of a circle spanned by the outer pinna margin) $<45°$, sporophore stalk about $1/4$ the length of the sterile blade. Go to 18.

18A. Pinna width increases toward the outer margin, which is lobed to shallowly cleft; largest pinnae in middle of sterile blade.
B. campestre (Prairie Moonwort), p. 262

18B. Pinna width not increasing toward outer margin, which is often cleft into 2–4 linear segments; lowest pinnae the largest.
B. lineare (Slender Moonwort)

17B. Lowest pinnae wedge-shaped to half-moon shaped, with a span >60°, sporophore stalk $^1/_2$ or more the length of the sterile blade. Go to 19.

19A. Lowest pinnae of sterile blade hatchet-shaped, wedge-shaped or broadly spoon-shaped with a pinna span of 60°–120°.

20A. Sterile blade distinctly stalked. Go to 21.

21A. Sporophore tall, its stalk (at time of spore release) equal to or exceeding the length of the sterile blade; branches bearing the sporangia not crowded; pinna pairs often 6 or more; sterile blade usually dull yellow-green. (Note: pinnae of some plants can have a wider spread; see below.) **B. minganense (Mingan Moonwort), p. 256**

21B. Sporophore short, its stalk (at spore release) $^1/_2$ (or less) the length of the sterile blade; sporophore branches crowded and dense with sporangia; usually 4–5 pinna pairs. Go to 22.

22A. Middle pinnae blocky to short mushroom-shaped, broadly attached to rachis; outer pinna margin entire to unequally notched into 2 (sometimes 4) nonspreading lobes, upper portion longer and broader than the lower portion; plants in the field whitish green. (Note: sterile blade stalks on some plants can be very short; see below.) **B. pallidum (Pale Moonwort), p. 263**

22B. Middle pinnae wedge-shaped, outer margins toothed to deeply cleft into spreading lobes, nar-

rowly attached to rachis, plants
deep bluish green to dark green.
B. gallicomontanum
(Frenchman's Bluff Moonwort), p. 262

20B. Sterile blade sessile (stalkless) or
nearly so. Go to 23.

23A. Pinnae hatchet-shaped to wedge-
shaped with toothed outer margins,
often deeply cleft into 2 (rarely 4)
spreading, nearly equal segments.
B. ascendens (Upswept Moonwort), p. 262

23B. Pinnae spoon-shaped with rounded
outer margins, rarely cleft into unequal segments. **B. spathulatum**
(Spatulate Moonwort), p. 264

19B. Lowest pinnae of sterile blade half-
moon– shaped, with a pinna span of
150°–180°. Go to 24.

24A. Plants in the field whitish green; middle pinnae broadly attached to rachis;
usually 4 or fewer pinna pairs (see additional characters above).
B. pallidum (Pale Moonwort), p. 263

24B. Plants in the field deep green to yellow-green, middle pinnae narrowly attached to rachis; usually 5 or more
pinna pairs. Go to 25.

25A. Sterile blade clearly stalked; lowest
pinnae similar in shape to middle
pinnae, green to yellow-green (see
other characters for this species).
B. minganense (Mingan Moonwort), p. 256

25B. Sterile blade stalkless or nearly so;
lowest pinnae broader than middle
pinnae, dark green to green.
B. lunaria (Moonwort), p. 252

SUBGENUS OSMUNDOPTERIS: RATTLESNAKE FERN

The subgenus name reflects an early placement of this group with
Osmunda due to superficial similarities among their sporangia.
This subgenus contains only 1 very large species, *Botrychium vir-
ginianum* (Rattlesnake Fern).

RATTLESNAKE FERN

Botrychium virginianum (L.) Swartz
Synonym: *Botrypus virginianus* (L.) Holub

HABIT: Largest, most common, and earliest of *Botrychium* species to appear in our area. Its thin-textured, bright green, triangular, horizontal, highly dissected sterile blade rises prominently above woodland floor and can persist into autumn. Called "Rattlesnake Fern" because, when first open, the sporangia-bearing tip of the sporophore resembles the tip of a rattlesnake's tail. Commonly found in groups of several to many stems. The small, potatolike gametophyte is sometimes found persisting at the base of the plant.

ECOLOGY: In rich, moist or dry woodlands and wet thickets on subacidic soil, mostly in shade but occasionally in sunny spots in the North or in mountains.

RANGE: Ranging in all areas of North America except the desert southwest. Also South America, Europe, China, Japan, the Himalayas.

STERILE BLADE: 4–12 in. long; to 12 in. wide. Triangular, divided and subdivided into pinnules (variably but distinctly lacy-cut), thin-textured, bright green, not green in winter. Reflexed to almost horizontal.

PINNAE: Narrow, cut into pinnules that are toothed, lobed, or cut, with semiblunt tips. Up to 12 pairs produced on large plants. Variable in shape from plant to plant and somewhat dependent on light. Pinnae may overlap when fern grows in high light; more spread out in shaded plants. Veins few and simple.

COMMON STALK: 4–8 in. long below the point where sterile blade and sporophore diverge; erect, smooth, fleshy, round, pink at base.

SPOROPHORE: Six or more tapering, spreading to ascending branches at the top of a slender stalk that overtops the sterile blade. Sporangia distinctly bright yellow. Soon withers after early summer.

NOTES: In some habitats, Rattlesnake Ferns and the Moonworts (subgenus *Botrychium*) may resemble each other. However, in general, Rattlesnake Ferns are much larger than Moonworts and have a distinctly triangular, glossy sterile blade. Little Triangle Moonwort differs from small Rattlesnake Ferns in that the stalk of its sporophore is shorter than or equal in length to the spore-bearing portion.

MARGINALIA: *A. Pinnules, showing veins and lobes.*

DIAGNOSTIC ARROWS: *1. Sporophore borne well above juncture of main stalk and sterile blade.*

1.

A.

BOTRYCHIUM VIRGINIANUM
RATTLESNAKE FERN

The common name of this group derives from their half-moon–shaped pinnae and the Anglo-Saxon word for "plant" ("wort"). The sporophore and sterile blade of many Moonworts diverge well above the surface of the ground, like those of the Rattlesnake Fern (*B. virginianum*). Unlike the Rattlesnake Fern, however, the Moonworts' sterile blades are simpler and less lacy.

LITTLE TRIANGLE MOONWORT AND LANCE-LEAVED MOONWORT

Botrychium lanceolatum (S. C. Gmelin) Ängstrom

Little Triangle Moonwort: *B. l.* ssp. *angustisegmentum* (Pease & Moore) R. T. Clausen.
Synonym: *B. angustisegmentum* (Pease & Moore) Fernald
Lance-leaved Moonwort: *B. l. ssp lanceolatum*

HABIT: 2–10 in. tall. *Botrychium lanceolatum* has a distinctly triangular sterile blade that diverges high on the slender common stalk; 4–5 pairs of pinnae. Divided into 2 subspecies: *B. l.* ssp. *angustisegmentum* (Little Triangle Moonwort) and *B. l.* ssp. *lanceolatum* (Lance-leaved Moonwort); ssp. *angustisegmentum* is not as robust as ssp. *lanceolatum*.

ECOLOGY: Moist, cool, rich, acidic or subacidic woodlands. Sometimes occurs with *B. matricariifolium* (Daisyleaf Moonwort); sometimes in northern white cedar (*Thuja occidentalis*) swamps. Emerges late spring–early summer; releases spores later than other Moonworts; green into mid-autumn.

RANGE: *B. l.* ssp. *angustisegmentum* is circumpolar; most common in alpine areas. In our area from Ont. south to Tenn. and W. Va. along Appalachian Mts. *B l.* ssp. *lanceolatum* occurs throughout mountains of w. North America; also e. Canada, Greenland, Europe; in our area, n. Me. and Gaspé Pen.

STERILE BLADE: *B. l.* ssp. *angustisegmentum:* 1 in. ± long. Triangular, semi-erect to horizontal, emerging high up on common stalk close to sporophore. Smooth, fleshy, dark green, very shiny; nearly sessile; 4–5 (rarely 7) pairs of deeply lobed pinnae often with pointed tips; margins of pinnae lobes curved upward (concave). *B. l.* ssp. *lanceolatum:* Medium green to yellow-green; lobes of pinnae blunt-tipped; margins of lobes less concave than ssp. *angustisegmentum*, some convex.

COMMON STALK: 1 1/2–8 in. long to where the sporophore and sterile blade diverge; slender, smooth. *B. l.* ssp. *angustisegmentum*: Dark brownish green. *B. l.* ssp. *lanceolatum:* reddish brown.

SPOROPHORE: Simply to elaborately branched, nearly sessile; slightly spreading; 3 main branches. Sporangia bright greenish yellow.

NOTES: Although eastern Little Triangle Moonworts are physically distinctive from Lance-leaved Moonworts, their level of genetic differentiation does not indicate a need to designate them as separate species. Little Triangle Moonwort can be confused with closely related *B. matricariifolium* (Daisyleaf Moonwort), but sterile blade of Little Triangle Moonwort is nearly sessile and its pinnae pairs closer together, with basal pinnae by far the longest. The sterile blade of Daisyleaf Moonwort is stalked and more trowel-shaped than triangular.

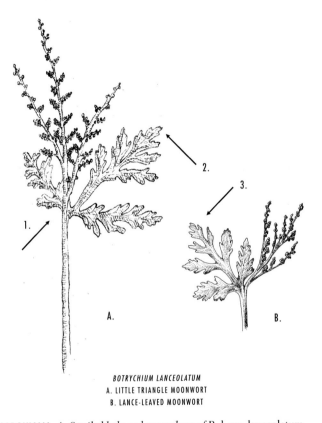

BOTRYCHIUM LANCEOLATUM
A. LITTLE TRIANGLE MOONWORT
B. LANCE-LEAVED MOONWORT

MARGINALIA: *A. Sterile blade and sporophore of* B. l. *ssp.* lanceolatum.
B. Sterile blade and sporophore of B. l. *ssp.* angustisegmentum.
DIAGNOSTIC ARROWS: *1. Sterile leaf and sporophore diverge high above ground, with sterile blade nearly sessile. 2. Blunt lobes of* B. l. *ssp.* lanceolatum. *3. Pointed tips of* B. l. *ssp.* angustisegmentum.

Botrychium lunaria (L.) Sw.

HABIT: Overall height usually less than 6 in. Sterile blade divided into 6 or more pairs of shiny, deep green pinnae shaped like half-moons or fans.

ECOLOGY: Dry pastures, meadows, hillsides, rocky ledges, under northern white cedar trees (*Thuja occidentalis*), damp quarry floors, road banks cut into calcium-rich soils, cliffs, or dunes. Prefers calcareous soils that have experienced enough disturbance to remove a deep litter layer or to prevent it from forming. Often associated with wild strawberry (*Fragaria virginiana*) and calcium-loving plants.

RANGE: Very widespread but rare in our region. Greenland south through the Canadian maritime provinces to Me., n. N.Y., Penn., west to the Great Lakes region and all Canadian provinces. In the West, extends from Alaska south to Ariz. Also cold climates of s. South America, New Zealand, Eurasia.

STERILE BLADE: 2–4 in. long, 3/4–2 in. wide. Narrow with a rounded end, erect; emerges from the common stalk at about half the height of the plant (although position is variable among sun and shade plants). Nearly sessile, thick, fleshy, smooth, shiny kelly green to deep green. Divided into 6–9 nearly opposite pairs of half-moon– or fan-shaped pinnae, which sometimes overlap with the next pair. Pinnae have entire to narrowly cleft, somewhat wavy margins. Topmost pinnae much narrower than lower ones, often reduced to a wedge shape. Veins arrayed like ribs of a fan.

COMMON STALK: 1–3 in. to divergence of sporophore and sterile blade.

SPOROPHORE: 1–5 in. long. Branching clusters. Tip may bend slightly downward.

NOTES: Moonwort figures in many northern European myths as a magical plant. Could be confused with the *Botrychium minganense* (Mingan Moonwort), but Mingan Moonwort has pairs of pinnae set well apart on the stem, and its sterile blade is distinctly stalked as opposed to sessile in Moonwort.

MARGINALIA: *A. Fan-shaped pinna.*

DIAGNOSTIC ARROWS: *1. Pendent sporophore. 2. Semiconcave, moon-shaped pairs of pinnae.*

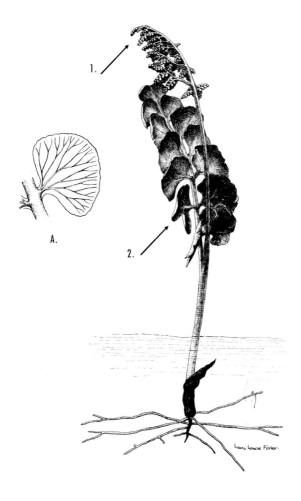

1.

2.

A.

BOTRYCHIUM LUNARIA
MOONWORT

DAISYLEAF MOONWORT

Botrychium matricariifolium (Döll) A. Br. ex W. D. J. Koch

HABIT: Rather stout; 2–10 in. tall; grows as scattered individuals. Sterile blade dull, pale green, trowel-shaped. Species and common names refer to resemblance of sterile blade to leaves of *Matricaria* (chamomile) in the daisy family.

ECOLOGY: Edges of rich moist woodlands, pastures, old-fields, roadsides, dunes, other areas with sparse grass cover in cooler regions; also alpine areas.

RANGE: Northern shore of Gulf of St. Lawrence and Nfld. south to Appalachian Mts. of N.C. and Tenn.; west to Que., Minn., and Wisc. Also Europe.

STERILE BLADE: $\frac{1}{2}$–4 in. long. Erect, stalked, 2–7 pairs rounded, narrow pinnae that are sometimes deeply lobed.

COMMON STALK: 1–8 in. long to where sterile blade and sporophore diverge; slender, fleshy, pale, chalky green; often with a pink stripe.

SPOROPHORE: Erect; 3 large branches, each bearing several small, branched clusters. Often longer than sterile blade. Sporangia yellow and prominent.

NOTES: Can be confused with closely related *Botrychium lanceolatum* spp. *angustisegmentum* (Little Triangle Moonwort), but the sterile blade is stalked rather than sessile where it meets the common stalk, and trowel-shaped rather than triangular.

MARGINALIA: *A. Sporophore. B. Sterile blade.*

DIAGNOSTIC ARROWS: *1 . Sterile blade on stalk close to clustered sporophore.*

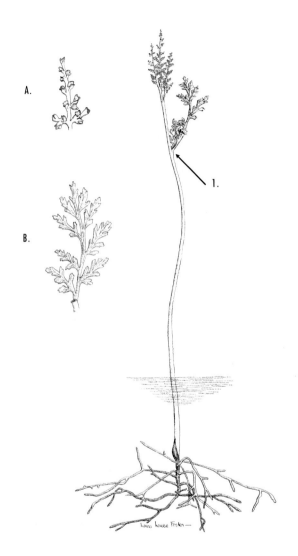

A.

B.

1.

BOTRYCHIUM MATRICARIIFOLIUM
DAISYLEAF MOONWORT

MINGAN MOONWORT

Botrychium minganense Victorin

HABIT: Yellowish green, upright. 3–10 in. tall.

ECOLOGY: Widely scattered; grassy meadows, second-growth maple woods, prairies, sand dunes, river banks on acid to near-neutral soils.

RANGE: Rare in our area. Que. and Nfld. south to n. N.Y. and Vt., west from n. Great Lakes across Canada to Alaska and south into mountains of w. U.S.

STERILE BLADE: ½–3 in. long. Emerges halfway up common stalk. Dull, yellowish green (sometimes grayish green in sun); fleshy; stalked. 2–10 (often 6 or more) pairs of fan-shaped or shallowly notched, ascending, stalked pinnae with entire margins.

COMMON STALK: 2½–4 in. long to the point where sporophore and sterile blade diverge.

SPOROPHORE: Pinnate; spreading branches; longer than sterile blade.

NOTES: "Mingan Moonwort" refers to Mingan Island in the Gulf of St. Lawrence, where the first specimens were collected. It is a tetraploid hybrid (4 sets of chromosomes), probably derived from *Botrychium lunaria* (Moonwort) and a species similar to *B. pallidum* (Pale Moonwort). In Mingan Moonwort, the basal pinnae are not cleft into 2 unequal lobes as they are in Pale Moonwort, and the blade is not pale whitish green. It can resemble Moonwort, but basal pinnae of Moonwort are broader (the outer margin of a pinna spanning an arc of about 180°) and Moonwort's sterile blade is sessile to the common stalk.

MARGINALIA: *A. Close-up of young sterile blade and sporophore.*

DIAGNOSTIC ARROWS: *1. Well-spaced pinnae on sterile blade. 2. Lowest pinnae symmetrical (not irregularly lobed). 3. Stalked sterile blade.*

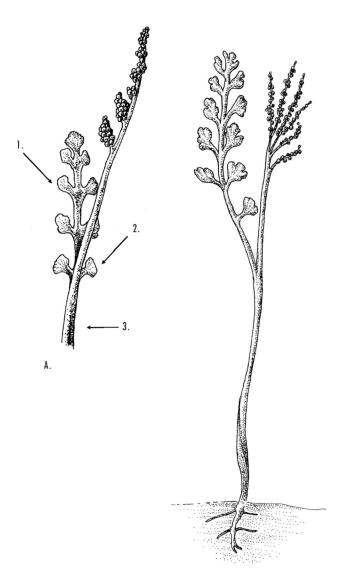

1.

2.

3.

A.

BOTRYCHIUM MINGANENSE
MINGAN MOONWORT

LEAST MOONWORT

Botrychium simplex E. Hitch. var. *simplex* (Lasch) R. T. Clausen

HABIT: Diminutive moonwort only 1 1/2–7 in. tall, often about the size of a thumb. The shape of the sterile blade in plants of our area is usually less lacy and lobed than other Moonworts, hence its name, *simplex*.

ECOLOGY: Damp meadows, moist woodlands, roadside ditches, and edges of pastures with rather poor, slightly acid soil. More common in our northern areas.

RANGE: Nfld. south to the Appalachian Mts. to W. Va., west to the Great Lakes states. Western varieties range from B.C. south to Calif. and inland to Wyo. and Utah; these are different in form and genetic composition from the eastern variety, var. *simplex*.

STERILE BLADE: 1/2–3 inches long. Very variable in shape, ascending close to where it emerges from common stalk. Sometimes appears to clasp the sporophore stalk, diverging with sporophore at variable heights, from near ground level to halfway up the height of the plant. Smooth, fleshy, pale to yellowish green, with 1–3 (rarely 5) pairs of rounded pinnae, the lowest ones often disproportionately larger and sometimes divided into pinnules.

COMMON STALK: 1 in. long. Fleshy, smooth, pale green.

SPOROPHORE: Long-stalked at maturity, usually overtopping the sterile blade and lengthening as spores ripen; sporangia small but prominent and widely spaced.

NOTES: Despite its "simple" name, the species has confounded taxonomists for a long time; its wide variability in form has caused many to name separate varieties, only to rethink and lump them again (e.g., see *Botrychium tenebrosum*, Shade-loving Moonwort, page 260).

MARGINALIA: *A. Sterile blade and sporophore.*
DIAGNOSTIC ARROWS: *1. Simple blade and simple unbranched sporophore.*

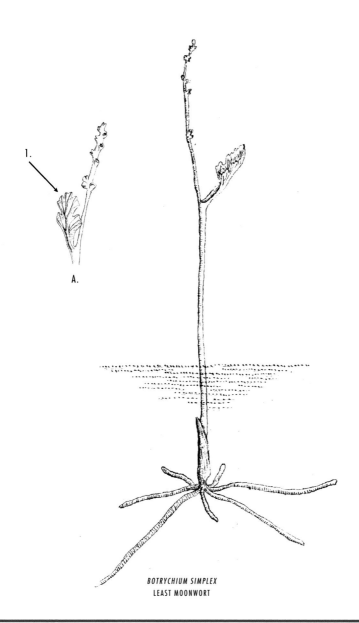

1.

A.

BOTRYCHIUM SIMPLEX
LEAST MOONWORT

SHADE-LOVING MOONWORT

Botrychium tenebrosum A. A. Eaton

Synonym: *Botrychium simplex* (E. Hitch.) var. *tenebrosum* (A. A. Eaton) R. T. Clausen

HABIT: A perplexing species that resembles *Botrychium simplex* (Least Moonwort), and was once thought to be a variety of that species. New scientific evidence shows that it is genetically distinct from Least Moonwort. The whole plant is small (1 1/2 – 4 in. tall) and slender.

ECOLOGY: Mostly in deep, moist woods and shaded margins of swamps or on hummocks in swamps. Outside New England, it also occurs in open sandy meadows.

RANGE: Ont. and Que. south to N.J. and Penn., west to Minn. Also in Iceland and Europe.

STERILE BLADE: 1/2 – 1 1/2 in. long. on a short stalk with 1 – 3 pairs of short, whitish green to yellow-green rounded pinnae; basal pinnae somewhat elongate; not greatly dissected or clasping the sporophore.

COMMON STALK: 1 – 3 in. to where sporophore and trophophore diverge, long, slender, pale green.

SPOROPHORE: Stalked and narrowly branched but not greatly surpassing the sterile blade in length.

NOTES: Can resemble *Botrychium simplex* (Least Moonwort), but the basal pinnae of Shade-loving Moonwort are rarely enlarged, nor does the sterile blade appear to clasp the sporophore stalk as in Least Moonwort. Furthermore, the sterile blade and sporophore of Shade-loving Moonwort are borne on shorter stalks and diverge high aboveground on a relatively long common stalk. Least Moonwort's long-stalked sporophore diverges from the sterile blade close to ground level.

MARGINALIA: *A. Close-up of sterile blade and sporophore.*

DIAGNOSTIC ARROWS: *1. Sporophore and sterile blade diverge aboveground. 2. Sterile blade with small basal pinnae, not clasping stalk.*

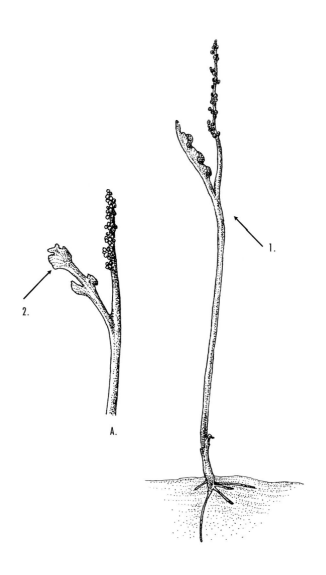

1.

2.

A.

BOTRYCHIUM TENEBROSUM
SHADE-LOVING MOONWORT

In addition to the more common Moonworts just described, 9 other species occur in the e. U.S. Because they have very limited distributions in our region, they receive only brief mention here.

UPSWEPT MOONWORT
Botrychium ascendens W. H. Wagner

A common western species of open fields. Grows in western mountains from Nev. to Alaska; only recently detected in Nfld., Ont., and Minn., but may be more widespread in our area. The sterile blade has upwardly angled, wedge-shaped pinnae with toothed outer margins often cleft into two spreading parts. Noted for unusual tendency to produce sporangia on the basal pinnae of the "sterile" blade.

PRAIRIE MOONWORT
Botrychium campestre W. H. Wagner & Farrar

Rare, cryptic Moonwort of prairies, inland dunes, and grassy areas associated with limestone; prefers drier habitats than other species do. Reported from Ont., N.Y., Mich., Wisc., Neb., Mont., the Dakotas, Colo., Alta., Sask., Wyo. Sterile blade is sessile, 1–2 in. with 5–9 pairs of widely spaced narrow pinnae. Sporophore often quite large relative to sterile blade. Plants produce masses of gemmae (tiny plantlets) on underground stems.

FRENCHMAN'S BLUFF MOONWORT
Botrychium gallicomontanum Farrar & Johnson-Groh

Tetraploid species, grows along with (diploid) *Botrychium campestre* (Prairie Moonwort) in native prairie grasslands. Currently known from only two sites in nw. Minn., it may be more common in the North and East and should be looked for. Resembles Prairie Moonwort but is larger and stouter. Yellow-green, 1 1/2-in.-long sterile blade is slightly stalked, and pinnae are more broadly wedge-shaped than those of Prairie Moonwort.

SLENDER MOONWORT
Botrychium lineare W. H. Wagner

Pale green with a narrow sterile blade and 4–6 pairs of thin, well-separated, forking pinnae. Last collected in 1942 along the St. John River in Canada, just a few miles from the northern tip of Me. It has not been seen in our area since, and despite the broad range of currently known populations from Calif. and Colo. to Alaska, it remains one of the rarer Moonworts. More sightings would add greatly to our understanding of this species. Look for it on limestone shelves and cliffs, in deep grass of meadows, and in woods in the northern reaches of our region.

MICHIGAN MOONWORT

Botrychium michiganense Gilman & F. S. Wagner

When this species was initially discovered by W. H. Wagner, he considered it to be an eastern population of the western species, *Botrychium hesperium* (Western Moonwort). However, later studies show the two to be genetically and morphologically distinct species. Michigan Moonwort ranges from Mich. and Minn. to the Black Hills of S.D., Wyo. west to e. Wash. and into Alta. In our area, it most closely resembles *B. matricariifolium* (Daisyleaf Moonwort), but it has a sessile, gray-green sterile blade to $2^1/_2$ in. long and makes an abrupt transition from deeply lobed basal pinnae to much less lobed middle pinnae.

LITTLE GOBLIN

Botrychium mormo W. H. Wagner

Known only from rich sugar maple, beech, or basswood forests of Wisc., Mich., and Minn., this very succulent Moonwort (the tiniest in our area) produces a 2 in.-long sterile blade with very short, squarish pinnae. Resembles a light green fungus more than a plant; most Little Goblins barely emerge above the leaf litter. Often remains dormant during dry years. Gametophytes sometimes found still attached to bases of sporophytes.

PALE MOONWORT

Botrychium pallidum W. H. Wagner

Very small Moonwort with whitish green pinnae; basal pinnae often cleft into two unequal lobes, with upper lobe larger. Recorded primarily in open fields in Me., Man., Ont., Que., S.D., Mont., Sask., Colo., Minn., and Mich. Produces masses of gemmae (tiny plantlets) on underground stem.

FALSE NORTHWESTERN MOONWORT

Botrychium pseudopinnatum W. H. Wagner

Only known Moonwort with 6 sets of chromosomes. Named for similarity to the western species *Botrychium pinnatum* (Northwestern Moonwort). In our region it is reported only from Lake Superior, though it may be more common as it is often confused with *B. matricariifolium* (Daisyleaf Moonwort). Distinguished from Daisyleaf and from *B. michiganense* (Michigan Moonwort) by pinnately branched sporophore and lustrous, deep green $2^1/_2$- in.-long sterile blade.

SPATULATE MOONWORT
Botrychium spathulatum W. H. Wagner

Resembles *Botrychium minganense* (Mingan Moonwort), but tends to appear later. Currently known only from fields and inland dunes of Mich. Sterile blade pinnate, leathery, shiny, dark green, to 3 1/2 in. long. Pinnately branched sporophores.

Note the lustrous dark green sterile blade of Botrychium lanceolatum *ssp.* angustisegmentum (*Little Triangle Moonwort*). (*Photo by Donald Farrar*)

Botrychium lunaria (*Moonwort*) *with its moon-shaped pairs of pinnae.* (*Photo by Donald Farrar*)

The Grape Ferns (the subgenus derived from the Greek word for "little scepter") are named for their spherical sporangia, which are borne on highly branched, upright sporophores. The whole reproductive structure resembles an upright bunch of tiny, yellow grapes. Grape Ferns produce sterile blades (often horizontally oriented) that appear to be divided into 3 parts with greatly enlarged lower pinnae—a bit like a small *Pteridium aquilinum* (Bracken Fern) or *Gymnocarpium* spp. (Oak Ferns) in overall architecture. The sterile blade and sporophore typically diverge underground, rather than sharing a common aboveground stalk like *Botrychium virginianum* (Rattlesnake Fern) and most species of the subgenus *Botrychium* (Moonworts). Grape Ferns emerge in early summer and are evergreen. Five species occur in our area. Grape Ferns differ from the Moonworts in their generally larger size (width of sterile blade usually >2 in.); leathery texture; attitude (sterile blade held about parallel to ground); and position of sporophore and sterile blade junction at or below ground level. (Only *B. simplex*, Least Moonwort, also diverges close to the ground, but it has fan-shaped pinnae.) Sterile blades of Moonworts are usually narrower than 2 in., fleshy or delicate in texture, and angle distinctly upward. Small plants with no sporophore are almost always Grape Ferns or Rattlesnake Fern.

Branched clusters of yellow sporangia on sporophore of Botrychium dissectum (*Cutleaved Grape Fern*). *(Photo by Frank Bramley/NEWFS)*

CUT-LEAVED GRAPE FERN
(DISSECTED GRAPE FERN)

Botrychium dissectum Spreng.
Synonym: *Sceptridium dissectum* (Spreng.) Lyon

HABIT: Extremely variable species. Triangular sterile blade diverges from sporophore at or below surface of ground. The blades appear in early summer and last through winter and into the next spring, though they turn bronze after frost.

ECOLOGY: Wide variety of habitats including dry or moist open woodlands, fields, abandoned pastures, cemeteries, floodplain forests, and sandy areas of pinelands and scrub oaks. Tolerates many soil types as long as they are slightly disturbed and not too dry. Sometimes occurs with a thick cover of Haircap Mosses (*Polytrichum* spp.).

RANGE: Our most common Grape Fern, found throughout our area from N.S. to Fla., west to Ark., north to s. Ont.

STERILE BLADE: 8–12 in. long and equally wide on a 1–7-in. stalk. Triangular; appears to be divided into 3 sections because basal pinnae are much enlarged. Semileathery, coarse, fleshy, reflexed, often borne parallel to soil. Pinnae trowel-shaped, often divided into pinnules with toothed, serrated, or lacy-cut edges and pointed tips—very variable. Also variable in color, green to dark blue-green, turning bronze in winter or in full sun.

SPOROPHORE: 2–8 in. ± long. Overtops sterile blade, with branched clusters of light yellow sporangia. Withers soon after spore release in late summer.

NOTES: Could be confused with *Botrychium virginianum* (Rattlesnake Fern) due to overall form of the dissected sterile blade, but much smaller size and divergence of sterile blade and sporophore at or near ground level distinguish Cut-leaved Grape Fern. Several forms are found throughout the range of this highly variable species.

MARGINALIA: *A. Highly dissected form of sterile pinna. B. Less dissected sterile pinna.*

DIAGNOSTIC ARROWS: *1. Sterile blade and sporophore diverging close to surface of ground. 2. Erect and slightly branched sporophore.*

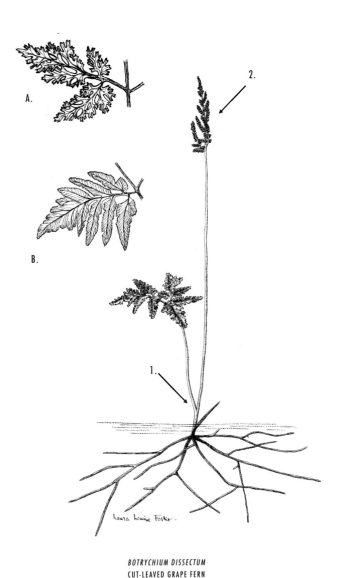

A.

B.

2.

1.

BOTRYCHIUM DISSECTUM
CUT-LEAVED GRAPE FERN

LEATHERY GRAPE FERN

Botrychium multifidum (Gmel.) Rupr.
Synonym: *Sceptridium multifidum* (Gmel.) Nishida ex Tagawa

HABIT: Largest of the Grape Ferns. Very leathery and succulent. Stout and coarse. Variable forms, depending on habitat. In early summer, new and old sterile blades sometimes found side by side, both green, with the old one limp and soon withering.

ECOLOGY: Often poor, acidic soils (even serpentine soils) in fields, blueberry barrens, and roadsides. Populations frequently small.

RANGE: Very broadly distributed from Nfld. south to Va. (generally more common in the northern mountains), west through the northern plains states and provinces to s. Alaska, midcoast Calif., and Rocky Mt. states.

STERILE BLADE: 2–6 in. long and equally wide. Broadly triangular; held horizontal or reflexed; thickly fleshy or leathery; shiny green to grayish green. Borne on a short stalk in open-growing plants, variously elevated on a longer stalk in shade plants. 3–5 pairs of pinnae, each on long, prominent stalks, with lowest pairs the largest; lobed or cut into pinnules. Terminal sections are about the same size as lateral sections. Individual pinnae somewhat concave on upper surface. Pinnules oval, sometimes overlapping, with rounded or blunt tips, margins entire or with small, rounded teeth.

SPOROPHORE: Wide-spreading, branching, prominent, taller than sterile blade, many sporangia. Grows slower than sterile blade, usually visible in late summer.

MARGINALIA: *A. Pinnule. B. Pinna segment.*
DIAGNOSTIC ARROWS: *1. Previous year's sterile blade. 2. Large, clustered sporophore. 3. Triangular sterile blade and overlapping pinnules. 4. Long prominent stalk.*

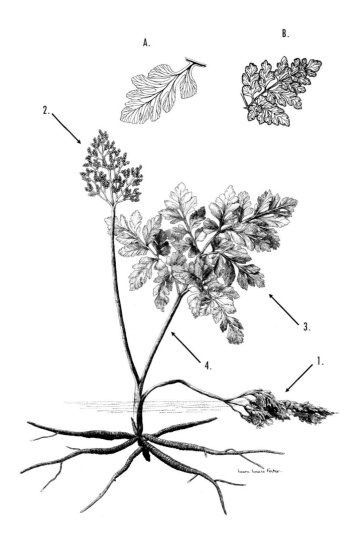

A.

B.

2.

3.

4.

1.

BOTRYCHIUM MULTIFIDUM
LEATHERY GRAPE FERN

SPARSE-LOBED GRAPE FERN
Botrychium biternatum (Savigny) L.

Found in more southern reaches of our area from Del. and N.J. south to Fla., west to e. Tex., north to Ky., Ill., and Mo. Distinguished by relatively simple pinnae, which are divided into pinnules with entire margins, giving it a less feathery look than other grape ferns. The sterile blade is dark green, herbaceous, and 7 in. long × 11 in. ± wide. Pinnules at tops of pinnae narrow and very elongated, with pointed tips. Sporophore is also branched, and 2–3 times taller than sterile blade. Can co-occur with *B. dissectum* (Cut-leaved Grape Fern) in sparse woods and shrubby fields.

BLUNT-LOBED GRAPE FERN
Botrychium oneidense (Gilbert) House
Synonym: *Sceptridium oneidense* (Gilbert) Holub

A bright green Grape Fern once considered a variety of *Botrychium multifidum* (Leathery Grape Fern). Blunt-lobed Grape Fern is a hybrid of Leathery Grape Fern and *B. dissectum* (Cut-leaved Grape Fern), with which it sometimes occurs. Prefers moist, shady young hardwood stands, floodplain forests, and swamps. Distinguished from Cut-leaved Grape Fern by pinnae, which are broader (to 8 in.) and much less pointed at the tips. Blunt-lobed's pinnules also usually slightly toothed or serrated, unlike those of Leathery, which are wavy and lobed. Considered rarer than either Leathery or Cut-leaved, with an overlapping but narrower range extending from N.B. south to interior S.C., and west to Mich., Wisc., Ohio.

ST. LAWRENCE GRAPE FERN
Botrychium rugulosum W. H. Wagner
Synonym: *Sceptridium rugulosum* (W. H. Wagner) Skoda & Holub

Narrowly distributed species, tends to occur in small populations, sometimes mixed with *Botrychium multifidum* (Leathery Grape Fern), *B. dissectum* (Cut-leaved Grape Fern), and *B. oneidense* (Blunt-leaved Grape Fern). Thin, herbaceous sterile blade 6–12 in. long and equally wide; divided into numerous delicate pinnae and trowel-shaped pinnules with coarse-toothed margins. Terminal pinnules about the same size as lateral pinnules. Pinnae can appear somewhat convex along upper surface (with edges turned downward). St. Lawrence Grape Fern does not venture far from the St. Lawrence River Valley and Great Lakes (hence its common name), but has been found in n. Vt., N.Y., Mich., and Minn., principally in sandy soils of pastures that are reverting to woods, sometimes under staghorn sumac (*Rhus typhina*) stands.

GENUS *OPHIOGLOSSUM*: ADDER'S-TONGUES

(Greek: *ophis*, "snake," + *glossa*, "tongue"; referring to the narrow, tonguelike shape of the sporophore)

Ophioglossum contains about 25 species worldwide, most of which are tropical or subtropical. Three species are recorded for our region. *Ophioglossum pusillum* (aptly called Northern Adder's-tongue) enjoys a broad northern range, in contrast to O. *engelmannii* (Limestone Adder's-tongue), which is found in the southern and western portions of the U.S., Mexico, and Central America. *O. vulgatum* (Southern Adder's-tongue) overlaps in range midway between these two species, extending from N.J. to Fla. and Mexico, as well as Eurasia. Adder's-tongues prefer open, grassy habitats and may be often overlooked or misidentified in passing because they resemble a nonflowering form of a lily or orchid. Look closely at the sterile blade (trophophore), however, and it quickly becomes apparent that it is not a lily or orchid leaf because it has netted (not parallel) veins and lacks a midvein. Leaf vein pattern is one of the first characters used to distinguish among *Ophioglossum* species. In our region's species, the succulent sterile blade is produced beneath the erect sporophore (a spore-bearing spike that contains deeply embedded sporangia, like two rows of beads, along its length).

Although the subterranean gametophyte of *Ophioglossum* has been described somewhat unattractively as a "contorted, worm-like object," modest beginnings give rise to beautiful sporophytes, which can produce colonies by proliferating off roots. Interestingly, *Ophioglossum* species have some of the highest numbers of chromosomes of all vascular plants, with up to 1,200 chromosomes packed into each cell. Clearly, simplicity in outer form belies internal complexity.

OPHIOGLOSSUM KEY

1A. Sterile blade has a tiny sharp point at tip; nets of larger veins encircle intricate nets of smaller veins; plants from southern edge of our region, restricted to limestone.
O. engelmannii
(Limestone Adder's-tongue)

1B. Sterile blade without a sharp-pointed tip; nets of larger veins encircle only linear segments of smaller veins; broader range in more diverse habitats. Go to 2.

2A. Sterile blade pale green and widest at the midpoint.

> ***O. pusillum* (Northern Adder's-tongue)**

2B. Sterile blade dark green and widest at its base near where it meets the stem.

> ***O. vulgatum* (Southern Adder's-tongue)**

LIMESTONE ADDER'S-TONGUE

Ophioglossum engelmannii Prantl

HABIT: 5–10 in. tall with 1–2 erect to spreading, sometimes slightly folded, sterile blades large in proportion to whole plant. Pale green, distinctly elliptical, with sharp-pointed tip. Often sends up new stems in late summer following rains.

ECOLOGY: Limey, gravelly depressions in pastures; woodlands, red cedar (*Juniperus virginiana*) glades, sometimes on ledges. Emerges in April, persists to August.

RANGE: Ill., Ohio, and Mo. south to Fla., Tex., Ariz., and into Central America.

STERILE BLADE: 3–4 in. long; ³/₄–1¹/₂ in. wide. Elliptical, distinctly pointed tip, abruptly narrowed base. Smooth, succulent, light green, sessile; upper half arches backward. Intricate venation, with netted larger veins encircling netted smaller veins. Occasionally two blades produced per plant.

SPOROPHORE: 2–5 in. long including stalk. Sporangia-bearing portion 1–2 in. long; bears 20–40 pairs of sporangia; comes to a narrow pointed tip on a bending stalk.

MARGINALIA: *A. Sterile blade.*

DIAGNOSTIC ARROWS: *1. Intricately netted veins. 2. Pointed tip.*

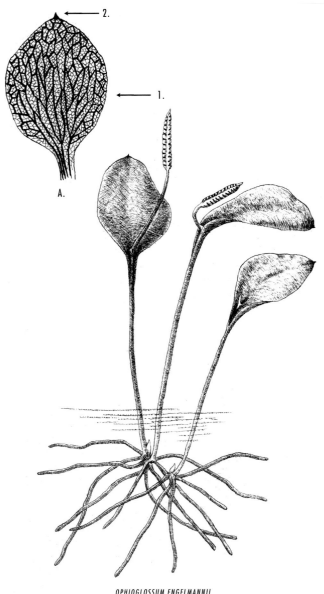

OPHIOGLOSSUM ENGELMANNII
LIMESTONE ADDER'S-TONGUE

Ophioglossum pusillum Rafinesque

HABIT: Only about 2–8 in. tall. Distinguished by light green sterile blade that is widest at midpoint.

ECOLOGY: Open swamps, marsh edges, grassy pastures, old-fields, roadside ditches, and floodplains in moderately acid soils.

RANGE: N.B. south to Va. and W. Va., west to Minn. and Mich. Also Ore., Wash., n. Calif., sw. Canada.

STERILE BLADE: 4 in. long. Erect, soft, with a gradually tapering base and an acute to rounded tip; widest at midpoint. Larger veins encircle mainly linear (not netted) segments of smaller veins. Membranelike sheath sometimes visible at the base of the plant, not persistent.

SPOROPHORE: 2–5 in. above the height of the sterile blade; sporangia-bearing portion 3/4– 2 in. ± long, bears 10–40 pairs of sporangia, and comes to a narrow tip.

NOTES: Similar to *Ophioglossum vulgatum* (Southern Adder's-tongue) but with a pale green (rather than dark green) sterile blade.

MARGINALIA: *A. Venation on sterile blade.*

DIAGNOSTIC ARROWS: *1. Gradually tapering tip of sterile blade. 2. Blade widest at midpoint.*

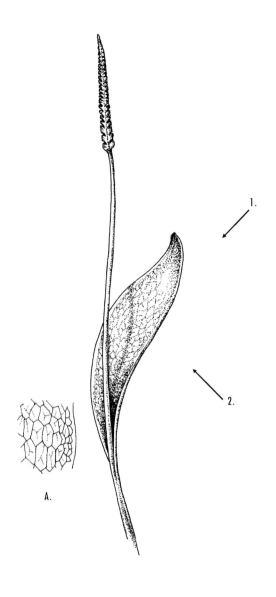

OPHIOGLOSSUM PUSILLUM
NORTHERN ADDER'S-TONGUE

Ophioglossum vulgatum L.

HABIT: Elusive; 4–10 in. tall. Single, simple, narrow grass green sterile blade emerges from a delicate, smooth, and fleshy common stalk, which is tipped by fertile spike (sporophore). Withers in midsummer.

ECOLOGY: Damp patches of turf in fields, woodlands, forested bottomlands, and floodplains. Appears in spring and early summer.

RANGE: N.J. south to Fla. and e. Tex., inland to Penn., Ky., and Ill. Also reported from Ariz., Mexico, Eurasia.

STERILE BLADE: 4 in. ± long; 1 1/2 in. ± wide. Widest near base; round-tipped, smooth, succulent, dark green, somewhat shiny; ascending or with upper half arching backward. Larger veins encircle mainly linear (not netted) segments of smaller veins.

SPOROPHORE: Borne on top of tall stalk that is 2–4 times the length of the sterile blade. Sporangia-bearing portion 1 1/2 in. ± long; narrow, comes to a pointed tip, and bears 10–35 pairs of sporangia. Persistent leathery sheath sometimes visible at base.

NOTES: Resembles *Ophioglossum pusillum* (Northern Adder's-tongue), but sterile blade is widest near stem and darker green.

MARGINALIA: *A. Sporophore. B. Sterile blade.*
DIAGNOSTIC ARROWS: *1. Blunt-tipped blade, widest near base. 2. Venation of sterile blade.*

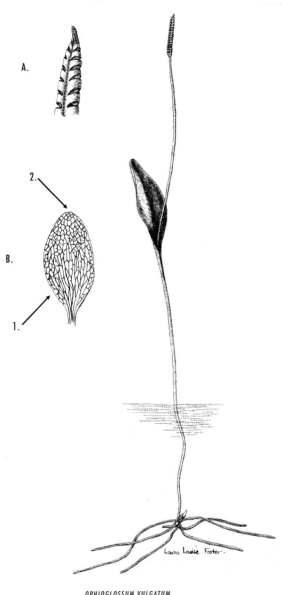

A.

B.

2.

1.

OPHIOGLOSSUM VULGATUM
SOUTHERN ADDER'S-TONGUE

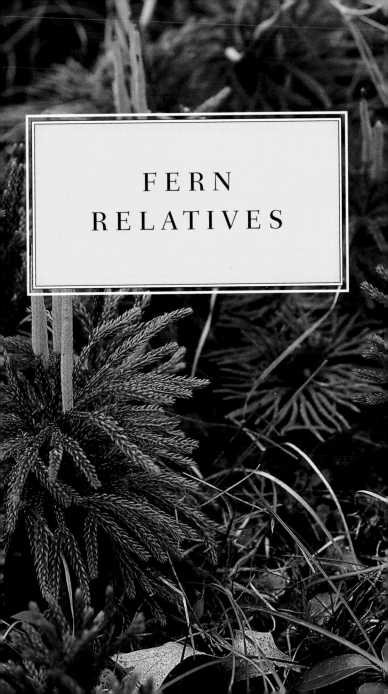

FERN
RELATIVES

FERN RELATIVES

GENERA *DENDROLYCOPODIUM, DIPHASIASTRUM, HUPERZIA, LYCOPODIELLA, LYCOPODIUM, PSEUDOLYCOPODIELLA, SPINULUM:* CLUB MOSSES AND FIRMOSSES

Clubmosses are some of the most familiar of the broad group traditionally called the "fern allies." Commonly known as Ground Pine, Firmoss, Princess Pine, or Running Pine, many Clubmosses look like diminutive relatives of pines, hemlocks, and cedars; others resemble giant mosses. All the common names call to mind the similarities among conifers, mosses, and clubmosses—the small, shiny, evergreen, somewhat needlelike leaves and the preference for woodland or moist, mossy habitats.

Clubmosses are small, usually evergreen, perennial plants of upright, trailing, or creeping habit. The many small, crowded leaves are narrow and pointed, simple, sessile (without a leaf stalk), and frequently all one size. On most species, they are arranged around the stem in 4–16 ranks (see explanation below) in pairs, spirals, or alternating overlapping patterns.

Clubmoss colonies expand primarily through growth of horizontal stems that "run" and

Dendrolycopodium dendroideum (*Prickly Tree Clubmoss*). (*Photo by Arthur Haines*)

sometimes even "leap" or arch over small obstacles (see Foxtail Bog Clubmoss, page 314). Each year, the horizontal stem, whether above- or belowground, branches and grows longer. Older stems (near the center of the colony) eventually wither and die, but the horizontal stem continues to grow, and the colonies expand in most species.

Today's Clubmosses are surprisingly similar to those found in Paleozoic fossil records dating back 390 million years. These ancient Clubmosses, together with giant ancestors of Horsetails and Quillworts, populated the vast forest jungles that have become today's coal beds.

Clubmosses belong to the family Lycopodiaceae, which was traditionally represented by just two genera: *Phylloglossum* (Australia and New Zealand) and *Lycopodium* (North America). *Lycopodium* was later divided into 3 genera: *Lycopodium*, *Lycopodiella*, and *Huperzia*. In that arrangement, *Lycopodium* was still a highly variable genus, and the use of "groups," such as the *Lycopodium complanatum* group, helped identify more closely related species within the genus. Now these groups are being recognized as separate genera and assigned new generic names. The original *Lycopodium* is now separated into 16 genera worldwide, 7 of which occur in the range covered by this Field Guide: *Dendrolycopodium*, *Diphasiastrum*, *Huperzia*, *Lycopodiella*, *Lycopodium*, *Pseudolycopodiella*, and *Spinulum*. These relatively new generic names may not yet be familiar to many botanists, but we expect they will become more common in the next few years. Clear field characters differentiate the genera, and for the most part, the species names remain the same. Older scientific names under the genus *Lycopodium* are included in the synonymy for each species.

OLD SCIENTIFIC NAME	NEW GENUS	COMMON NAME
L. obscurum group	Dendrolycopodium	Tree Clubmosses
L. complanatum group	Diphasiastrum	Ground Cedars
L. selago group	Huperzia	Firmosses
L. inundatum group	Lycopodiella	Bog Clubmosses
L. clavatum group	Lycopodium	Clubmosses
L. carolinianum group	Pseudolycopodiella	Slender Bog Clubmoss
L. annotinum group	Spinulum	Bristly Clubmosses

The common names are as confusing as the scientific names; Ground Pine, Running Pine, Princess Pine, or Running Cedar are often used interchangeably and extensively as common names for the Clubmosses, which gives rise to considerable confusion in a field guide. In this Field Guide, we have made an effort to apply one common name to each genus, as listed in the preceding table, although it may not be the most familiar common name. As with the synonyms, a few of the alternative common names are listed under each species description. In this Field Guide, "Clubmosses" refers to all of the above genera.

A number of characters distinguish Clubmosses from Horsetails, Quillworts, and other fern allies. All of the genera listed in the table have spores of one size. All the Clubmoss genera except *Huperzia* reproduce by spores borne in sporangia on more or less distinct strobili (conelike structures) above the uppermost leaves. Some strobili are on the end of a distinctive branched or unbranched stalk while others are sessile (without stalks). The sporangia develop at the base of highly modified, reduced leaves (called sporophylls) on the strobili. The sporophylls are stalked in most North American genera, and turn light brown after the spores mature. Most Clubmoss genera also have horizontal stems, with upright stems arising from them. Firmosses (*Huperzia*), unlike the other genera, do not have strobili (sporangia are borne at the base of sporophylls on the upright stem); have unstalked, evergreen sporophylls, and produce gemmae (plantlets) near the top of the upright stem.

Sporangia of all Clubmosses are numerous, tiny, spherical or kidney-shaped, and yellow. They are produced in enormous quantities and mature in late summer or early fall. When mature, sporangia open by means of a transverse slit, and powdery spores are widely dispersed by the smallest currents of air. The released spores are so minute and uniform in size that they were at one time used as units for microscopic measurements. They are also water-repellent and dustlike, so they were once used as soothing powders for chafes and wounds. Enormous quantities were also used to coat pills. Because of their high oil content, they give off a flash explosion when ignited, so they were also used for fireworks and for photographic flashes.

The gametophytes formed by the spores are tiny, and range in shape from disclike to conical, often with semi-overlapping lobes on top that encase the antheridia and archegonia. The gametophytes of *Lycopodium, Huperzia, Spinulum, Dendroly-*

Conical gametophyte

copodium, and *Diphasiastrum* are subterranean, contain no chlorophyll, and depend on mycorrhizal fungi for sustenance. Gametophytes of *Lycopodiella* and *Pseudolycopodiella* develop on the surface, are green and photosynthetic but also depend to some extent on mycorrhizal fungi. It has been reported that the photosynthetic gametophytes of *Lycopodiella* may develop within a year or two, but nonphotosynthetic gametophytes take at least 8 years to develop to perceptible size. It is still unknown how much time is needed to develop mature sporophyte plants.

Hybrids of species within a genus do occur. The hybrids tend to exhibit characteristics of both parents; however, the best method for confirming hybrids is through observing large numbers of malformed spores (except in *Diphasiastrum* and *Lycopodiella* hybrids), and this requires a 50× magnification. More detailed information about hybrids is noted in the discussion of each genus.

CLUBMOSS TERMINOLOGY

SPOROPHYLLS (LITERALLY, "SPORE-LEAF"): Leaves associated with the sporangia. Sporophylls of most Clubmosses with strobili look very different from the other leaves on the stem. (*Lycopodiella* is the exception.)

TROPHOPHYLL: Botanists use the term *trophophyll* to describe the leaves not associated with sporangia. We use the less accurate but more familiar term *leaf* to describe these structures. In *Huperzia* (Firmosses), sporophylls and trophophylls look similar and are found in alternating zones on the upright stem.

STROBILUS (PLURAL, STROBILI): A localized region of the stem, usually terminal, that bears only sporophylls.

BRANCHING means a branch divides, then divides again and again, up to the number listed (e.g., 4–7 times) like a spreading tree branch.

ANNUAL CONSTRICTIONS, or WINTER BUD CONSTRICTIONS, are terms that describe a stem or section of stem that looks narrower than the rest of the stem due to the presence of smaller, sometimes more congested leaves. These indentations mark the start (and end) of seasonal (annual) growth, when colder temperatures and other conditions limit growth, just as tree growth rings do.

RANKS, as in "leaves 6-ranked," often describe and distinguish Clubmosses. When you look down a stem with the tip pointed directly toward your eyes, the leaves line up in rows or ranks, like parading soldiers or a marching band viewed from the front of the band. If a pair of leaves is oriented 90° from the pair above or below, then from above it looks (and is) 4-ranked. Three alternating pairs offset from each other would be 6-ranked. Sometimes three leaves emerging close together (called a pseudowhorl) alternate with a pair of leaves, creating a 5-ranked pattern, as in *Diphasiastrum sitchense* (Sitka Clubmoss). Sometimes leaves are folded or keeled, like the keel of a boat, but these are still counted as a "rank." In this Field Guide, leaves on the "upper side," "lateral," or "underside" of the branch refer to the position if the branch were horizontal. "Lower" refers to the placement of a leaf along a stem, as in *Huperzia appressa* (Mountain Firmoss), where the leaves in the lower portions of the stem are more spreading and half the size of the leaves in upper portions of the stem.

REFLEXED, ASCENDING, SPREADING, AND APPRESSED describe the position or posture of a leaf relative to the stem. Reflexed means bent backward, ascending is growing at an upward angle, and appressed is lying close to or pressed against the stem or stipe. Spreading is at an angle from ascending to perpendicular to the stem.

KEY CHARACTERS OF CLUBMOSS GENERA

Dendrolycopodium: Treelike (main axis with forked branches), branches mostly round in cross-section, leaves often similar size, strobili sessile.

Diphasiastrum: Treelike (main axis with forked branches), branches flattened or 4-sided, leaves keeled and not keeled, strobili on long stalks (one species, *D. sitchense*, has unusual characters for genus).

Huperzia: Bristly (no strobili) upright stem bears sporangia in distinct zones, sporophylls stay green; gemmae produced at end of stems; no true horizontal stem.

Lycopodiella: Diminutive, single, slender upright stem and strobilus; horizontal stem not flattened and leaves of horizontal stem all similar (sporophylls resemble trophophylls), plants deciduous except for small tip of horizontal stem.

Lycopodium: Upright bristly stems with 1–6 branches; leaves have long, colorless hair at tip; branches round in cross-section; strobili on elongated branched stalks.

Pseudolycopodiella: Upright slender stem unbranched, one strobilus per stem, horizontal shoots flattened and lateral leaves of horizontal stem wider than others, horizontal stem evergreen.

Spinulum: Upright shoot branching near base, leaves with minute spine on tip, branches round in cross-section, strobili sessile.

GENUS *DENDROLYCOPODIUM*: TREE CLUBMOSSES

(Greek: *dendro*, "tree"; description of treelike *Lycopodium*)

The genus *Dendrolycopodium* is one of the more recently recognized genera of the older, more encompassing *Lycopodium* genus. *Dendrolycopodium* species have a branched, treelike form (with a distinct central axis and 2–4 fan-shaped lateral branching systems emerging from that upright axis) and deeply buried horizontal stems. Branches are round or compressed in cross-section; with 6 ranks of leaves that are pointed but without spines or hairlike bristles on the leaf tips. Horizontal stems do not have annual constrictions, but upright stems in some species have visible annual constrictions. Sessile strobili are produced at the end of the central stem and often also on the upper branches. Most plants produce 1–7 strobili per upright stem. Gametophytes are disc-shaped, subterranean, and not photosynthetic.

There are 4 species of *Dendrolycopodium* worldwide, 3 of which are common in our area. Hybrids of these species may produce well-formed spores; they are rare and difficult to distinguish.

DENDROLYCOPODIUM KEY

1A. Leaves of the upright stem below the branches spreading and prickly to the touch.   ***D. dendroideum* (Prickly Tree Clubmoss)**

1B. Leaves of upright stem below the branches appressed or nearly so, and upright stem not prickly to the touch. Go to 2.

    2A. Leaves on underside of lateral branches minute compared to others; leaves on the upper side appressed. Lateral branches flat in cross-section.   ***D. obscurum* (Flat-branched Tree Clubmoss)**

    2B. Leaves on underside of lateral branches nearly same size as rest of leaves; leaves on upper side not appressed. Lateral branches round or elliptic in cross-section.   ***D. hickeyi* (Hickey's Tree Clubmoss)**

PRICKLY TREE CLUBMOSS

Dendrolycopodium dendroideum (Michx.) A. Haines
Synonyms: *Lycopodium obscurum* L. var. *dendroideum; Lycopodium dendroideum* Michx.

HABIT: Treelike, evergreen Clubmoss, each stem with many spreading branches and prickly, needlelike leaves. Stems sprout upward every 6 in. or so from the underground horizontal stems.

ECOLOGY: Common in rich hardwood and mixed forests, and successional shrubby areas; moist to dry, acidic soils.

RANGE: Nfld. and N.S. south to Va., west to Wyo. and Wash., north to Alaska and across Canada. Also e. Asia.

HORIZONTAL STEMS: Creeping and branching well below surface of ground; scalelike leaves but without annual constrictions.

UPRIGHT STEMS: To 12 in. tall. Erect and treelike, branches 4–5 times to form fanlike lateral branches.

LATERAL BRANCHES: Often round in cross-section, with inconspicuous annual constrictions.

LEAVES: ¼ in. ± long. Numerous, spreading to ascending; leaves on main stem below lateral branches are pale green, needlelike, stiff, and spreading (thus the common name "prickly"). Leaves of lateral branches 6-ranked—2 ranks of leaves on upper side of branch, 2 ranks of lateral leaves (1 on each side), 2 ranks on underside of branch—all equal size.

STROBILUS: 1½ in. long. Sessile, borne singly on ends of upper branches, with 1–7 + (up to 14) per upright stem.

SPOROPHYLL: Almost round; flat base; short, abruptly tapering tip.

NOTES: Similar to *Dendrolycopodium obscurum* (Flat-branched Tree Clubmoss) and *D. hickeyi* (Hickey's Tree Clubmoss), but spreading, prickly leaves on lower portion of upright stem and arrangement of leaf ranks on lateral branches (2 above, 2 below, and 1 on each side) make Prickly Tree Clubmoss distinctive.

MARGINALIA: *A. Enlarged view of branchlet. B. Cross-section of branchlet.*

DIAGNOSTIC ARROWS: *1. Main stem prickly. 2. 6-ranked leaves all equal and arranged as indicated. 3. Strobilus sessile.*

A.

B

1.

2.

3.

DENDROLYCOPODIUM DENDROIDEUM
PRICKLY TREE CLUBMOSS

HICKEY'S TREE CLUBMOSS

Dendrolycopodium hickeyi (W. H. Wagner, Beitel, & Moran)
A. Haines

Synonyms: *Lycopodium hickeyi* W. H. Wagner, Beitel, & Moran; *Lycopodium obscurum* L. var. *isophyllum* Hickey

HABIT: Treelike, evergreen Clubmoss with many spreading branches and dark green leaves that are ascending but not appressed.

ECOLOGY: Mainly in hardwood forests and second-growth, shrubby habitats. Also in dry open sites such as power line rights-of-way; more frequent than other species in dry sandy sites.

RANGE: Nfld. south to Va., and Appalachian Mts. to N.C., west to Minn. and s. Ont.

HORIZONTAL STEMS: Creeping and branching below surface of ground, without annual constrictions.

UPRIGHT STEMS: To 6 in. tall. Erect, treelike; branched 4–5 times to form fanlike lateral branches. Leaves on main stem below branches are dark green, narrow, and tightly appressed.

LATERAL BRANCHES: Round to elliptic in cross-section, with inconspicuous annual constrictions.

LEAVES: To ¼ in. long. Linear and widest in the middle, entire, pointed at apex. Leaves of lateral branches 6-ranked—1 rank of leaves on upper side of branch, 1 rank on underside, and 4 lateral ranks (2 on each side)—all the same size and equally spreading.

STROBILUS: ⅓–2½ in. long. Sessile, 1–7 per upright stem.

SPOROPHYLL: Almost round, abruptly to gradually tapers to apex.

NOTES: Easily confused with *Dendrolycopodium obscurum* (Flat-branched Tree Clubmoss). In *D. hickeyi* (Hickey's Tree Clubmoss), all leaves on the lateral branches are similar in size and not twisted (in Flat-branched Tree Clubmoss, leaves are different sizes and some are twisted); branches of Hickey's are generally round to elliptic in cross-section (somewhat flattened in Flat-branched). Range of Hickey's Tree Clubmoss overlaps Flat-branched Tree Clubmoss but extends considerably north and west of that species. In areas where the two species overlap, individual species are still distinct.

MARGINALIA: *A. Close-up of lateral branch. B. Rounded cross-section of branchlet.*

DIAGNOSTIC ARROWS: *1. Base of upright stem not prickly. 2. All leaves on lateral branches are same size and spreading or ascending (not appressed or twisted). 3. Strobilus sessile.*

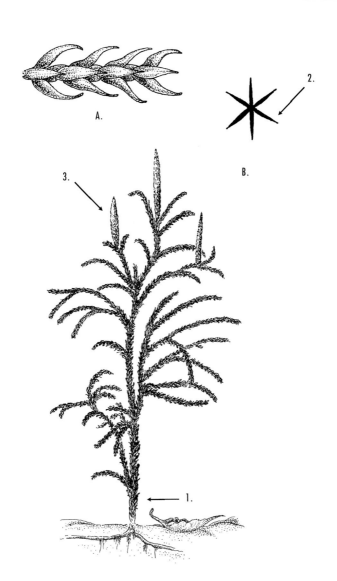

A.

2.

B.

3.

1.

DENDROLYCOPODIUM HICKEYI
HICKEY'S TREE CLUBMOSS

FLAT-BRANCHED TREE CLUBMOSS
(PRINCESS PINE)

Dendrolycopodium obscurum (L.) A. Haines
Synonym: *Lycopodium obscurum* L.

HABIT: Treelike, evergreen Clubmoss with many spreading, some-what flattened branches.

ECOLOGY: Common in rich hardwood and mixed forests, and suc-cessional shrubby areas; moist to dry, acidic soils.

RANGE: N.B. and N.S. south to Va., south to Ga. in the Ap-palachian Mts., west and north to Wisc. and Ont.

HORIZONTAL STEMS: Creeping and branching well below surface of ground; no annual constrictions.

UPRIGHT STEMS: To 12 in. tall. Erect, treelike; branched 4–5 times to form fanlike lateral branches. Tightly appressed leaves on main stem below lateral branches. Stems arise at intervals from subsur-face horizontal stem.

LATERAL BRANCHES: Somewhat flattened in cross-section, with leaves on underside very small. Conspicuous annual constrictions.

LEAVES: ¼ in. ± long. Narrow, lance-shaped; smooth sides taper to sharp-pointed tips. All leaves ascend (pointed toward end of branch); leaves of lateral branches 6-ranked—1 rank of leaves on upper side of branch (same size as lateral ones but appressed), 4 ranks of lateral leaves (2 on each side) spreading and twisted so flat surface of leaf is parallel to ground, and 1 rank on underside of branch much smaller than others.

STROBILUS: 1½ in. long. Sessile (no stalk), borne singly on ends of upper branches, 1–6 per upright, branched stem.

SPOROPHYLL: Rounded, flat base and long, gradually narrowing tip.

NOTES: *Dendrolycopodium obscurum* (Flat-branched Tree Club-moss) is similar to *D. dendroideum* (Prickly Tree Clubmoss), but the lower portion of the main stem below the branches is not prickly, and the branches are often flattened, not rounded, in cross-section. It is also confused with *D. hickeyi* (Hickey's Tree Clubmoss), but leaves of the lateral branches are not all equal in size (the leaves on the underside of the branch are much smaller) and the branches are more flattened in cross-section.

MARGINALIA: *A. Branchlet cross-section. B. Enlarged view of branchlet. C. Leaf. D. Sporophyll with sporangia.*

DIAGNOSTIC ARROWS: *1. Treelike growth form from deep-in-the-ground horizontal stem. 2. Main stem not prickly. 3. Branches flattened in cross-section since upper and underside leaves are appressed. 4. Leaves on underside of branch much smaller than others.*

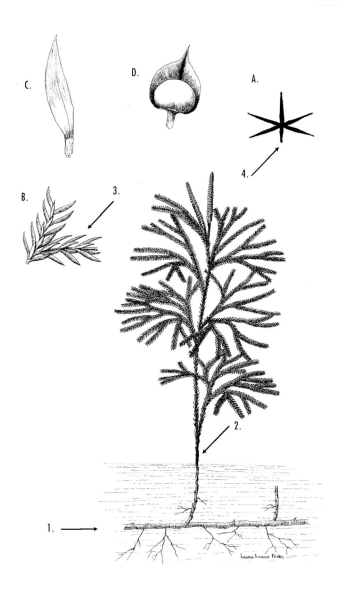

C.

D.

A.

4.

3.

B.

2.

1.

DENDROLYCOPODIUM OBSCURUM
FLAT-BRANCHED TREE CLUBMOSS

(Latin: *Diphasium,* a different genus in the family Lycopodiaceae, + *astrum,* "incomplete re-semblance")

Diphasiastrum species most often grow in dry, upland habitats, and most are relatively easy to recognize. They have a miniature tree form (a main upright "stem" with "side branches"); the narrow branches of most species have a flat or quadrangular cross-section; and the strobili stalks, when present, have branches of equal length on each fork. The 4-ranked arrangement of the leaves is also distinctive: the leaves of the upper- and underside ranks lie flat, and the lateral ranks (leaves on the "edges" of the flattened branch) are folded or keeled. Only *Diphasiastrum sitchense* (Sitka Clubmoss) has round branches with a 5-ranked pattern. The leaves of *Diphasiastrum* species have no spinelike or hairlike tips. Most branches and stems have visible annual constrictions (short sections with smaller and more congested leaves than the rest of the stem). Sporangia are kidney-shaped. Gametophytes are subterranean and carrot-shaped.

Diphasiastrum hybrids can be found in areas where more than 1 species occurs. Hybrids of this genus often produce fertile spores, so hybrids are not easily identified by the presence of abortive spores.

DIPHASIASTRUM KEY

1A. Strobili sessile or stalks <½ in. long; plants less than 4½ in. tall (without strobili). Go to 2.

    2A. Branches round in cross-section; leaves all about same size and 5-ranked. Sporophylls at base of strobilus with same spacing as those above.   **D. sitchense (Sitka Clubmoss)**

    2B. Branches somewhat flattened (oval in cross-section); leaves all the same size and 4-ranked. Sporophylls at base of strobilus widely spaced.

                D. sabinifolium (Savin-leaved Clubmoss)

1B. Strobili stalked, 1–4 strobili per stalk; plants usually more than 4½ in. tall (without strobili); branches flattened or 4-angled in cross-section; leaves of different sizes and 4-ranked. Go to 3.

    3A. Branches nearly 4-angled in cross-section; usually blue-green; leaves on underside of branch equal in size to upper-side leaves but less than half the size of lateral leaves; horizontal stems deeper than 2 in. underground.

D. tristachyum (Blue Ground Cedar)

3B. Branches flattened in cross-section; usually green; leaves on underside of branch much smaller than others; horizontal stems at or near surface. Go to 4.

4A. Lateral branches not all oriented in same plane; with conspicuous annual constrictions; usually 1–2 strobili per stalk. **_D. complanatum_ (Northern Ground Cedar)**

4B. Lateral branches lie in the same plane, giving it a fan shape; without annual constrictions; 2–4 strobili per stalk, branches often close together, sometimes appear as a whorl. **_D. digitatum_ (Southern Ground Cedar)**

(Above) Diphasiastrum complanatum (*Northern Ground Cedar*) *has long, slender strobilus stalks.* (Above, right) *Dense cluster of* Diphasiastrum sitchense (*Sitka Clubmoss*) *with mostly sessile strobili.* (*Photos by Arthur Haines*) (Right) *Strobili of* Diphasiastrum tristachyum (*Blue Ground Cedar*) *are on branched candelabras.* (*Photo by Janet E. Novak*)

NORTHERN GROUND CEDAR
(Flat-branched Clubmoss)

Diphasiastrum complanatum (L.) Holub
Synonym: *Lycopodium complanatum* L.

HABIT: Creeping, treelike, with wide, flattened, bright green branches at various angles, giving it a slightly scraggly appearance. Conspicuous annual constrictions on stems and branches.

ECOLOGY: Dry, open, coniferous or mixed forest; boreal and subalpine slopes.

RANGE: Greenland and across Canada, south to Me., N.H., Vt., west across n. U.S. to Minn. and again in Wash. and Idaho, and up to Alaska. Circumboreal.

HORIZONTAL STEMS: Creeping on surface or buried in leaf litter.

UPRIGHT STEMS: 3–17 in. tall (with strobili). Branching up to 5 times to form arching, semirounded irregular sprays. Conspicuous annual constrictions on stems and branches.

LATERAL BRANCHES: Flattened in cross-section, conspicuous annual constrictions. Upper surface green and slightly shiny; underside pale and dull.

LEAVES: Tiny, 4-ranked, all appressed and attached to stem for more than ½ their length. Upper rank of leaves very narrow, ¹⁄₁₆ in. ± long; lateral leaves keeled and much larger than upper rank of leaves (up to ¼ in. long); leaves of underside rank even smaller than upper leaves and elongate triangular.

STROBILUS: ⅓–1 in. long. Slender stalks sometimes forked, bearing 1 or 2 strobili. Usually 1–2 stalks per upright stem.

SPOROPHYLL: Light yellow, triangular with abruptly pointed tip; edges rough and chaffy. Sporangia almost round.

NOTES: *Complanatum* comes from *complanatus*, which means "flattened." *Diphasiastrum complanatum* (Northern Ground Cedar) hybridizes with *D. tristachyum* (Blue Ground Cedar) to form *D. × zeilleri* when they occur together, mostly north and west of our range (fairly frequent in n. cen. and w. Minn.).

MARGINALIA: *A. Branch stem showing annual constrictions. B. Upper surface of branchlet. C. Undersurface of branchlet. D. Sporophyll with sporangia.*

DIAGNOSTIC ARROWS: *1. Straggly growth form. 2. 1 or 2 strobili per stalk. 3. Conspicuous annual constriction. 4. Leaves on underside of branch much smaller than others.*

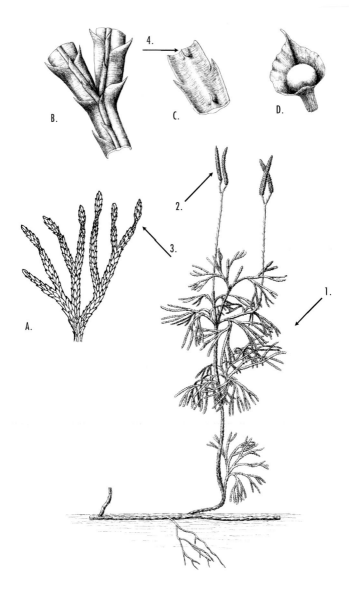

DIPHASIASTRUM COMPLANATUM
NORTHERN GROUND CEDAR

SOUTHERN GROUND CEDAR
(SOUTHERN RUNNING PINE)

Diphasiastrum digitatum (Dill. ex A. Braun) Holub

Synonyms: *Lycopodium digitatum* Dill. ex A. Braun; *Lycopodium complanatum* var. *flabelliforme* Fern

HABIT: Creeping; treelike, flattened, dark green, fanlike lateral branches. Inconspicuous annual constrictions on upright stems. Very common species.

ECOLOGY: Mixed coniferous or hardwood forests, dry woods, or scrubby and open fields.

RANGE: Nfld. to Ont. south to mountains of n. Ga., west to Ark., north to e. Minn. Endemic to e. North America.

HORIZONTAL STEMS: Creeping on soil surface or in leaf litter.

UPRIGHT STEMS: 6–20 in. tall (with strobili); branching up to 3 times.

LATERAL BRANCHES: Flattened in cross-section, no annual constrictions. Underside of branch dull and pale, upper side green and shiny.

LEAVES: Tiny, 4-ranked, attached to stem for more than ½ their length. Upper rank of leaves appressed and narrow (¹⁄₃₂ in. long); lateral rank of leaves keeled, spreading at tips, and much larger than upper leaves (⅛–¼ in. long); leaves of underside rank smallest, triangular, with pointed tip.

STROBILUS: Mostly 1 in. ± long. Many strobili with elongate, sterile tip up to ½ in. long. Stalk usually twice-forked at nearly the same point, mostly near top of stalks, bearing 2–4 strobili in a false whorl. Stalks 1½–5 in. tall, 1 or 2 stalks per upright stem.

SPOROPHYLL: Greenish yellow, triangular with abruptly pointed tip.

NOTES: Another common name for Southern Ground Cedar is "Fan Clubmoss." This name describes this species well, because the compact branching pattern creates fanlike sprays. *Diphasiastrum × habereri* (House) Holub is a hybrid of *D. digitatum* (Southern Running Pine) and *D. tristachyum* (Ground Cedar).

MARGINALIA: *A. Upper side of branch stem. B. Underside of branch stem.*

DIAGNOSTIC ARROWS: *1. Flattened, fanlike branches. 2. 2–4 strobili in a false whorl. 3. Leaves on underside of branch triangular and much smaller than others.*

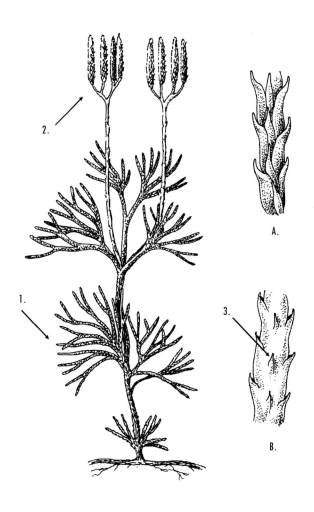

DIPHASIASTRUM DIGITATUM
SOUTHERN GROUND CEDAR

Diphasiastrum sitchense (Rupr.) Holub

Synonym: *Lycopodium sitchense* Rupr.

HABIT: Creeping, dense, fine-textured stems mostly branching near base, giving it a more mosslike appearance than other *Diphasiastrum* species.

ECOLOGY: Alpine meadows, open rocky barrens, subalpine and boreal conifer forests. Also open, disturbed borrow pits and fields.

RANGE: Lab. and Nfld. west across s. Canada, south into Me., N.H., N.Y., the Pacific Northwest, and north into Alaska. Also Kamchatka, Japan.

HORIZONTAL STEMS: Creeping on or near soil surface.

UPRIGHT STEMS: Clustered, 2–6 in. tall (with strobili). Lateral branches emerge from base, oriented vertically.

LATERAL BRANCHES: Dark green, somewhat shiny. Round in cross-section, $\frac{1}{16}$ in. wide; inconspicuous annual constrictions.

LEAVES: Small, mostly equal in size, 5-ranked. Spreading, attached less than $\frac{1}{10}$ their length, widest in the middle; sharply pointed tip.

STROBILUS: $\frac{1}{4}$–$1\frac{1}{2}$ in. long. Usually not stalked, although a short stalk, less than $\frac{1}{2}$ in., is common in New England; usually solitary at tips of upright stems.

SPOROPHYLL: Triangular; rounded tip.

NOTES: Rare in our region, has been confused with *Diphasiastrum sabinifolium* (Savin-leaved Clubmoss) but distinguished by having leaves in 5 ranks.

MARGINALIA: *A. Close-up of lateral branch, round in cross-section.*

DIAGNOSTIC ARROWS: *1. Upright stems clustered and branching near base. 2. Sporophylls on strobilus all close together.*

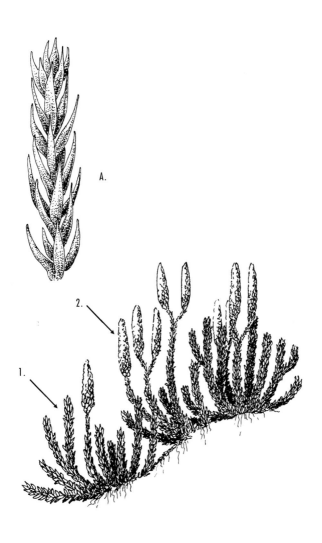

A.

1.

2.

DIPHASIASTRUM SITCHENSE
SITKA CLUBMOSS

BLUE GROUND CEDAR
(GROUND PINE, SLENDER GROUND CEDAR)

Diphasiastrum tristachyum (Pursh) Holub
Synonym: *Lycopodium tristachyum* Pursh

HABIT: Low, upright plants growing in dense clusters with thin-stemmed candelabras of strobili rising above the foliage. Lateral branchlets form well-balanced fans, reaching upward with ultimate branchlets ending at or near the same point, giving the plant a flat-topped appearance. Distinctly blue-green.

ECOLOGY: Dry, acid soils of open oak and conifer woodlands. Also open, abandoned pastures, pine barrens, along power lines, and clearings.

RANGE: Nfld. to Ont. south to Va., and in Appalachian Mts. south to Ga. and Tenn., northwest to Ohio, Mich., Minn., and s. Man. Also, Europe, disjunct in w. China.

HORIZONTAL STEMS: 2–5 in. below surface. Widely creeping.

UPRIGHT STEMS: 7–14 in. tall (with strobili). Erect, treelike, branching 4–7 times.

LATERAL BRANCHES: Fan-shaped and flattened, oriented upward. Lowest branches emerge near base of stem. Blue-green to green but usually with a fine, whitish powdery coating. Individual branches 4-sided, with small but distinct annual constrictions.

LEAVES: Tiny, evergreen, narrow, pointed. Attached to stem for more than ½ their length, 4-ranked. Upper rank of leaves very narrow, appressed, 1/16 in. long; lateral rank of leaves keeled and twice the size of upper leaves; underside rank of leaves similar in size to leaves of upper rank.

STROBILUS: Blunt-tipped, ½–1 in. long. Slender stalks once- or twice-forked; when twice-forked, branching points are separated along stalk, forming a candelabra of 3–4 strobili per stalk. Usually 2–3 stalks per upright stem.

SPOROPHYLL: Light yellow, triangular, tapering at tip; edges rough and chaffy. Sporangia almost round.

NOTES: Blue Ground Cedar forms hybrids with all other species of this genus in New England. Some hybrids are common in certain areas; all produce at least some normal spores.

MARGINALIA: *A. Underside of branchlet. B. Upper surface of branchlet. C. Sporophyll with sporangia.*

DIAGNOSTIC ARROWS: *1. Flat-topped growth form. 2. Candelabra usually of 3–4 strobili. 3. Leaves of upper side and underside are equal and half the size of lateral, keeled leaves.*

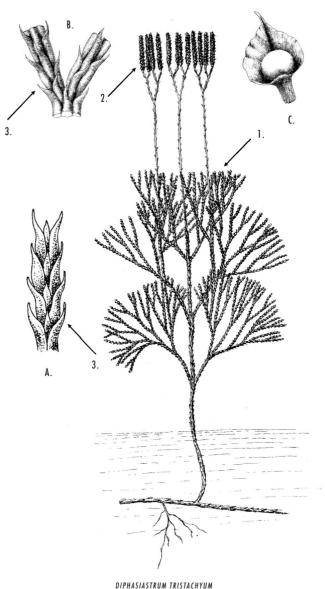

DIPHASIASTRUM TRISTACHYUM
BLUE GROUND CEDAR

ANOTHER INTERESTING GROUND CEDAR

SAVIN-LEAVED CLUBMOSS
Diphasiastrum sabinifolium (Willd.) Holub

Synonym: *Lycopodium sabinifolium* (Willd.) Holub

A hybrid between *Diphasiastrum sitchense* (Sitka Clubmoss) and *D. tristachyum* (Blue Ground Cedar), but usually grows where its parents do not. More common in northern parts of our area and often confused with Sitka Clubmoss. Horizontal stems surface-creeping, with upright stems and leaves like Sitka Clubmoss, but branchlets are compressed (oval) in cross-section (not round like Sitka Clubmoss or flat like Blue Ground Cedar), and leaves are of equal length in 4 ranks (instead of 5 in Sitka Clubmoss). Most distinctive character is that lower portion of strobilus has widely spaced sporophylls that look like the leaves on the stalk: the strobilus base is not clearly differentiated.

Sporophylls on lower portion of strobilus are widely spaced.

The leaves of Savin-leaved Clubmoss are all the same length and 4-ranked.

GENUS *HUPERZIA:* FIRMOSSES

(Named for Johann Peter Huperz, a German fern horticulturist)

Huperzia species are distinguished from other Clubmosses in our area by four distinctive characters: they have no strobili (spore-bearing cones); they have no true elongated horizontal stems (although with age, older stems lean over and appear to grow horizontally); sporophylls are found in distinct zones on the evergreen, upright stems; and gemmae are produced in the upper portion of mature stems.

In our area, *Huperzia* leaves (both sporophylls and trophophylls) are small, pointed, evergreen, and without stalks. The presence or absence and relative number of stomates (air pores) on the upper surface of these leaves helps distinguish one species of *Huperzia* from another. These can be seen as light-colored dots on fresh leaves at 20× magnification. Yellow, kidney-shaped sporangia that develop at the base of the sporophylls are found in distinct zones along the stem, mostly in the upper portions, and are clearly visible with a 10× hand lens. Sporophylls in *Huperzia* look like the other leaves (trophophylls) on the plant although they may be smaller. Unlike other Clubmosses, the sporophylls of *Huperzia* species do not wither and die after spore release.

Gemmae at base of leaves

Although many ferns and fern allies reproduce vegetatively as fragments break off from the elongated, horizontal stems, most *Huperzia* species do not. (Technically, *Huperzia* species do not produce distinct, horizontal stems, but *H. lucidula* will produce roots from several points along the prostrate part of the stem and, therefore, can use fragmentation of stems as a method of vegetative reproduction.) All *Huperzia* species, however, do produce miniature 6-leaved plantlets called gemmae in the upper portion of the stem. Gemmae mature in mid- to late summer; most fall off by the end of the growing season. Carried by wind or water to new sites, they readily develop roots and grow into new individuals. This mechanism provides an opportunity for vegetative propagules to spread to new sites and allows sterile hybrids to persist and spread in a given locality. *Huperzia* also reproduce sexually by spores. *Huperzia* gametophytes are cylindrical, subterranean, nonphotosynthetic, and dependent on mycorrhizal fungi for survival.

This genus contains 10–15 species worldwide; 7 species in North America, 4 of them in our region. Several hybrids occur in our region, with at least 2 relatively common ones. *Huperzia × josephbeitelii,* a hybrid between *H. appressa* (Mountain Firmoss) and *H. selago* (Northern Firmoss), occurs in New England above treeline; *Huperzia × bartleyi,* a hybrid between *H. porophila* (Rock Firmoss) and *H. lucidula* (Shining Firmoss), occurs throughout the range of Rock Firmoss. Mountain Firmoss also hybridizes (rarely) with Shining Firmoss to produce *H. × protoporophila,* which is found only in Mountain Firmoss habitats. Shining Firmoss hybridizes (rarely) with Northern Firmoss to form *H. × buttersii.* In most cases, hybrid characteristics are intermediate between the parents. Because *Huperzia* species reproduce vegetatively by gemmae as well as spores, hybrids may flourish in favorable conditions without repeated hybridization.

Huperzia Key

1A. Largest leaves long and narrow, but distinctly widest above the middle, 1–8 teeth; stomates only on lower surface. Stems with conspicuous annual constrictions. Plants of moist, acidic woods.   *H. lucidula* **(Shining Firmoss)**

1B. Largest leaves long and narrow but with sides parallel or narrowly triangular (widest at base). Leaves without teeth or only weakly toothed; stomates on both surfaces. Stems with barely noticeable or no annual constrictions. Go to 2.

  2A. Largest leaves long and narrow with sides parallel much of length; stomates 1–25 per half-leaf on upper surface. Found only on sandstone cliffs and outcrops.   *H. porophila* **(Rock Firmoss)**

  2B. Largest leaves long and narrow to narrowly triangular; more than 30 stomates per half-leaf on upper surface. Go to 3.

    3A. Gemmae in 1 whorl at end of annual growth; leaves all about same size. Found in open, wet habitats or moist, low areas.   *H. selago* **(Northern Firmoss)**

    3B. Gemmae borne throughout upper portion of stems; basal leaves much longer and more spreading than those near stem tip. Found only in exposed, high-altitude sites above treeline, and on cliffs and talus slopes.   *H. appressa* **(Mountain Firmoss)**

(Above) Huperzia appressa (*Mountain Fir-moss*) *grows* in alpine and exposed cliff habitats. (Photo by Arthur Haines) (Right) *Dense, flat-topped clusters of* Huperzia se-lago (*Northern Firmoss*). *(Photo by Frank Bramley/NEWFS)*

(Below left) *Bristly-looking* Huperzia lucidula (*Shining Firmoss*) *has kidney-shaped sporangia in distinct zones on stem* (below right). *(Photos by Arthur Haines)*

MOUNTAIN FIRMOSS
(Appalachian Fir Clubmoss)

Huperzia appressa (Desv.) A. & D. Löve
Synonym: *Huperzia appalachiana* Beitel & Mickel

HABIT: Very short, evergreen plant of exposed and alpine habitats; upright, clustered stems, densely covered with small, green to yellow-green leaves.

ECOLOGY: Damp, acidic rock in alpine areas, exposed cliffs, and talus slopes.

RANGE: From Greenland, Nfld., and Que. south to Ga. along Atlantic Coast and higher elevations of Appalachian Mts. Also near Lake Superior in Mich., Minn., and Ont.

STEMS: 2–4 in. tall. Erect, clustered stems, no annual constrictions.

LEAVES: Narrowly triangular, or with parallel sides, with entire margins. Leaves of upper portion are ½ the size of leaves in lower portions of stem. All leaves ascend, but lower ones spread more than upper ones. Green to yellow-green, not lustrous. Numerous stomates on both surfaces (35–60 per half-leaf on upper surface). Plants in shade have longer, wider-spreading leaves than those growing in sun.

SPORANGIA: In distinct zones of upper stem.

GEMMAE: Numerous and borne throughout upper portions of mature stem.

NOTES: Similar to *Huperzia selago* (Northern Firmoss), but gemmae scattered throughout upper portion of stem, and upper and lower leaves are different lengths. Unlike most *Huperzia* species, Mountain Firmoss is determinate, which means the whole plant dies after 12–15 years of spore production.

MARGINALIA: *A. Leaf. B. Close-up of gemma.*

DIAGNOSTIC ARROWS: *1. Gemmae scattered along upper stem (not clustered at top). 2. Leaves on upper portions of stem are half the size of lower leaves. 3. Leaf with entire margin.*

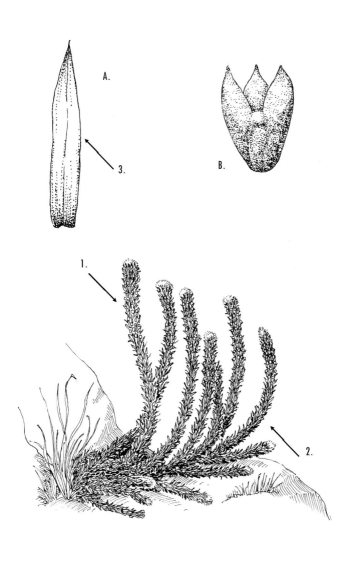

HUPERZIA APPRESSA
MOUNTAIN FIRMOSS

SHINING FIRMOSS (Shining Clubmoss)

Huperzia lucidula (Michx.) Trevisan
Synonym: *Lycopodium lucidulum* Michx.

HABIT: Low-growing, bristly-looking plant with dense covering of bright to dark green, shiny, small, evergreen leaves. Stems somewhat irregular or undulating in outline because of annual constrictions. Grows in loose clumps, sometimes forming "fairy rings" as the older trailing stems turn brown.

ECOLOGY: Shady, cool, moist, coniferous or mixed hardwood forests with moist, acid soils.

RANGE: Common throughout the region. Nfld and N.S. to s. Man., south to S.C., inland to Ga., west to e. Mo., north to Minn.

STEMS: 6–8 in. tall. Single or with a few branches, erect stems a continuation of the prostrate stem often hidden under leaf litter. Stem with conspicuous annual constrictions, giving it a slightly ragged profile.

LEAVES: ⅜ in. ± long. Lustrous; leaves are spreading to slightly reflexed. Largest leaves (both trophophylls and sporophylls) narrow, broadest at or above middle, with distinctively toothed edges, especially above the middle. Smaller leaves narrowly triangular. Stomates seen only on lower leaf surface.

SPORANGIA: In distinct zones of upper stem.

GEMMAE: Borne in 1 whorl on uppermost leaf axils, so the stem looks thick at the tip.

NOTES: Shape of the leaf (widest above the middle), toothed margins, and absence of stomates on the upper surface are distinguishing characters of this species.

MARGINALIA: *A. Leaf. B. Close-up of gemmae.*

DIAGNOSTIC ARROWS: *1. Upright stems with shiny leaves. 2. Annual constrictions. 3. Larger leaves widest above middle with toothed margins. 4. Gemmae clustered at tip.*

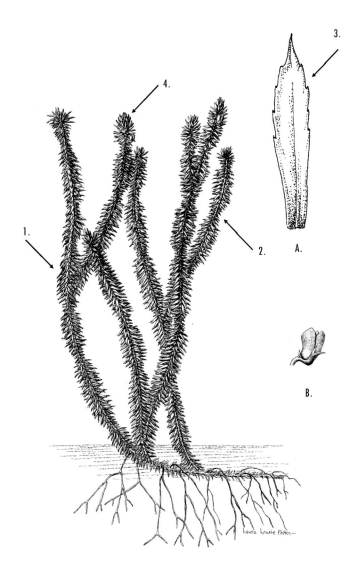

1.
2.
3.
4.
A.
B.

HUPERZIA LUCIDULA
SHINING FIRMOSS

Huperzia selago (L.) Bernh. ex Mart. & Schrank
Synonym: *Lycopodium selago* L.

HABIT: Low-growing plant with dense, small, green leaves. Stems grow in short, tight, flat-topped clusters.

ECOLOGY: Boreal, primarily cool, damp sites, including ditches, low fields, and lakeshores as well as conifer forests, swamps, and seepage slopes. Rarely at cliff bases and in ravines.

RANGE: Limited to northern portions of our region. Greenland, Nfld., and Lab. across much of n. and cent. Canada, south to Mass., Conn., and N.Y., west to Minn.

STEMS: 3–5 in. tall. Erect stems approximately the same height (plant appears flat-topped). Barely noticeable annual constrictions.

LEAVES: ⅛–¼ in. long. Narrow with sharp-pointed tips. Leaves linear (sides nearly parallel) or wider at the base. Leaf margin mostly smooth (short obscure teeth sometimes seen with a 10× hand lens). Stomates on both surfaces, 30–90 per half-leaf on upper surface. Leaves spreading to ascending, all about the same size.

SPORANGIA: In distinct zones of upper stem.

GEMMAE: Borne in 1 whorl at the end of the annual growth, thus the stem looks thick at the very tip.

NOTES: Northern Firmoss was considered a confusing complex of highly variable forms and subspecies. Separating *H. appressa* (Mountain Firmoss) and Northern Firmoss into distinct species has contributed to our understanding of the group, but research is still needed to clarify relationships of taxa and hybrids in this complex.

MARGINALIA: *A. Leaf. B. Gemmae at stem tip.*

DIAGNOSTIC ARROWS: *1. Upright stems with flat-topped form. 2. Leaf margin mostly entire, leaves all about same size. 3. Stems without annual constrictions.*

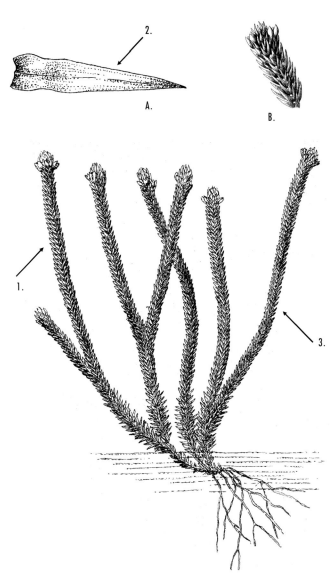

2.

A.

B.

1.

3.

HUPERZIA SELAGO
NORTHERN FIRMOSS

ROCK FIRMOSS
Huperzia porophila (Lloyd & Underwood) Holub
Synonym: *Lycopodium porophilum* Lloyd & Underwood

Leaf with
few teeth

A compact, clustered Firmoss with dense, lustrous, green leaves. Limited to damp, shady, acidic sandstone cliffs and ledges, or rarely on shale. Often found in disjunct populations in areas of Penn. south to Ala., west to Mo., north to Wisc. and Minn. Clustered stems are 5–6 in. tall, erect or with a curved base and erect tip; annual constrictions are slight and may or may not be visible. Largest leaves are narrow and long (¼ in.); smallest leaves are triangular and widest at base. This species is thought to be a fertile hybrid originating from *Huperzia appressa* (Mountain Firmoss) and *H. lucidula* (Shining Firmoss). Unlike Shining Firmoss, Rock Firmoss has few if any teeth on the leaf margin, rather inconspicuous annual constrictions, and is found only on sandstone cliffs, not on the forest floor.

GENUS *LYCOPODIELLA*: BOG CLUBMOSSES

(Latin: *Lycopodium,* a related genus, + *ella,* a diminutive suffix)

Lycopodiella species favor wet habitats: hence the genus's common name, Bog Clubmoss. Leafy horizontal stems creep along the surface, and roots usually emerge all along their length, except *Lycopodiella alopecuroides* (Foxtail Bog Clubmoss) and its hybrids, whose arching, horizontal stems root only where they contact the ground. Unlike most Clubmosses, stems of our *Lycopodiella* species survive only one season, overwintering as small, thickened tips of horizontal stems. *L. inundata* (Northern Bog Clubmoss) is the exception; the horizontal stem is more or less evergreen.

All upright stems are fertile and the strobili form on the upper section of the upright stem. Both strobili and the upright stems are covered with green leaves in many ranks, although the sporophylls are often longer and often held more horizontally, so that the strobili resembles a "bushy tail." Sporangia at the base of the sporophylls are almost spherical and yellow. Gametophytes are disclike, grow on the surface, and are photosynthetic.

This genus contains 8–10 species, 3 species in our area. Hybrids of these species are fairly common but difficult to recognize in part because some hybrids produce well-formed spores. The most common hybrid is a cross between *L. appressa* (Appressed Bog Clubmoss) and *L. inundata* (Northern Bog Clubmoss) and has been named Gilman's Bog Clubmoss (*L. × gilmanii*). *L. subappressa* (Northern Appressed Bog Clubmoss) and *L. margueritae* (Northern Prostrate Bog Clubmoss) are tetraploid species (4 sets of chromosomes) that are rare and occur only in Mich. in wet, acidic ditches and borrow pits. These are likely hybrids with Appressed Bog Clubmoss as one parent.

LYCOPODIELLA KEY

1A. Fertile stems usually <4 in. tall; leaves of horizontal stems without teeth; each segment of horizontal stem usually produces only 1 upright stem.
        L. inundata (Northern Bog Clubmoss)

1B. Fertile stems usually >4 in. tall; leaves of horizontal stems toothed; each segment of horizontal stem usually produces 1–5 upright stems. Go to 2.

  2A. Horizontal stems arch, rooting where stems contact the ground; sporophylls spread, thus strobili appearing wider (⅛–¼ in.) than upright stem.
        L. alopecuroides (Foxtail Bog Clubmoss)

2B. Horizontal stems not arching; sporophylls ascending to appressed, thus strobili appear barely wider (less than ¹⁄₁₆ in.) than upright stem.

L. appressa (Appressed Bog Clubmoss)

FOXTAIL BOG CLUBMOSS

Lycopodiella alopecuroides (L.) Cranfill
Synonym: *Lycopodium alopecuroides* L.

HABIT: Leafy, deciduous Bog Clubmosses easily recognized by bushy "foxtail" and distinctively arching horizontal stems.

ECOLOGY: Bogs, marshes, ditches, especially in saturated sandy areas with some organic matter.

RANGE: Mostly along coastal plain, Mass. south to Fla. and west to Tex., disjunct in Me. Also West Indies.

HORIZONTAL STEMS: Commonly arching 3–14 in. Rooting at tips.

UPRIGHT STEMS: 3–12 in. tall. Erect; leafy, with 1–3 upright stems close together.

LEAVES: Leaves of upright stems ⅜ in. long, narrow, somewhat spreading to ascending, with 1–8 sharp, distinct, divergent teeth along each side. Leaves of horizontal stems ¼ in. ± long, oriented to point upward, with 1–7 teeth along each side.

STROBILUS: 1–2 in. long, ½ in. ± wide. Looks like a bushy tip, ½–⅓ of stem length.

SPOROPHYLL: Green, awl-like, widely spreading; 1–5 teeth per side, mostly on lower half of leaf.

NOTES: Arching horizontal stems are distinctive in this species and are also present in its hybrids.

MARGINALIA: *A. Leaf. B. Enlargement of bushy strobilus.*
DIAGNOSTIC ARROWS: *1. Leaves distinctly tooth-edged. 2. Arching horizontal stem.*

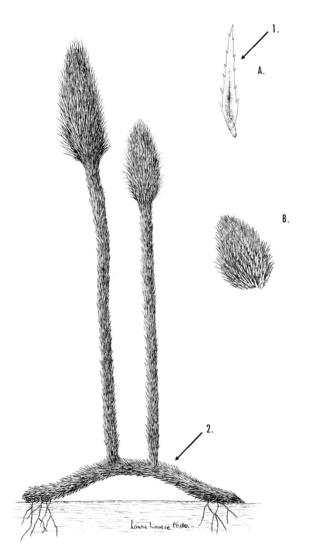

A.

B.

1.

2.

LYCOPODIELLA ALOPECUROIDES
FOXTAIL BOG CLUBMOSS

APPRESSED BOG CLUBMOSS

Lycopodiella appressa (Chapman) Cranfill
Synonyms: *Lycopodium inundatum* var. *bigelovii* Tuckerm.;
Lycopodium inundatum var. *appressum* Chapman; *Lycopodium appressum* (Chapman) Lloyd & Underwood

HABIT: Deciduous Bog Clubmoss with narrow strobilus and upright stems more clustered together than other *Lycopodiella*.

ECOLOGY: Bogs, marshes, ditches, especially in saturated sandy areas with some organic material.

RANGE: Primarily along Atlantic coastal plain. Nfld. south to Fla., west to Tex., but also inland north into Okla., Mo. Disjunct in Vt.

HORIZONTAL STEMS: Surface-creeping; rooting along stem.

UPRIGHT STEMS: 5–16 in. high. Erect; densely leaved; deciduous, usually 2–6 upright stems.

LEAVES: Leaves of upright stems ⅛ in. long. Narrow and appressed. Leaves of horizontal stems with 0–7 teeth per side.

STROBILUS: 1–2 in. tall. Narrow, with appressed sporophylls. Barely wider than sterile section of stem. ⅙–⅓ stem length.

SPOROPHYLL: Appressed with no teeth on margins, or a low, broad tooth on 1 or both margins.

NOTES: Distinguished from other *Lycopodiella* species by tightly appressed sporophylls and the larger number of upright stems. Also, horizontal stem is ½ in. ± thick (thicker than *Lycopodiella inundata* [Northern Bog Clubmoss]).

MARGINALIA: *A. Appressed leaves on upright stem.*
DIAGNOSTIC ARROWS: *1. Appressed sporophylls. 2. Usually 2–6 upright stems.*

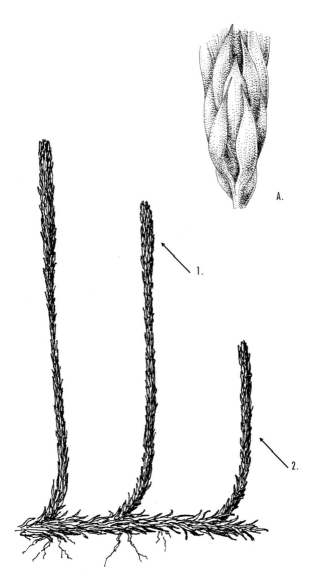

A.

1.

2.

LYCOPODIELLA APPRESSA
APPRESSED BOG CLUBMOSS

BOG CLUBMOSS (Marsh Clubmoss)

Lycopodiella inundata (L.) Holub
Synonym: *Lycopodium inundatum* L.

HABIT: Small, creeping, deciduous plant with erect, bushy-tailed fertile stems.

ECOLOGY: Cool, shaded bogs; lakeshores, marshes, disturbed sites; along edges of wet, sandy ditches and other watery spots.

RANGE: Nfld. to s. Ont., south to Va., west to Wisc., Minn. In w. U.S., Wash., Mont. north to Alaska. Also Eurasia.

HORIZONTAL STEMS: Surface-creeping; leafy, rooting along length, very slender (less than $\frac{1}{25}$ in. thick without leaves).

UPRIGHT STEMS: 1–5 in. tall. Erect; only 1 or sometimes 2 unbranched, upright stems; variable heights.

LEAVES: $\frac{1}{4}$ in. ± long. Narrow; leaves of upright stems ascending or spreading, sometimes with toothed edges; leaves of horizontal stems with smooth margins and oriented to point upward.

STROBILUS: Mostly 1 per stem. Looks like a narrow bushy tail, encompassing $\frac{1}{3}$–$\frac{1}{2}$ upright stem length.

SPOROPHYLL: Spreading to ascending, green.

NOTES: Distinctive characters are its very slender horizontal stems and leaves of horizontal stem with entire margins.

MARGINALIA: *A. Leaf of horizontal stem. B. Sporophyll with sporangia. C. Enlargement of bushy strobilus.*

DIAGNOSTIC ARROWS: *1. Horizontal stem flat to ground and very slender. 2. Leaves seldom toothed.*

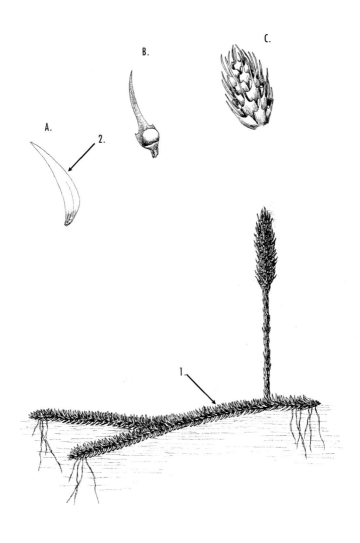

A.

2.

B.

C.

1.

LYCOPODIELLA INUNDATA
BOG CLUBMOSS

GENUS *LYCOPODIUM*: CLUBMOSSES

(Greek: *lykos*, "wolf" + *pous*, *podes*, "foot"; referring to resemblance of branch tips to a wolf's paw)

Recent taxonomic work has reorganized the highly diverse *Lycopodium* genus into multiple genera. According to this newer taxonomic scheme, *Lycopodium* species have upright stems that are round in cross-section with 12–20 ranks of leaves. Each upright stem has 1–6 spreading to ascending branches (but not in a treelike arrangement with a central stem and horizontal branches). Stems and branches have visible annual constrictions. The horizontal stems are on or near the surface. Leaves have a long, hairlike bristle on the tip. Strobili are on long stalks, and the branching pattern of the strobili stalks, when present, usually resembles a main, central axis with side branches (see illustration) rather than the equally forked branches of *Diphasiastrum*. Gametophytes of species in our area are disc-shaped, subterranean, and nonphotosynthetic.

Two species of this genus occur in our area: *Lycopodium lagopus* (One-cone Clubmoss) and *L. clavatum* (Common Clubmoss).

strobilus branching
pattern of
Diphasiastrum

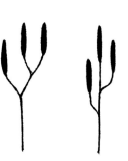

strobilus branching
pattern of *Lycopodium*

LYCOPODIUM KEY

1A. Strobili mostly single, on a long stalk or, if 2 strobili, then they are attached at nearly the same point on stalk; upright stem with 2–3 mostly upright branches; only in northern parts of our area. **L. lagopus (One-cone Clubmoss)**

1B. Strobili, 1–5, each borne on alternating separate branches of stalk; upright stem with 2–3 mostly spreading to ascending branches; throughout our area.

L. clavatum (Common Clubmoss)

Lycopodium clavatum *(Common Clubmoss) often forms dense colonies.*
(Photo by Cheryl Lowe)

Strobilus stalks of Ly-
copodium lagopus
(One-cone Clubmoss)
are mostly un-
branched. (Photo by
Janet E. Novak)

COMMON CLUBMOSS (Running Clubmoss)

Lycopodium clavatum L.

HABIT: Trailing, evergreen Clubmoss with clustered, upright, medium green stems densely covered with small, pale green leaves.

ECOLOGY: Common in open fields and thickets, moist and well-drained wooded areas; occasionally swamp and bog edges.

RANGE: East of the Rocky Mts., from Nfld. south to Va., and in Appalachian Mts., s. to Ga, northwest to Wisc., Minn., into s. Ont. and Man. West of the Rocky Mts., Mont. to n. Calif. and north to s. Alaska. Nearly cosmopolitan: South America, Europe, Asia, Africa.

HORIZONTAL STEMS: Near the surface; semi-arching or prostrate and creeping; branching and interlacing, often forming dense colonies; rooting at intervals; densely covered with leaves.

UPRIGHT STEMS: 4–10 in. tall. Densely leafy; evergreen; clustered, branched 3–6 times, with the branches emerging mostly from the lower half of the stem; branches of various lengths.

LATERAL BRANCHES: Similar to upright stems, but somewhat spreading, with conspicuous annual constrictions.

LEAVES: ⅓ in. long. Narrow, tapering upward to a thin, colorless, bristle; edges smooth to toothed. Leaves usually spreading, sometimes ascending along upper portions of branches.

STROBILUS: 3 in. ± long. Long, slender stalks with 1–5 alternate branches. (Plants with only 1 strobilus can be found within a given population, so look at all the stems.) One strobilus on the end of each branch of the stalk; stalks 6 in. ± long, covered with reduced, scattered leaves.

SPOROPHYLL: Yellow-tan; with abrupt, hairlike tip; sides irregularly toothed.

NOTES: *Lycopodium clavatum* has many common names, including Running Pine, Staghorn, and Wolf's Claw Clubmoss. It was once overcollected—used for Christmas decorations and listed as an herbal remedy. Extended hairlike bristles on leaves differentiate even sterile plants from similar Clubmosses (except *L. lagopus* (One-cone Clubmoss), which has mostly single strobili and only 2–3 branches per upright leafy stem.

MARGINALIA: *A. Sterile leaf with hairlike tip. B. Sporophyll with sporangia.*

DIAGNOSTIC ARROWS: *1. 1–5 strobili on end of each branch of long stalk.*
2. Leaves spread or point upward.

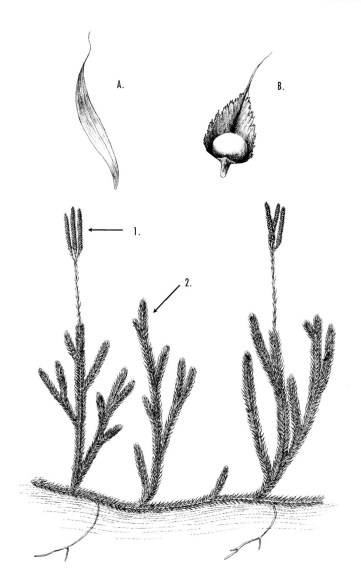

A.

B.

1.

2.

LYCOPODIUM CLAVATUM
COMMON CLUBMOSS

Lycopodium lagopus (Lestad. ex. Hartm.) Zinserl. ex Kuzen.

Synonym: *Lycopodium clavatum* L. var. *lagopus* Lestad. ex Hartm.

HABIT: Trailing, evergreen Clubmoss with clustered, upright, medium green stems densely covered with small leaves.

ECOLOGY: Open, grassy fields; woodland openings and edges. More northern, higher elevation sites than *Lycopodium clavatum* (Common Clubmoss).

RANGE: Greenland south to Conn., west through Mich. and Minn., west across Canada up into Alaska. Also Eurasia.

HORIZONTAL STEMS: On or near surface; often branching and overlapping; rooting at intervals; with annual constrictions. Densely covered with evergreen leaves.

UPRIGHT STEMS: 4–10 in. tall. Densely leafy; evergreen; with 1–2 branches clustered and emerging mostly from the lower ½ of stem.

LATERAL BRANCHES: Similar to upright stems; very upright; with conspicuous annual constrictions.

LEAVES: ⅛ in. long. Narrow, tapering upward to tiny hairlike tip; edges smooth to toothed. Leaves usually ascending to appressed.

STROBILUS: 3 in. long. Strobilus at end of each long, slender, mostly unbranched stalk. If 2 strobili per stalk, then strobili are attached at the same point. Stalks 6 in. long with a few scattered leaves.

SPOROPHYLL: Yellow-tan; gradually tapering to hairlike tip.

NOTES: Once considered a variety of *Lycopodium clavatum* (Common Clubmoss), but One-cone Clubmoss usually has only 1 strobilus at the end of the strobilus stalk, and narrower and more tapering sporophylls.

MARGINALIA: *A. Sporophyll with sporangia. B. Leaf.*

DIAGNOSTIC ARROWS: *1. Usually 1 strobilus at end of strobilus stalk.*
2. Upright stems all very vertical. 3. Leaves ascending or appressed.

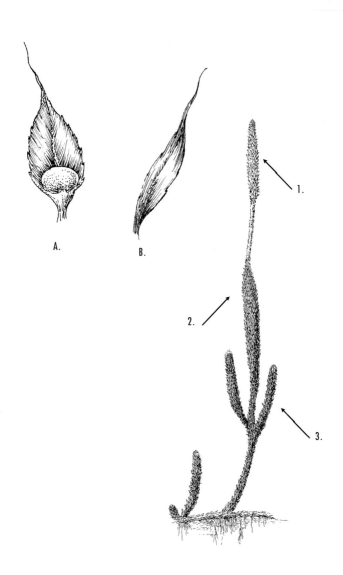

LYCOPODIUM LAGOPUS
ONE-CONE CLUBMOSS

GENUS *PSEUDOLYCOPODIELLA:* SLENDER BOG CLUBMOSS

(Greek: *pseudo,* "false," + *Lycopodiella,* a similar, related genus)

This genus and species has been separated from *Lycopodiella* based on the differentiated, almost leafless stalk of the strobilus, the evergreen character of the horizontal stems, and the small, yellow-brown sporophylls. This genus contains 12 species, with only one in our area. Gametophytes tuber-shaped, lobed, and photosynthetic, and they grow on the ground surface.

SLENDER BOG CLUBMOSS
(FALSE BOG CLUBMOSS)

Pseudolycopodiella caroliniana (L.) Holub
Synonyms: *Lycopodiella caroliniana* (L.) Pichi-Sermolli; *Lycopodium carolinianum* L.

HABIT: Evergreen, horizontal stems, with a few, tall delicate stalks per plant.

ECOLOGY: Sandy bogs, wet meadows, pinelands, ditches, often with Sphagnum Moss, in very acidic soils.

RANGE: In our area along coastal plain, N.Y. south to Fla. and west to Tex. Also Mexico, Central and South America, Asia, Africa.

HORIZONTAL STEMS: Creeping on surface, rooting along length; appear flattened in cross-section, evergreen.

UPRIGHT STEMS: 2–6 in. tall. Not branched; scattered along horizontal stem. Slender, sparse leaves.

LEAVES: Narrow; larger leaves (⅛ in. long) of horizontal stems with entire margins, appear 2-ranked and are held horizontal to ground. Much smaller leaves on upper and lower sides of horizontal stems are appressed. Upright stem nearly naked, with only tiny leaves.

STROBILUS: ⅜–1 in. tall. Solitary at end of upright stem.

SPOROPHYLLS: Shorter and broader than leaves of upright stem.

NOTES: Reaches northernmost edge of its range in our area, but is rarely found in our area.

MARGINALIA: *A. Enlargement of strobilus. B. Sporophyll with sporangia. C. Leaf of upright stem. D. Leaf of horizontal stem.*

DIAGNOSTIC ARROWS: *1. Tall, slender, almost naked upright stem. 2. Evergreen, bristly leaved and frequently horizontal-rooting stem creeping on surface of ground.*

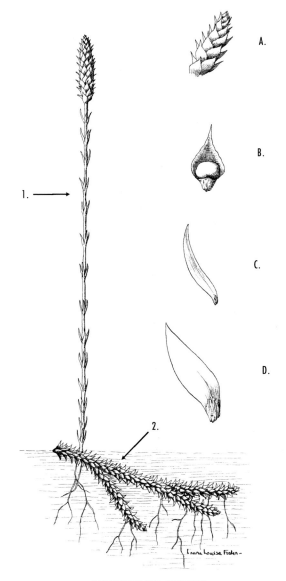

1. ⟶

2. ⟶

A.

B.

C.

D.

PSEUDOLYCOPODIELLA CAROLINIANA
SLENDER BOG CLUBMOSS

GENUS *SPINULUM:* BRISTLY CLUBMOSSES

(Latin: *spinula*, "diminutive spine"; as found on the tips of the leaves)

Spinulum is one of the more recently recognized genera resulting from the division of the older, more encompassing *Lycopodium* genus, with 3 species of *Spinulum* worldwide, 2 of which grow in our region. *Spinulum* species have upright stems that are mostly round in cross-section, with 8–10 ranks of leaves each with a small but firm spinelike tip. It is stiff and prickly to the touch. The horizontal stems run along the surface, not underground, and stems branch near the ground, so the plants do not have a distinct central stem or axis. *Spinulum* species have sessile strobili. Gametophytes are disc-shaped, subterranean, and nonphotosynthetic.

The 2 species in our area are *Spinulum annotinum* (Bristly Clubmoss) and *S. canadense* (Northern Interrupted Clubmoss). Some taxonomists question whether the characters of Northern Interrupted Clubmoss are determined by environmental conditions or are genetically distinct, and whether it should be considered a distinct species. It is found only on the northern edges of our range and is just briefly described here.

Note: When examining leaves for identification, it is best to look at leaves growing midway between the annual constrictions and leaves found just above an annual constriction. The leaves midway between constrictions show distinct differences in stomate numbers, whereas those closer to the annual constrictions do not. Stomates can be seen as light-colored dots on fresh leaves at 20× magnification.

SPINULUM KEY

1A. Leaves just above annual constrictions broadest at or near base of leaf; margins entire or with very small teeth; leaves midway between annual constrictions with abundant stomates on upper surface (25–53 per half-leaf). Strobili mostly ⅜–⅝ in. long. **S. canadense (Northern Interrupted Clubmoss)**

1B. Leaves just above annual constrictions broadest at or above middle; leaf margins slightly to clearly toothed; leaves midway between annual constrictions with no stomates on upper surface. Strobili mostly ⅝–1 ¾ in. long.
S. annotinum (Bristly Clubmoss)

(Above) Spinulum annotinum (*Bristly Clubmoss*, photo by Frank Bramley/ NEWFS), *and* (Right) S. canadense (*Northern Interrupted Clubmoss*, photo by Arthur Haines*). Both have prickly, evergreen stems and sessile strobili. Bristly Clubmoss is much more common.

BRISTLY CLUBMOSS (Interrupted Clubmoss)

Spinulum annotinum (L.) Haines

Synonyms: *Lycopodium annotinum* L.; *Lycopodium annotinum* L. var. *acrifolium* Fern.

HABIT: Evergreen, stiff, prickly; light to dark green stems resemble a narrow bottlebrush. Individual strobili without stalks; leaves mostly spreading to reflexed.

ECOLOGY: Common in moist to dry coniferous or mixed forests; also in exposed grassy or rocky sites, in acid soils; above treeline in protected areas.

RANGE: Greenland south to Va., along Appalachian Mts. south to N.C. northwest to Minn., throughout Canada, south along Rocky Mts. to N.M. and Ariz.

HORIZONTAL STEMS: Near surface, at or just below humus layer; with annual constrictions.

UPRIGHT STEMS: 6 in. tall. Branching at base; round in cross-section, bristly leaved, with annual constrictions.

LEAVES: ⅓ in. long. Narrow, broadest above the middle, with very sharp-pointed tip and a narrowed base; 10-ranked, ascending to reflexed; margins slightly to distinctly toothed. Leaves midway between annual constrictions with no stomates on upper surface.

STROBILUS: 1½ in. long. Sessile (no stalk); usually 1 strobilus per branch stem.

SPOROPHYLL: Yellow-tan; triangular ovate with abruptly tapering to sharp pointed tip.

NOTES: Another common name for Bristly Clubmoss is "Interrupted Clubmoss" (*annotinus* means "belonging to the year," referring to the annual constrictions that interrupt the stems). Might be confused with *Huperzia lucidula* (Shining Firmoss), but Bristly Clubmoss has spine tips on the leaves and strobili, whereas Shining Firmoss has neither spine tips nor strobili, but does have gemmae.

MARGINALIA: *A. Sterile leaf with toothed edges. B. Sporophyll with sporangia.*

DIAGNOSTIC ARROWS: *1. Strobilus sessile. 2. Leaves spreading. 3. Annual constrictions. 4. Leaves with sessile stiff bristle on tip.*

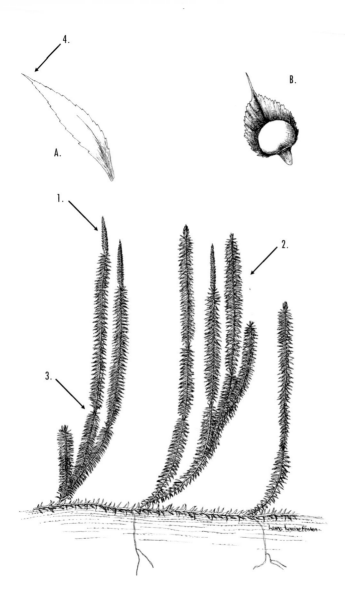

SPINULUM ANNOTINUM
BRISTLY CLUBMOSS

NORTHERN INTERRUPTED CLUBMOSS

Spinulum canadense (Ness) Haines.

Synonyms: *Lycopodium annotinum* L. var. *pungens* La Pylaie ex Desv.;
Lycopodium canadense Ness.

Similar to *Spinulum annotinum* (Bristly Clubmoss) with ever-green stems resembling a narrow bottlebrush, individual strobili without stalks. Primarily of northern and alpine communities, in open, exposed areas, but also at lower elevations at the northern edge of our range. Leaves just above annual constrictions triangular or at least broadest at or near base of leaf; ascending to loosely appressed; margins entire or with very small teeth; leaves midway between annual constrictions with abundant stomates on upper surface (25–53 per half-leaf). 8-ranked. Northern Interrupted Clubmoss and Bristly Clubmoss sometimes occur together, and do hybridize.

Note the differences between the sterile leaves of Spinulum annotinum *(left) and* S. canadense *(right).*

GENUS *EQUISETUM:* HORSETAILS AND SCOURING RUSHES

(Latin: *equis,* "horse," + *seta,* "bristle"; referring to resemblance to horse's tail)

The Horsetails of today are plants of a single genus, *Equisetum,* in the family Equisetaceae. They are considered one of the oldest of the Pteridophytes (fern families), being closely allied to the prehistoric Calamitales, large and abundant treelike plants that flourished nearly 300 million years ago in the Carboniferous Period.

Horsetails are most abundant in the northern temperate zones, although several species are found in the tropics. They grow in wet, sandy, gravelly, and clay soils from stream and pond edges to wet meadows and damp woods. Even when they appear to be growing in drier sites, their roots often reach down to the water table.

Equisetum species in our area are small to medium-sized plants with slender, round, hollow stems and distinct nodes (a swollen point on stem, or where branches attach to stem). The stem or branch section between the nodes is called the internode. Growth is symmetrical; when branches are present, they are whorled.

The pale brown, succulent fertile stems of Equisetum arvense *(Field Horsetail) are visible only in the spring. (Photo by Frank Bramley/ NEWFS)*

Feathery, delicate Equisetum pratense *(Meadow Horsetail). (Photo by David M. Stone/ NEWFS)*

Stems and branches are green and photosynthetic, although some species have nonphotosynthetic, tan, short-lived fertile stems. Both stems and branches have ridges and grooves on the surface; the ridges often have gritty silica particles that form rows, bands, teeth, or even rosettes, depending on the species. This silica is also embedded in the tissue, which is why *Equisetum* species were often used to scour pans (thus the common name, Scouring Rush) and as a fine abrasive for burnishing brass and finishing violins.

The leaves are tiny and fused into small sheaths surrounding each node; the sheath looks like a toothed band circling the node. Characters such as length and color of the sheath and its teeth are used in identification. Some *Equisetum* species have branches, which develop from the base of the sheath at the node; the branches in turn have nodes, internodes, and sheaths. Many a child (and adult) has enjoyed pulling apart a Horsetail stem at the node, and then "putting it back together." Although the broken stem fits neatly back into the sheath "socket," the connective tissue has been broken and the upper segment will stop growing and eventually turn brown.

Stems and branches in most species have a large hollow center. In the tissue surrounding the central hollow are two rings of smaller tubes: the outer set (the vallecular canals) is embedded under each groove, and the inner set (the carinal canals) is located under the ridges. Viewed in cross-section, the sizes and shapes of the central and vallecular canals are also characters used to identify the species.

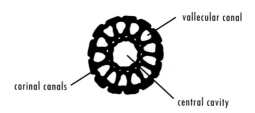

Cross-section of *Equisetum* stem with central cavity, small inner carinal canals, and outer circle of larger vallecular canals

The rhizomes of *Equisetum* species are structurally similar to the stems and branches (i.e., composed of nodes, internodes, and sheaths). Ranging in length from a few inches to many feet, they often spread extensively underground, sometimes reaching depths of 12 ft. with new stems or rootlets sprouting from the nodes. The rhi-

Cone of Equisetum palustre *(Marsh Horsetail) showing sporangia on edges of small hexagonal plates. (Photo by Adelaide Pratt/NEWFS)*

zomes of some species develop small underground tubers that store and supply additional nourishment if necessary, and these tubers can be the source of new plants.

A spore-bearing cone forms at the top of each fertile stem (and rarely on branches). (In *Equisetum*, this structure is defined as a cone, not a strobilus, because the central stem (axis) has side branches of stem tissue. See Morphology section, page 21.) It is often yellow and looks a bit like an armored, upright catkin, with its outer surface composed of tightly fitting hexagonal plates. These plates are actually greatly modified leaves, called sporangiophores. A stalk or stem connects the center of each plate to the main axis of the cone, like a flat umbrella with its handle embedded in the central stem. The rather large sporangia form on the outer edge of the underside of the hexagonal plates. When the cone is mature, it lengthens slightly, splitting the armor and allowing the sporangia to expand outward, split open, and release the spores. In some *Equisetum* species, the fertile stem disappears after the spores are dispersed. In others, the fertile stem emerges early, is light brown and unbranched until the spores are dispersed, then it turns green and branches develop as the cone withers and disappears.

Equisetum species have only one kind of spore, but two kinds of gametophytes—male and female. *Equisetum* spores contain chlorophyll and are moist. When ripe, they live only a few days and germinate within 10–12 hours of landing in an appropriate site. The spore's outer coating splits into 4 ribbons, which stay attached to the spore at one end. These ribbonlike strips with spatulate (spoonlike) tips are called elaters. They are extremely responsive to moisture, curling and uncurling around the spore as they become exposed to more or less moisture in the air. Their curling and twisting action aids not only in dissemination of the spores, but also in keeping enough of the spores tangled together to ensure that both male and female gametophytes will develop in the same tiny bit of moisture.

Spores with curled (left) and uncurling (right) elaters

The male gametophytes are usually yellow-green, numerous, and very small. The antheridia (male organs) usually develop first, and each antheridium produces several hundred sperm, which are larger and more numerous than in any of the fern genera. The less numerous female gametophytes are much larger (almost ½ in.), with many distinct lobes and a dark green color. The archegonia (female organs) are formed along the edges of the undersides of the female gametophyte. As they develop, they push up and around the edge of the gametophyte, with a protruding neck to open and receive the sperm.

Female gametophyte (above) and sperm (below)

The genus *Equisetum* contains about 15 species throughout the world, often divided into 2 groups or subgenera: *Hippochaete*, or Scouring Rushes, and the subgenus *Equisetum*, or Horsetails. In our region, Scouring Rushes have evergreen stems (except *E. laevigatum*, Smooth Scouring Rush), are unbranched, and, except for Smooth Scouring Rush, have pointed cones. Horsetails in our region have blunt-tipped cones and whorled branches and are not evergreen. Diagnostic characters for species of *Equisetum* include pointed or blunt-tipped cones, whether or not the stems have branches, the size of the central cavity, the size of the vallecular canals, the number of ridges, and characters of the sheath teeth. For many species, the number of sheath teeth equals the number of ridges and can be an alternative characteristic to count.

There are 9 species in our region. Far and away the most common Horsetail is *E. arvense* (Field Horsetail). Not only is it extremely common, but it also occurs in many forms that often delude us into believing we have found a different species. The forms are often a response to environmental conditions; for example, plants in exposed sites are more prostrate. In addition to environmentally induced variations, Horsetail hybrids are not uncommon and usually exhibit characters intermediate between the two parents. Hybrids do not form, however, between the subgenera *Hippochaete* (Scouring Rushes) and *Equisetum* (Horsetails).

Most hybrids are sterile, reproducing only by spreading underground roots. Four of the more common hybrids are briefly described at the end of the section, but not included in the key. *Equisetum* hybrids have white, misshapen spores instead of the green, spherical, fertile spores of the species. Although individual spores are too small to see with a 10× hand lens, the color of the many dustlike particles is visible.

EQUISETUM KEY

1A. Stems primarily unbranched, persisting more than 1 year (evergreen); cone with sharp pointed tip. (*E. laevigatum* [Smooth Scouring Rush] has unbranched stem, but cone with rounded tip and stems not persistent in our area.) Go to 2.

   2A. Cone tip rounded; stems usually annual (not persisting more than 1 year). ***E. laevigatum* (Smooth Scouring Rush)**

   2B. Cone tip pointed; aerial stems persisting. Go to 3.

      3A. Stems with 14–50 ridges; central cavity more than ½ stem diameter; cones ⅜–1 in. long.
      ***E. hyemale* ssp. *affine* (Common Scouring Rush)**

      3B. Stems with 3–12 ridges; central cavity absent or up to ⅓ stem diameter; cones ¹⁄₁₆–⅜ in. long. Go to 4.

         4A. Stems upright to half-recumbent, 3–12 ridges; sheath teeth number same as ridges; central cavity ⅓ of stem diameter.
         ***E. variegatum* ssp. *variegatum* (Variegated Scouring Rush)**

         4B. Stems curling, prostrate, and entwined with 6 ridges and 3 teeth on sheath; no central cavity.
         ***E. scirpoides* (Dwarf Scouring Rush)**

1B. Stems commonly with whorls of branches; deciduous at end of growing season; cone blunt-tipped. (Stems sometimes unbranched in *E. palustre* and *E. fluviatile*.) Go to 5.

   5A. Usually unbranched, but sometimes with a few branches.
   ***E. laevigatum* (Smooth Scouring Rush)**

   5B. Commonly with whorls of branches. Go to 6.

      6A. Length of lowest internode of branch shorter than adjacent stem sheath. Go to 7.

         7A. Central cavity ¾ or more of stem diameter, making it easy to compress when squeezed; stems with 12–24 shallow ridges; sheaths have 12–24 teeth that are dark throughout or sometimes with narrow white border. ***E. fluviatile* (Water Horsetail)**

7B. Central cavity less than ⅓ stem diameter; stems with 5–10 strong ridges; sheaths have 5–10 dark teeth with prominent white borders.

E. palustre (Marsh Horsetail)

6B. Length of lowest internode of branch equal or longer than adjacent stem sheath. Go to 8.

8A. Sheath teeth reddish brown, papery, attached into 3–4 larger groups; branches of stem often branch again. Cones appear in spring on unbranched, succulent light brown stems that branch and turn green after spores released.

E. sylvaticum (Woodland Horsetail)

8B. Sheath teeth brown to black, firm, and separate or attached into more than 4 larger groups; branches not branching again. Go to 9.

9A. Central cavity ⅓–½ stem diameter; branch sheath with triangular, clasping teeth; stem internodes rough to the touch; branches delicate and spreading. Cones appear in spring on unbranched, succulent light brown stems that branch and turn green after spores released.

E. pratense (Meadow Horsetail)

9B. Central cavity ¼–⅓ of stem diameter; branch sheath teeth taper gradually to a slender tip; stem internodes smooth or slightly rough; branches ascending. Cones appear in spring on unbranched, succulent light brown stems that disappear after spores released.

E. arvense (Field Horsetail)

The smooth stem of Equisetum fluviatile (*Water Horsetail*) compresses easily when squeezed. (*Photo by Frank Bramley/NEWFS*)

Evergreen shoots of Equisetum hyemale (*Common Scouring Rush*) feel like fine sandpaper. (*Photo by Cheryl Lowe*)

(Left) The beautiful cone and black-and-white sheath of Equisetum variegatum (*Variegated Scouring Rush*). (*Photo by Arthur Haines*) (Above) Equisetum scirpoides (*Dwarf Scouring Rush*) is easily recognized by its small, curly stems. (*Photo by Dorothy Long/NEWFS*)

Equisetum arvense L.

HABIT: Most common bushy Horsetail and most variable in form, from upright to spreading, small to medium large. Weedy. Unbranched fertile stem and cone appear early in the season; wither and disappear by May.

ECOLOGY: Fields, woods, glades, marshes, roadsides, and waste places. Thrives in any soil, but prefers damp, sandy, semishaded areas. Throughout our area.

RANGE: Throughout Canada and U.S. except Fla., La., Miss., S.C. Also Eurasia, China, Korea, Japan.

FERTILE STEMS: 6–12 in. tall. Erect, pale brown, unbranched, succulent, with cone; short-lived (appearing March–May). Sheaths ½ in. ± with large, dark, lance-shaped teeth.

STERILE STEMS: 6–24 in. tall. Green; 4–14 ridges; sheaths with small (⅛ in. ±), dark brown teeth with white margins, often connected in pairs. Stems solitary or close together.

BRANCHES: Regular whorls ascending or somewhat spreading, giving bushy appearance. Solid (not hollow) with 3–4 strong ridges and grooves. Lowest internode of branch longer than adjacent stem sheath. Branch sheath green, with 3–4 sharp-pointed, dark-tipped teeth spreading outward.

CAVITIES: Central cavity relatively small, ¼–⅓ stem diameter. Vallecular canals relatively large (⅓–½ width of central cavity).

CONE: 1–1½ in. long. Long-stemmed, blunt-tipped.

RHIZOME: Slender, dark brown, branching and creeping; covered with a brown felt; tubers sometimes present.

NOTES: Environmental conditions such as exposure, habitat, and season affect growth habit; for example, plants in windy exposed sites tend to be more prostrate while those in sheltered sites are much taller. Sometimes confused with *Equisetum pratense* (Meadow Horsetail) and *E. palustre* (Marsh Horsetail). Meadow Horsetail has more delicate branches and teeth are triangular rather than lancelike. Unlike Field Horstail, the lowest branch internode of Meadow Horsetail is shorter than adjacent stem sheath, and the branch teeth have black tips and clasp the stem.

MARGINALIA: *A. Cross-section of main stem. B. Sheath and teeth of main stem. C. Sheath of branch. D. Sheath and branches. E, G. Immature sterile stems. F. Fertile stem.*

DIAGNOSTIC ARROWS: *1. Sheath is shorter than first branch internode. 2. Many ascending branches. 3. Branch teeth sharp-pointed and slightly flared.*

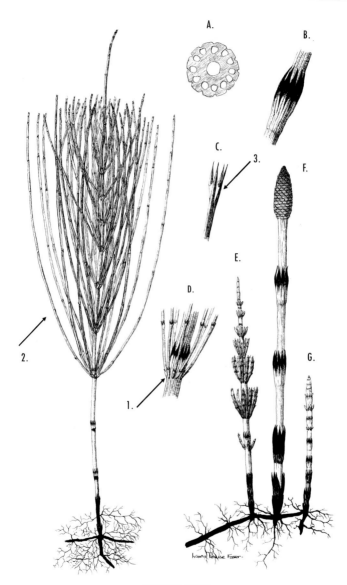

A.

B.

C.

3.

F.

D.

E.

1.

2.

G.

EQUISETUM ARVENSE
FIELD HORSETAIL

Equisetum fluviatile L.

HABIT: Smoothest and hollowest Horsetail. Variable form, with many, few, or no branches.

ECOLOGY: Common in sluggish waters, marshes, ponds, and ditches, shallow to deep water (*fluviatile* means "river").

RANGE: Throughout Canada, south to Va., west to Ore. (except in Rocky Mts.), north to Alaska. Also Eurasia.

STEMS: 14–46 in. tall. All alike, green, erect, mostly solitary; very hollow, very smooth. 12–24 flat obscure ridges. Sheaths ⅓ in.± wide, green, clasping, often tinged with orange; 12–24 narrow, black, sharp-pointed teeth, sometimes with narrow white border. Stems sometimes branching after cone has formed.

BRANCHES: Up to 6 in. long. Variable length and number of branches; spreading to ascending, usually only from midstem nodes; 4–6 smooth, slender, hollow ridges. Branch internode nearest stem shorter than adjacent stem sheath. Teeth narrow.

CAVITIES: Central cavity ⅘ stem diameter or more. Vallecular canals lacking.

CONE: 1 in. ± long. Blunt tip, short-stemmed, maturing in summer.

RHIZOME: Reddish, hollow, same size as stems, wide-creeping.

NOTES: Distinguished from other species by thin stem walls that easily compress when squeezed. Formation of branches seems to be related to environmental factors, especially shade and shelter (more branching in shaded, sheltered locations). Often confused with Shore Horsetail (*Equisetum* × *litorale*), which is described on page 358; comparative drawings are here.

MARGINALIA: *A. Sheath of main stem. B. Cross-section of stem. C. Cone. D. Shore Horsetail* (E. × litorale) *sheath of main stem. E. Shore Horsetail cross-section.*

DIAGNOSTIC ARROWS: *1.Two forms: with and without branches. 2. Very thin stem walls. 3. Shallow ridges. 4. Branches, if present, only form midstem nodes. 5. Shore Horsetail: first branch internode is equal in length to sheath. 6. Shore Horsetail: stem less hollow and more deeply ridged than Swamp Horsetail.*

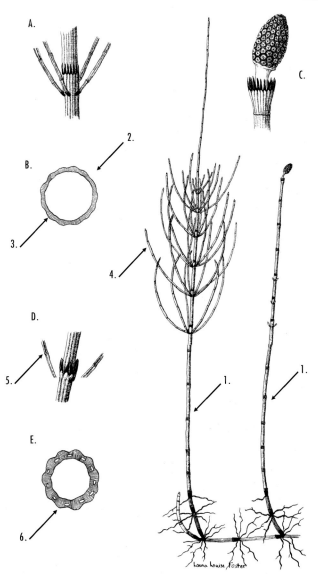

A.

C.

2.

B.

3.

D.

5.

E.

6.

4.

1.

1.

EQUISETUM FLUVIATILE
WATER HORSETAIL

COMMON SCOURING RUSH
(Rough Horsetail)

Equisetum hyemale L. ssp. *affine* (Engelm.) Calder & Taylor
Synonyms: *Equisetum robustum* A. Braun var. *affine* Engelmann;
Hypochaete hyemalis (L.) Bruhin ssp. *affinis* (Engelm.) Holub

HABIT: Tall, slender, hollow, dark green stems. Surfaces are rough; ash gray sheaths outlined above and below by dark edges. Evergreen, thicketlike growth particularly noticeable in winter woods.

ECOLOGY: Common. Moist soils in woods, fields, swamps, riverbanks, roadsides.

RANGE: Nfld. to Alaska across s. Canada, south throughout U.S. Eurasian species is *Equisetum hyemale* ssp. *hyemale*.

STEMS: 7–86 in. tall. ½ in. ± thick at base; erect, evergreen, mostly unbranched. Second-year stems more likely to branch than first-year stems, as are stems with tips damaged in some other way. If present, branches tend to be nearly vertical. Fertile and sterile stems alike. Rough surface with 14–50 broad ridges. Sheaths 1–2 times longer than wide (including teeth); tight to stem, green at first, then gray with dark bands at base and top. Sharp-pointed, brown-edged teeth usually soon wither and disappear.

CAVITIES: Central cavity ⅔ ± stem diameter. Vallecular canals much smaller than central cavity.

CONE: ½–1 in. Short-stemmed, with sharp-pointed tip, maturing in summer.

RHIZOME: Branching and widely creeping.

NOTES: Internodes often bulge with age, so stem looks constricted at nodes. Sometimes confused with *Equisetum laevigatum* (Smooth Scouring Rush), but Smooth Scouring Rush does not have evergreen stems; has a narrow, dark band only on the upper edge of the sheath (not the bottom edge as well); and its sheaths stay green, rather than becoming ash gray as in Common Scouring Rush. Also, sheaths of Smooth Scouring Rush are flaring rather than tight to the stem.

MARGINALIA: *A. Cone, stem, and sheath. B. Cross-section of stem.*
DIAGNOSTIC ARROWS: *1. Rough stem. 2. Sharp-pointed cone. 3. Clasping sheath that becomes gray with dark bands at base and top.*

EQUISETUM HYEMALE
COMMON SCOURING RUSH

Equisetum laevigatum A. Br.

HABIT: Tall, slender Scouring Rush with smooth, hollow stems. Grows in clusters and is usually not evergreen.

ECOLOGY: Sandy soils in moist prairies, riverbanks, roadsides. Primarily central and w. U.S.

RANGE: S. Ont. south through Ohio to Tex., west to Pacific Coast, north into s. Canada.

STEMS: 8–60 in. tall; ¼ in. ± thick at base. Slender, erect, very hollow, usually not evergreen, seldom branched; 10–32 rounded ridges; smooth surface. Sheaths elongate, green or with some brown in old stems, ⅓ in. ± wide. Sheaths constricted at base, flaring toward top, with 10–32 sharp-pointed, dark brown teeth with rough edges. Teeth wither quickly, leaving dark upper rim on sheath.

CAVITIES: Central cavity large, ¾ ± stem diameter. Vallecular canals very small compared to central cavity.

CONE: ½–1 in. Short-stemmed, rounded or with small sharp tip.

RHIZOME: Branching and widely creeping.

NOTES: More slender, paler green, more fragile than *Equisetum hyemale* (Common Scouring Rush).

MARGINALIA: *A. Cone, stem, and sheath. B. Cross-section of stem.*
DIAGNOSTIC ARROWS: *1. Smooth stem. 2. Cone tip rounded or with tiny point. 3. Flared sheath that stays green with only an upper dark band after teeth wither.*

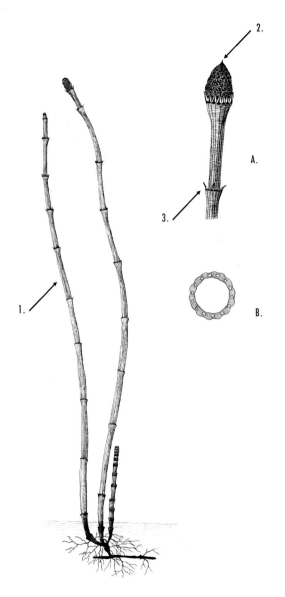

1.

2.

A.

3.

B.

EQUISETUM LAEVIGATUM
SMOOTH SCOURING RUSH

MARSH HORSETAIL

Equisetum palustre L.

HABIT: Medium-sized Horsetail with slender, upright stems growing solitary or in clusters. Stems usually with whorls of stout, upward curving branches, but in some conditions, not branched.

ECOLOGY: Marshes, swamps, ditches, stream banks, and open, wet woods. Rare and local.

RANGE: Throughout Canada and Alaska south to Pa., west through Minn. to Ore. Also Eurasia to China, Korea, Japan.

STEMS: 8–32 in. tall. Erect; branched mostly from midstem nodes, sometimes unbranched. Fertile stems have cone at tip; sterile stems have long, thin, tapering, unbranched tip. 5–10 prominent ridges. Sheaths green, elongate, sometimes flared outward and then constricted again at teeth; 5–10 long, narrow, pointed, persistent teeth, black with broad, white, rough margins.

BRANCHES: Short, fairly thick, curving upward, hollow, 4–6 ridges with rounded grooves. Lowest internode of each branch shorter than adjacent stem sheath. Branch sheaths with 5–6 green, clasping teeth with tiny black tips.

CAVITIES: Central cavity small (⅛–⅓ stem diameter). Vallecular canals about same size as central cavity.

CONE: 1 in. ± long. Blunt tip; on slender medium-short stem.

RHIZOME: Slender, solid, dark; deeply creeping and branching, sometimes with tubers.

NOTES: Variable; in exposed sites, branches may emerge only from lower nodes and become thin and whiplike near ends or be absent altogether. Sterile unbranched stems resemble *Equisetum variegatum* (Variegated Scouring Rush), but the latter has rather rough stems and is evergreen.

MARGINALIA: *A. Cone and sheath. B. Joint of side branch. C. Sheath and base of branches on main stem. D. Cross-section of stem.*

DIAGNOSTIC ARROWS: *1. Ascending flat-topped branches; sterile stem has long unbranched tip; fertile stem bears cone. 2. Cone stem relatively short with prominent white margins on teeth of sheath. 3. Lowest branch internode shorter than sheath. 4. Central cavity and vallecular cavity both about same size.*

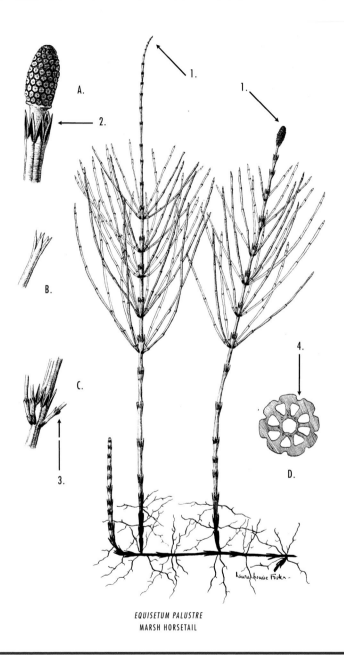

EQUISETUM PALUSTRE
MARSH HORSETAIL

Equisetum pratense Ehrh.

HABIT: Feathery with delicate, thin branches that spread horizontally outward in perfect whorls, usually in small, scattered colonies.

ECOLOGY: Moist, sunny meadows to cool, moist woodlands.

RANGE: Across Canada and south to N.J., west to Iowa, N.D., B.C. Also Eurasia to China. Mostly in northern parts of our area.

FERTILE STEMS: 15 in. ± tall. Erect; first appear pale pink to brown and without branches, branching and turning green after spores discharge. Not common.

STERILE STEMS: 6–20 in. tall. Erect; green; slightly rough. 8–18 ridges that are broader than grooves. Sheaths clasping, elongate, ⅓ in. ± wide; urn-shaped. 8–18 narrow, persistent, sharp-pointed teeth with dark brown centers and distinct white margins.

BRANCHES: 5 in. ± long. Whorled; spreading to horizontal or slightly drooping; solid, thin, delicate, and 3-angled; lowest branches a little shorter than others; no rebranching. Lowest internode of branch equal to or longer than adjacent stem sheath. Branch teeth triangular and clasping.

CAVITIES: Central cavity ⅙–⅓ stem diameter. Vallecular canals small compared to central cavity.

CONE: 1 in. ± long. Long stems (1–2 in.), blunt tip. Matures late spring.

RHIZOME: Black, slender; horizontally creeping deep in soil with wiry roots.

NOTES: Most often confused with *Equisetum arvense* (Field Horsetail), but Meadow Horsetail is more delicate and has more teeth on stem sheath, and the branch teeth are triangular rather than lance-shaped.

MARGINALIA: *A. Sheath of sterile stem. B. Sheath of fertile stem. C. Fertile stem with cone. D. Cross-section of stem. E. Sheath and first sections of branches.*

DIAGNOSTIC ARROWS: *1. Spidery and more delicate growth form than Field Horsetail. 2. White-margined, dark, clasping teeth on sterile stem sheath. 3. Long-stemmed cone.*

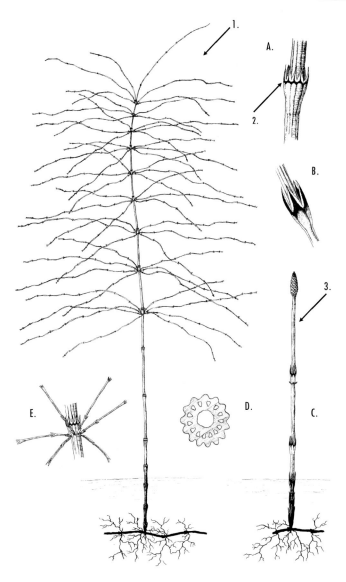

1.

A.

2.

B.

3.

E.

D.

C.

EQUISETUM PRATENSE
MEADOW HORSETAIL

DWARF SCOURING RUSH

Equisetum scirpoides Michx.
Synonym: *Hippochaete scirpoides* (Michx.) Farw.

HABIT: Smallest *Equisetum* species. Grows in curling, entwining, evergreen mats. Usually well hidden in the tangled grasses or deep mosses with which it grows. Black, sharp-pointed cones of the more erect fertile stems often give away its hiding place.

ECOLOGY: Moist, coniferous woods, hummocks in swamps, mossy banks, peat bogs, tundra. A forest species of cooler areas, mostly rare and local in our area, common above Canadian border. Mostly in subacid soils.

RANGE: Across Canada, south to Conn., west to Iowa, north to Minn. and S.D., west to n. Wash. Also n. Eurasia, Siberia, n. China.

STEMS: 1–8 in. tall. Evergreen, ascending, prostrate, coiling, and entwined. 6 broad ridges with deeply concave grooves; mostly dark green and unbranched. Fertile stems usually more erect. Sheaths long, green, flared, with 3 teeth (rarely 4); teeth triangular and sharp-pointed. Teeth have dark center and lighter-colored edges, forming a dark band on the sheath.

CAVITIES: No central cavity; 3 large vallecular canals about middle of stem.

CONE: Small, black, stemless cone with a sharp-pointed tip; matures in summer or overwinters and disperses spores in early spring.

RHIZOME: Creeping, slender, widely branching.

NOTES: Distinctive character is its small, curling, entwining stems.

MARGINALIA: *A. Cone and sheath. B. Cross-section of stem.*
DIAGNOSTIC ARROWS: *1. Curling growth (usually less upright than shown here). 2. Three vallecular cavities, but 6 ridges.*

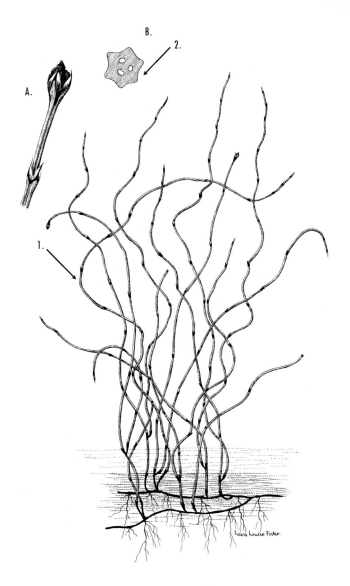

B.

2.

A.

1.

EQUISETUM SCIRPOIDES
DWARF SCOURING RUSH

WOODLAND HORSETAIL

Equisetum sylvaticum L.

HABIT: An elegant Horsetail, emerald green; delicate lacy branches in horizontal whorls gracefully droop toward the tips.

ECOLOGY: Moist forests, wet meadows, wooded swamps. Common in rich, moist, subacid soil.

RANGE: Across Canada, south to Va., west through Ohio, S.D., Wash. Also Eurasia to n. China.

FERTILE STEMS: 8 in. ± tall. Erect; first appear pale pink to brown and without developed branches, branching and turning green after spores discharge.

STERILE STEMS: 10–27 in. tall. Erect; brownish to green, branched, mostly solitary; slightly rough; hollow. 8–18 ridges, each with 2 rows of tiny spikes. Sheath green at base and chestnut brown above; long, narrow, somewhat urn-shaped (spreading then clasping below teeth). 10–18 reddish, persistent teeth connected into 3–4 large groups resembling large, broad teeth.

BRANCHES: 6 in. ± wide. Numerous, in delicate, arching whorls; 3–4 ridges, often rebranching into tiny 3-ridged branchlets; teeth narrow, pointed, and spreading. Lowest internode of branches longer than adjacent stem sheath. No branches from lower nodes.

CAVITIES: Central cavity ⅙–⅓ stem diameter. Vallecular canals large and prominent, up to ½ the width of the stem tissue.

CONE: 1 in. ± long. Rounded tips, long-stemmed; matures late spring, then disappears.

RHIZOME: Slender, branching, creeping deep in soil; sometimes with large tubers.

NOTES: Delicate branches that branch again to create lacy effect makes this species distinctive.

MARGINALIA: *A. Cross-section of stem. B. Sheath on stem. C. Immature sterile stem. D. Fertile stem with cone.*

DIAGNOSTIC ARROWS: *1. Branches often rebranching. 2. Diverging and then clasping sheaths. 3. Late-developing branches on fruiting fertile stem.*

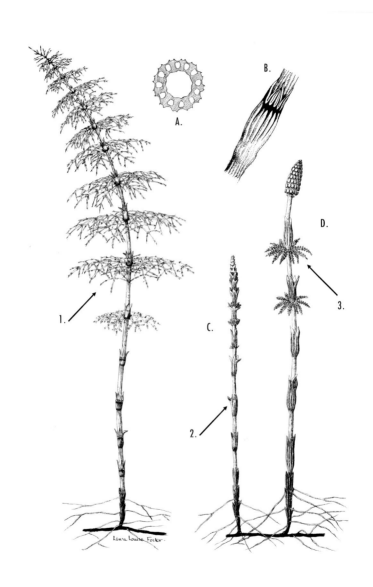

A.

B.

C.

D.

1.

2.

3.

Laura Louise Foster

EQUISETUM SYLVATICUM
WOODLAND HORSETAIL

VARIEGATED SCOURING RUSH
(VARIEGATED HORSETAIL)

Equisetum variegatum Schleich. ex F. Webber & D. M. H. Mohr ssp.
variegatum
> Synonym: *Hippochaete variegata* (Schleich. ex F. Webber &
> D. M. H. Mohr) Bruhin ssp. *variegata*

HABIT: Slender, evergreen, dark green species that seldom branches and grows in twisting, half-recumbent to upright tufts from a semi-exposed rhizome. Called "variegated" because of its distinct black-and-white sheaths.

ECOLOGY: Cool, shady spots in open woods, tundra, river banks, and wet meadows. Often moist, sandy, circumneutral to subalkaline soils. Primarily a more northern species.

RANGE: Greenland and throughout Canada, south to N.J., west to Ill., Minn., also in Rocky Mts. south to Utah and west to Wash., Ore. Also Eurasia to n. Asia.

STEMS: 3–19 in. tall. Unbranched; rough, slender; 3–12 ridges, with broad grooves. Sheaths green and spreading, with black apical band; 3–12 short, prominent, sharp-pointed teeth with brown centers and distinct white margins, sometimes also with deciduous hairlike tip.

CAVITIES: Central cavity ⅓ stem diameter. Vallecular canals distinct and almost ½ the diameter of the central cavity.

CONE: Small, greenish; short-stemmed with sharp-pointed tip; matures late summer or overwinters and disperses spores in spring.

RHIZOME: Near surface; slender, black, branching, creeping.

NOTES: Distinguished from *Equisetum laevigatum* (Smooth Scouring Rush) by sharp-pointed cone, distinct black-and-white sheaths, and persistent sheath teeth.

MARGINALIA: *A. Cross-section of stem. B. Cone and white-margined teeth on sheath.*

DIAGNOSTIC ARROWS: *1. Round flattish-topped cone with sharp tip.*
2. Sheath green and spreading with black apical band. 3. Sharp teeth with white margin and dark centers. 4. Large vallecular cavities.

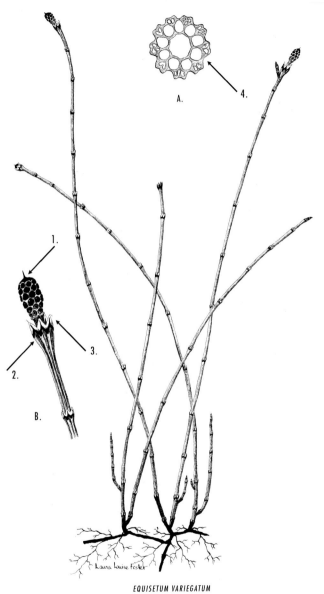

A.

B.

1.

2.

3.

4.

EQUISETUM VARIEGATUM
VARIEGATED SCOURING RUSH

INTERMEDIATE SCOURING RUSH
Equisetum × ferrisii Clute

This hybrid between *Equisetum hyemale* (Common Scouring Rush) and *E. laevigatum* (Smooth Scouring Rush) is relatively common in the western parts of our region, but rare in New England. Tends to be rougher and stouter than Smooth Scouring Rush, with similar green upper sheaths. Lower sheaths turn gray like Common Scouring Rush. Stems unbranched and lower stems tend to be evergreen. Sheaths elongated, with 14–32 teeth that usually drop off early. Cone has a pointed tip.

SHORE HORSETAIL
Equisetum × litorale Kühl. ex Rupr.

A hybrid between *Equisetum fluviatile* (Water Horsetail) and *E. arvense* (Field Horsetail), occurs where both species are present. Variable in form, usually smaller (to 27 in.), thinner (¼ in.), rougher, smaller cavity (⅔–⅗ stem diameter), and with more pronounced ridges than Water Horsetail. Teeth on sheaths dark and narrow. Although usually sterile, it spreads abundantly by rhizomes. Branches, if present, emerge from midstem nodes, have 4 ridges, and are not hollow. Cones small but rarely present; spores misshapen and abortive. Water Horsetail best distinguished from *E. × litorale* by very thin stem walls and flat ridges. *E. × litorale* is best distinguished from Field Horsetail by the first internode of lowest whorl of branches, which is equal in length to the sheath (this internode is longer than the sheath in Field Horsetail) and by white, misshapen spores of the hybrid.

EQUISETUM × MACKAII (Newm.) Brichan

A hybrid of *Equisetum variegatum* (Variegated Scouring Rush) and *E. hyemale* var. *affine* (Common Scouring Rush). Unbranched, 7–16 ridges and teeth. Teeth have dark centers and thin, white margins (in contrast with wide, prominent white margins in Variegated Scouring Rush). Sheaths have an upper black band or are more or less black throughout, rather than having an ash gray central band like older stems of Common Scouring Rush. As in other *Equisetum* hybrids, spores are white and misshapen. Not common, but found from Me. to N.J., west to Minn.

EQUISETUM × NELSONII (A. A. Eaton) J. H. Schaffner

This hybrid between *Equisetum variegatum* (Variegated Scouring Rush) and *E. laevigatum* (Smooth Scouring Rush) has unbranched stems with pointed cones and dark green sheaths like its parents. Does not persist through the winter (unlike Variegated Scouring Rush). The 6–14 teeth are persistent (unlike the deciduous 10–32 teeth of Smooth Scouring Rush), with dark brown centers, white margins, and brown tips that are long and threadlike. Spores white and misshapen. Relatively common in the Great Lakes region, a few disjunct sites farther west.

Pointed cone of Equisetum × ferrisii *(left) and elongated sheath (right), which turns gray.*

Equisetum × mackayi *cone and black sheath.*

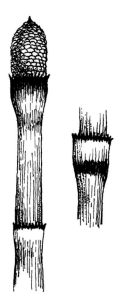

GENUS *ISOËTES*: THE QUILLWORTS

(Greek: *iso*, "equal," + *etos*, "year"; referring to some species that are evergreen)

Quillworts belong to the genus *Isoëtes* and are the only member of the family Isoëtaceae. The genus contains about 300 species worldwide. *Isoëtes* species are small, perennial, summer-fertile aquatic plants. Often they are totally submerged, although they are sometimes amphibious or terrestrial. Some that are only periodically inundated go dormant during dry spells, reviving when water becomes available. Quillworts grow throughout the world wherever there are bodies of still, fresh or somewhat salty waters, such as backwaters, river edges, ponds, lakes, and ditches. In our area, there are approximately 10 species with 5 recognized hybrids. As the group is studied more thoroughly, we will undoubtedly see many changes in the taxonomy of this complex group of plants.

Isoëtes are not at all like ferns in appearance. They look like small tufts of chives or young onions. Their slender, unbranched, quill-like leaves are awl-shaped, rounded, quadrangular, or triangular in cross-section. Their leaves are seldom more than 12 in. long, and they grow straight or in twisting spirals from a central swollen base at the juncture with the fleshy, subterranean corm. The slim, pointed leaves are brittle and have 4 vertical air channels that are interrupted frequently and irregularly by horizontal walls, which can give the leaves a jointed appearance. The leaf bases flatten and widen abruptly into spoonlike shapes, convex on their outer sides and concave on the inner sides; they overlap one another, somewhat like the leaves on the head of an artichoke. The youngest leaves are on the inside. The outer, oldest leaves wither and fall off seasonally or as new leaves are added. Below these leaves is a fleshy, brownish, globe-shaped corm from which the leaves originate and from which the long, fleshy, tubular, forking, and abundant roots grow downward. The leaves and corms of some species are edible and are consumed by geese, muskrats, and other aquatic animals.

Like the Spikemosses (*Selaginella*) and the Water Ferns (*Azolla* and *Marsilea*), *Isoëtes* species have 2 types of spores: a large megaspore and a tiny microspore. *Isoëtes* sporangia (cases containing the spores) are the largest of any known living plant. They are borne in a

MARGINALIA: *A. Diagram of megaspore showing proximal ridges.*
B. Swollen base of leaf with artichoke-like imbrication containing velum and sporangia.
DIAGNOSTIC ARROWS: *1. Spiral-like growth form from bulbous base.*

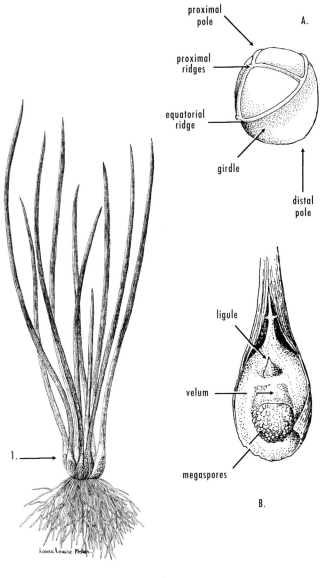

proximal
pole

A.

proximal
ridges

equatorial
ridge

girdle

distal
pole

1.

ligule

velum

megaspores

B.

ISOËTES
THE QUILLWORTS

pocket within the concavity of the lower spoon-shaped part of the leaf and are wholly or partly covered by a velum, a thin layer of tissue. The degree to which the velum covers the sporangium can be a helpful diagnostic feature.

The innermost, youngest leaves are usually sterile. The next outermost leaves usually feature a single pocket containing the sporangium, which contains the microspores. The outside leaves contain the megaspores in their pockets. In some species, the 2 types of spores are borne in the middle and outer leaves.

The megaspores are numerous, from several to hundreds per sporangium. They are chalky white, crusted with silica, and globe-shaped. On the upper surface of each megaspore are 3 radial "proximal ridges" that radiate from a common point to about ⅓ to halfway around the spore, where they come into contact with the "equatorial ridge," which encircles the spore. The hemisphere with the 3 proximal ridges is denoted as the "proximal pole," and the hemisphere with no ridges is called the "distal pole." The surface texture of *Isoëtes* megaspores is fundamental to species identification. These spore textures or ornamentation patterns result from various types of elaborated structures: crests or muri (wall-like ridges that stand out from the spore surface, which always have a narrow, sharp apex); rugulae (low, moundlike ridges with a rounded, smooth apex); spines (like those on a sea urchin); and tubercles (bumps). Common textures for the megaspores of species in our area include (numbers in parentheses refer to figure on opposite page):

(1) *reticulate* (pitted)—a honeycomb arrangement of crests
(2) *cristate* (crested)—crests only occasionally join together; do not form a honeycomb arrangement
(3) *rugulate*—covered with rugulae (large, moundlike ridges) that don't form a honeycomb
(4) *echinate*—covered with separate and distinct spines
(5) *tuberculate*—covered with low, rounded tubercles (bumps)
(6) *smooth*—without obvious ornamentation

In addition to ornamentation, it is important to notice if there is a dramatic change in surface texture bounding the equatorial ridge just on the distal side. This region of difference in ornamentation is called the "girdle" and its form and appearance are often unique to particular species.

The microspores are minute, grayish, powdery, usually oval, and with smooth or slightly roughened surfaces. They are extremely numerous; in some species, several hundred thousand microspores are contained in 1 sporangium.

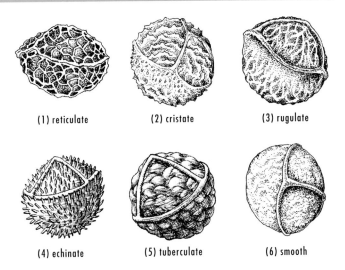

(1) reticulate (2) cristate (3) rugulate

(4) echinate (5) tuberculate (6) smooth

Both the microspores and the megaspores produce their own gametophytes. The sperm-bearing gametophyte produces 4 spermatozoids, which are tiny and slender with long, hairlike appendages (flagellae) at one end, by which they propel themselves. The egg-bearing gametophyte is a round, many-celled structure on top of which are 1 or more shallow channels surrounded by little funnel-like necks, called archegonia. The solitary eggs are embedded at the base of the funnels. The necks open when the eggs are ready for fertilization and close after the spermatozoid enters. The young plants develop directly from the fertilized egg within the archegonium.

Although several species of Quillworts are found in most of our own watery areas, the group is unfamiliar to most people, even to those interested in ferns. Because the species are so similar in habit and growth form and superficially resemble some common aquatic and amphibious grasses or rushes, they are frequently overlooked; they are also hard to distinguish when they grow intermingled with other plants. Furthermore, because several *Isoëtes* species are usually submerged, they are often less accessible than upland plants. Quillworts often hybridize with each other, producing confusing forms with intermediate characteristics.

The great similarity in growth, form, and ecological preferences of most species of Quillworts makes it necessary to examine characteristics of the megaspores to identify species accurately. With experience, many species can be identified with a good 15–20× hand lens in the field. The megaspore ornamentation is much more obvious when the spores are dry. This can be accomplished by gently removing a single outer leaf (without destroying the whole plant), breaking open a sporangium, and spreading the spores on the back of your hand. There, they can be dried by wind or your breath, while the hairs of your hand hold them neatly in place! For some species, you may need a binocular microscope fitted with an ocular micrometer to measure spore size in order to see the characteristic surface areas for identification. Megaspores are best collected at the end of the growing season when they are well-developed but have not dispersed from the sporangium. Be aware, however, that many Quillworts are rare because their aquatic habitats have been so heavily used and altered by people; avoid collecting or damaging the whole plant. Some species are endemic to particular regions of our area or to particular habitats, and hence easier to identify nondestructively in the field.

Though the Quillworts are a challenging group, they are fascinating and much more common than most people would believe. Recent studies in the genus have added 6 species to our area since the first edition of this book. In addition, several Quillworts that were not recognized as distinct have been shown to be separate species. Hybrids are very common in areas where several species co-occur. Hybrids are generally readily identified by megaspores of quite variable size (some of which may be deformed) and often by very dense and intricate ornamentation. Although individual, interspecific hybrids are sterile, historically they have given rise to many new fertile species by chromosome doubling, a process known as allopolyploidy. The species in our area have 2–10 sets of chromosomes. The following descriptions focus on true species in our area, rather than these hybrids, but point out the taxa that do hybridize and give the nomenclature of their progeny.

ISOËTES KEY

Note: Isoëtes megaspores are too small to give in inches, and if you use an ocular micrometer, sizes will be read in metric. Spore diameter is a crucial measure and it is important to be accurate, so megaspore sizes are shown in millimeters rather than inches.

1A. Velum (thin, leafy tissue covering the sporangia) covers entire sporangium; very small species found as deep as 3–6 ft. in water of deep, cold lakes.   *I. prototypus* **(Prototype Quillwort)**

1B. Velum does not entirely cover the sporangium; plants found in a variety of habitats. Go to 2.

2A. Megaspores have distinct spines; leaves deciduous (not lasting more than 1 season). **I. echinospora (Spiny-spored Quillwort)**

2B. Megaspores not spiny; leaves evergreen. Go to 3.

3A. Leaves usually black at base of plant; found in damp flooded woodlands in mostly acidic soil of the Midwest and southeast coast; megaspore has smooth girdle. **I. melanopoda (Black-footed Quillwort)**

3B. Leaves not tinged or grading only to red-brown at base. Go to 4.

4A. Species of limestone areas, cedar glades, temporary pools of interior portion of our area (Ky., Mo., Tenn., Tex., Kans.). **I. butleri (Butler's Quillwort)**

4B. Species of other habitats and ranges. Go to 5.

5A. Species of sandy clay in seasonally wet depressions, principally around granite, under deep shade, restricted to Va. **I. virginica (Virginia Quillwort)**

5B. Species of other habitats and ranges. Go to 6.

6A. Species lacking a well-defined girdle on the megaspore. Go to 7.

7A. Megaspores reticulate (netted), averaging less than 0.5 mm in diameter; velum covers 10–15% of sporangium; plants of subacidic clay banks and ditches. **I. engelmannii (Engelmann's Quillwort)**

7B. Megaspores cristate (with crests resembling broad spines), averaging larger than 0.5 mm; plants of tidal shores, lakes, and ponds. **I. riparia (Riverbank Quillwort)**

6B. Species with well-defined girdle (not obscure). Go to 8.

8A. Megaspore girdle with tiny projections. Go to 9.

9A. Leaves fleshy and coming to a short-tapering tip; deeply submerged in cool, low-nutrient waters. **I. lacustris (Lake Quillwort)**

9B. Leaves thin, long-tapering; growing on shallow, muddy shores in full sun.
I. tuckermanii **(Tuckerman's Quillwort)**

8B. Megaspore girdle smooth. Go to 10.

10A. Leaves thin, soft-textured, longer than 5 in.; megaspores generally less than 0.6 mm in diameter.
I. acadiensis **(Acadian Quillwort)**

10B. Leaves fleshy, rigid and erect, 5 in. long or shorter; megaspores averaging more than 0.6 mm in diameter.
I. hieroglyphica **(Carved Quillwort)**

ACADIAN QUILLWORT

Isoëtes acadiensis Kott

Submerged aquatic plants of shallow waters in slightly acid lakes and streams. Leaves rigid and dark olive green to reddish brown; to 8 in. tall. Velum covers less than half the sporangium. Megaspores 0.45–0.65 mm in diameter, rugulate (with smooth ridges, sometimes appearing to join together in the distal regions), girdle smooth. A rare species found most commonly along the coast from Nfld. south to N.Y. Also reported in Va.

BUTLER'S QUILLWORT

Isoëtes butleri Engelm.

Terrestrial plants to 8 in. tall, growing on calcareous soil of white cedar (*Thuja occidentalis*) glades, barrens, temporary pools, and muddy depressions in limestone areas. Leaves very narrow, triangular in cross-section, dull grayish or yellowish green, paler at base. Velum covers less than ¼ of the sporangium. Megaspores tuberculate, 0.36–0.65 mm in diameter; girdle obscure. Restricted to calcareous soils and cedar glades in interior North America from Mo. and Kans. to Ky., Okla., Tenn., Tex.

SPINY-SPORED QUILLWORT

Isoëtes echinospora Durieu
Synonyms: *Isoëtes braunii* Durieu; *Isoëtes echinospora* ssp. *muricata* (Durieu) A. Löve & D. Löve

Most common northeastern Quillwort, often submerged and sometimes emergent out of shallow water along wet shores of low-nutrient ponds and slow-moving streams with sandy or gravelly substrates. Leaves bright green to reddish green and often deciduous, to 10 in. ± long. Velum covers less than ½ the sporangium. Megaspores 0.35–0.55 mm in diameter, echinate (covered with distinct sharp spines); girdle absent. Ranges broadly from Greenland south to N.J., west through the Great Lakes states and Canada to Alaska.

ENGELMANN'S QUILLWORT

Isoëtes engelmannii A. Br.
One of the larger Quillworts in our area, with bright green, evergreen, somewhat sprawling leaves to 36 in. ± tall. Aquatic or emergent along clay banks of shallow streams, ponds, or roadside ditches, often in subacidic to calcareous substrate. Velum covers 10–15% of sporangium. Megaspores reticulated (with a honeycomb network) of sharp, regularly spaced ridges, 0.38–0.51 mm in diameter; girdle absent. N.H., Vt., and e. Ont. south to n. Fla., inland to Ark., Mo., and Ill. Hybridizes readily with other species, including *Isoëtes echinospora* (Spiny-spored Quillwort) to produce *I. × eatonii* Dodge (Eaton's Quillwort), and with *I. tuckermanii* (Tuckerman's Quillwort) to produce *I. × foveolata* (Pitted Quillwort).

I. engelmannii was formerly thought to be a very broad-ranging and variable species. However, it is now known that this taxon originally included several distinct entities, which have now been elevated to new species. These include:

I. valida (Engelm.) Clute (formerly *I. engelmannii* var. *caroliniana*, *Isoëtes caroliniana*): inhabits lakes, streams, bogs, and swamps of the Blue Ridge and Piedmont of N.C., Va., Penn., Del., and Tenn. Velum covers ⅓–⅔ of the sporangium.

I. appalachiana (a new species): Sporangia have brown streaks; velum covers ⅕–¼ of the sporangium; has an irregular pattern of high, ragged crests on the megaspore. Grows along creek banks, boggy woodland pools, and lakes in acidic substrates in the Appalachian regions and coastal plain of Penn., Ga., N.C., S.C., Fla.

CARVED QUILLWORT

Isoëtes hieroglyphica A. A. Eaton

Small, rare species with stout but short, recurved, stiff, abruptly tapering, olive to dark green leaves up to 4½ in. long. Found mainly in sandy or rocky substrates in cold, clear lakes. Velum covers less than ½ the sporangium. Megaspores 0.58–0.70 mm, rugulate (at proximal end) with low, rounded ridges that join together at the distal end; girdle smooth. Endangered or threatened in many parts of its range; isolated localities from n. New England to adjacent Canada, with a disjunct population in Wisc. Some authors recognize Carved Quillwort as a distinct species; others lump the species with *Isoëtes lacustris* L. (Lake Quillwort).

LAKE QUILLWORT

Isoëtes lacustris L.
Synonyms: *Isoëtes macrospora* Durieu

Dark green, fleshy leaves to 10 in. long; can persist more than 1 season. As the name implies, they grow deeply submerged in the still waters of cool, low-nutrient lakes (and sometimes streams); in clear water, they can grow at depths of 10 ft. Velum covers less than ½ the sporangium. Megaspores 0.55–0.75 mm in diameter, cristate at proximal end and cristate to weakly reticulate distally, with a distinct girdle of dense spines and short ridges. From Greenland south to N.Y., west to Mich. and Minn., north to Sask., disjunct populations in Va.

BLACK-FOOTED QUILLWORT
(Black-based Quillwort)

Isoëtes melanopoda Gay & Durieu

To 16 in. tall with fleshy, bright green leaves, often blackish toward base (hence common name). Grows in flooded woodlands along the coast from Va. south to S.C. In these habitats, typically lacks black leaf base. Also terrestrial in meadows, vernal pools, temporary ponds, fields, and ditches in acidic soil. Velum covers less than ¾ of sporangium. Megaspores smooth to tuberculate to short-rugulate with low ridges, 0.28–0.44

mm in diameter; girdle smooth. Primary range in s. Midwest, including Mo., Ky., and Minn., south to La., Ark., Tex. Disjunct populations in N.J., Va., and the Carolinas.

PROTOTYPE QUILLWORT
(CANADIAN QUILLWORT, BIG QUILLWORT)

Isoëtes prototypus D. M. Britton

Rare, submerged, small plants to 6 in. tall, with stiff, dark green leaves that are reddish brown toward the base. Found only in deep waters of cold, low-nutrient lakes. Velum entirely covers sporangium. Megaspores rugulate with low, rounded ridges, 0.43–0.57 mm in diameter; girdle obscure. Reported only from N.B., N.S., and e. Me.

RIVERBANK QUILLWORT
(SHORE QUILLWORT)

Isoëtes riparia Engelm. ex Braun

Slender, evergreen, bright green, frequently twisted leaves to 16 in. tall. Found at tidal shores, estuaries, and lake, pond, and stream margins. Often submerged but can become emergent on calcareous or subacidic sand and silt. Velum covers less than ½ the sporangium. Megaspores 0.34–0.65 mm ± in diameter, variable size; cristate to echinate (crests can resemble broad spines); girdle obscure. Once viewed as wide-ranging, Riverbank Quillwort in the narrow sense may occupy only a narrow range around N.J. and environs.

Like members of the *Isoëtes engelmannii* "complex," the species formerly recognized as *I. riparia* in the broad sense is now viewed as consisting of several distinct species, including:

I. canadensis (Engelmann) A. A. Eaton: principally New England northward. Very distinctive megaspores with no girdle and widely spaced crests separated by open, smooth spore surface.

I. saccharata Engelmann: coastal species with densely cristate megaspores and a wide girdle of short spines and crests; restricted to Md., Va., D.C. area.

I. hyemalis (a new species): a species of ephemeral, often fast-moving woodland streams from Va. to Ga. with violin-shaped wings near the leaf bases.

These are all tetraploid hybrids (4 sets of chromosomes) of diverse parentage resulting from hybridization among several species; differences and relationships are still being investigated and clarified.

TUCKERMAN'S QUILLWORT

Isoëtes tuckermanii A. Braun ex Engelmann

Aquatic plants with olive green to reddish, tapering, reflexed leaves of variable texture; 8 in. tall. Inhabits shallow, mucky, or rocky edges of lakes, ponds, estuaries, and streams in full sun. Prefers slightly acidic waters. Velum covers less than ½ the sporangium. Megaspores 0.40–0.65 mm; reticulate mesh of roughly crested ridges in both proximal and distal hemispheres; girdle with tiny projections. Occurs from Ont. and N.B. south through New England and N.Y. to N.J. Like *Isoëtes riparia* (Riverbank Quillwort), a tetraploid (4 sets of chromosomes) of uncertain parentage. Hybridizes with *I. echinospora* (Spiny-spored Quillwort); with *I. engelmannii* (Engelmann's Quillwort) to form *I.* × *foveolata* (Pitted Quillwort); and with *I. lacustris* (Lake Quillwort) to form *I.* × *harveyi* (Harvey's Quillwort).

VIRGINIA QUILLWORT

Isoëtes virginica Pfeiffer

Semiterrestrial plants to 11 in. tall. Slender, delicate, often weak leaves, dull green to pale brown at base. Resembles *Isoëtes melanopoda* (Black-footed Quillwort) but has larger megaspores. Plants are ephemeral and most leaves are withered by mid-July. In sandy-clay soils in deeply shaded ephemeral woodland streams or sinkhole ponds. Velum covers about ¹⁄₁₀ the sporangium, which is covered with brown dots or streaks. Megaspores tuberculate to rugulate with smooth-crested ridges, 0.40–0.48 mm in diameter; girdle obscure. Local to Va.

GENUS *SELAGINELLA:* SPIKEMOSSES

(Latin: *Selago,* an old name for the similar genus *Huperzia,* + *ella,* "diminutive")

Spikemosses belong to 1 currently recognized genus, *Selaginella* (Family Selaginellaceae), which contains more than 800 species. Future taxonomic treatments may eventually recognize 2 or 3 genera in this family, but the genus *Selaginella* encompasses the species of our area. The great majority of the species are found in the tropics. They are semiprostrate or creeping plants that resemble in many ways the damp-loving mosses and liverworts with which they are often confused. (Unlike mosses, they have a true vascular system.) Other species prefer drier, higher, more rocky, and less tropical regions. These "stiff" Spikemosses resemble a diminutive *Huperzia selago* (Northern Firmoss).

Many of the 800 *Selaginella* species have fascinating characteristics. Some are gorgeously iridescent, with leaf surfaces that capture tiny amounts of light and channel it efficiently to photosynthetic tissues. Others are "resurrection plants," which can dry up during drought periods only to rehydrate and come alive again when rain falls. Much remains to be discovered about the lifestyles of our own native Spikemosses.

Like some Clubmosses, Spikemosses bear their spores in the axils at the bases of the leaves (sporophylls) in strobili at the ends of fertile stems. Unlike Clubmosses, however, Spikemosses have two types of spore: the microspores, which germinate into the sperm-bearing gametophytes, and the megaspores, which germinate into the egg-bearing gametophytes. These two types of spore are contained in separate spore cases, or sporangia. The sporangia with microspores are usually produced above the sporangia with megaspores on the stem, but this placement can vary. The microspores look like orange dust to the naked eye and are somewhat spiny when seen under a microscope. Megaspores are lighter in color, rather large, pitted or ridged, and round-pyramidal; they occur in groups of 4 in each sporangium. The sperm-bearing gametophyte, which is extremely small, consists usually of a single antheridium, and the egg-bearing gametophyte (which is much larger though still tiny) consists of a mass of green tissue with several archegonia. The archegonia develop while the megaspore is still inside the sporangium. When the female gametophytes are nearly fully developed, the sporangium cracks open, exposing the eggs to fertilization. The fertilized egg produces a new plant (sporophyte). In some species, the embryo of the sporophyte maintains a nutritional connection with the maternal gametophyte.

Two species of this genus are common and range throughout our area: *Selaginella rupestris* (Rock Spikemoss) and *S. apoda* (Meadow Spikemoss). Another two species, *S. selaginoides* (Northern Spikemoss) and *S. eclipes* (Hidden Spikemoss), have more restricted ranges and are reported mainly from along and north of the Canadian border. (A few species native to Asia, including *S. uncinata*, *S. braunii*, and *S. kraussiana*, are in wide cultivation in the Southeast, with some escapes into the wild; these are not treated here.) The species of our area are relatively easy to distinguish. Identification depends on measurements of sterile leaf shape and arrangement, the size and shape of the strobilus, and other characteristics that are readily observed on fresh or dried specimens using a hand lens.

SELAGINELLA KEY

1A. Sterile leaves all same length and width, spirally arranged around stem. Go to 2.

> **2A.** Sterile leaves come to a point at the end, but do not bear a distinct bristle; strobilus cylindrical with widely spreading sporophylls (leaves that bear the sporangia). Known only from very northern reaches of our area (e.g., n. N.Y., Me., Mich.); most often in damp, alkaline soil.
> **S. selaginoides (Northern Spikemoss)**

> **2B.** Sterile leaves have bristles at tips; strobilus has 4 ranks of tightly appressed sporophylls (creating a squarish shape overall); wide-ranging throughout our area; often in thin, dry soil. **S. rupestris (Rock Spikemoss)**

1B. Sterile leaves of 2 sizes, arranged in 4 discernible ranks around the stem. (For a definition of "ranks," see page 283.) Go to 3.

> **3A.** Sterile leaves along the middle portion of stem keeled (shaped like a boat hull) along underside of the leaf toward tip; they come to an abrupt tip; midvein does not extend all the way to tip. **S. apoda (Meadow Spikemoss)**

> **3B.** Sterile leaves not keeled; they narrow gradually to long, tapering tip, and midvein extends all the way to tip.
> **S. eclipes (Hidden Spikemoss)**

Selaginella apoda (*Meadow Spikemoss*) *grows in moist to wet soils.* (*Photo by Cheryl Lowe*)

Selaginella rupestris (*Rock Spikemoss*) *prefers dry, exposed soils on cliffs, ledges, and gravelly slopes.* (*Photo by Jean Baxter/NEWFS*)

Selaginella selaginoides (*Northern Spikemoss*) *is found in damp, alkaline soils of cool northern sites.* (*Photographer unknown/NEWFS*)

Selaginella apoda (L.) Spring

HABIT: Delicate, weak, evergreen, pale yellow-green. Creeping; forms an open, matted tracery of tiny, translucent, acutely pointed flat leaves on tiny, pale green, threadlike, branching stems. Often mistaken for moss, but has true veins in the leaves.

ECOLOGY: Fairly common in muddy, seepy, or damp limy soil in meadows and open swamps, along stream banks, in pastures; often in damp patches in lawns or in previously tilled land.

RANGE: Me. to Fla., west to Tex. (and n. Mexico), north to Ohio, Mo., Penn.

STEMS: To ½ in. ± long. Creeping and lying close to ground; very slender; branching alternately, forming flat mats; smooth.

STERILE LEAVES: Arranged alternately on stem at right angles on all 4 sides (4-ranked). Of 2 sizes: with 2 lateral rows of larger leaves (⅛ in. ± long) and 2 rows of smaller leaves appressed and pointing forward (¹⁄₁₆ in. ± long). Larger leaves yellow-green, oval-shaped; broadest ones occur toward the tip of the stem; very thin, membranous; margins finely toothed; distinct midrib and keel on the underside near tip. Tip of leaf comes to acute tip, ending in teeth but not in a bristle; midvein does not extend to the tip.

SPOROPHYLLS: Arrayed in 4 rows.

STROBILUS: ½ in. ± long. Semiquadrangular; found at ends of branches.

SPORANGIA: Separate for microspores and megaspores. Usually paler green than rest of plant.

MEGASPORES: Dull white; tightly netted (reticulate) texture (best seen under a microscope).

MARGINALIA: *A. Matted growth form. B. Strobilus at end of branch. C. Section of stem. D. Reticulate megaspore.*

DIAGNOSTIC ARROWS: *1. Leaves of two different sizes, with keeled midribs and pointed tip. 2. Translucent leaves on threadlike stems.*

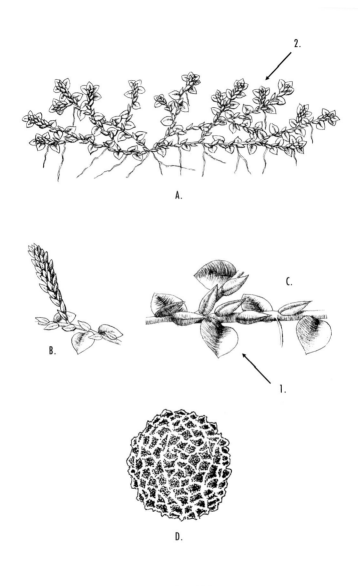

SELAGINELLA APODA
MEADOW SPIKEMOSS

Selaginella eclipes W. R. Buck

HABIT: Creeping, mat-forming, terrestrial plant with small, papery sterile leaves.

ECOLOGY: In moist or wet, calcium-rich habitats, including swamps; open woods, pastures, damp meadows; rarely on rocks.

RANGE: Restricted to a narrow band in the nw. edge of our area, from Que. south to N.Y., Ill., Iowa, Mich., Mo., Wisc., Okla., Ark.

STEMS: ¼–½ in. long. Smooth, creeping, with very thin branches.

STERILE LEAVES: Two types. Lateral leaves elliptical or oval; ⅛ in. ± long; arrayed at a right angle to the stem; with tiny teeth along margins best seen under a hand lens. The other type of leaf smaller with a rounded base and a long transparent bristle. Leaves not keeled (boat-shaped on underside). Midrib of leaf extends all the way to tip.

SPOROPHYLLS: Oval; with toothed margins and pointed tip.

STROBILI: ½–2 in. long. Loose, flattened; solitary or paired.

MEGASPORES: Shiny; a loosely netted (reticulate) texture.

NOTES: Closely related to (possibly a subspecies of) and resembling *Selaginella apoda* (Meadow Spikemoss), but with shiny, slightly larger megaspores and no keels on the sterile leaves.

MARGINALIA: *A. Loosely netted texture of megaspore. B. Close-up of sporophylls.*

DIAGNOSTIC ARROWS: *1. Sterile leaves of two different sizes and 4-ranked. 2. Sterile leaves not keeled and with long tapering tip.*

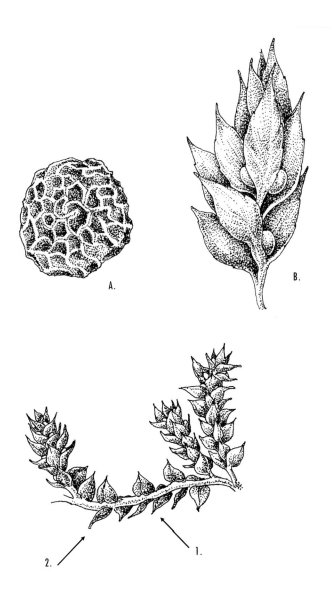

A.

B.

1.

2.

SELAGINELLA ECLIPES
HIDDEN SPIKEMOSS

ROCK SPIKEMOSS (Dwarf Spikemoss)

Selaginella rupestris (L.) Spring

HABIT: Small, gray-green, evergreen, tough, upright, rigid; often grows as a spreading, dense mat of several square feet.

ECOLOGY: Thin, dry soil on outcrops, dry ledges, or sea cliffs of acidic bedrock; mossy rocks; gravelly slopes, or semimoist sand hills; and other exposed dry and thin-soiled locations. Often with *Polytrichum* (Haircap) mosses and well hidden.

RANGE: Broadest distribution of all Spikemosses in North America. From N.B. west to Sask., south through the Great Lakes and Midwest to Neb. and n. Miss., and all eastern states.

STEMS: 2 in. ± long. Rounded; rigid; runners fork upward into tufts. Stems covered by appressed and overlapping sterile leaves, except at fertile tips.

STERILE LEAVES: ⅛ in. ± long. All same size; green (occasionally red-tinged), narrow, convex, with deeply grooved keel, densely appressed on stem. Margins prominently spiny. Each tip with long, pointed, white or transparent bristle. Stomata (pores) only along a groove on underside of sterile leaf.

SPOROPHYLLS: Broader at base, oval, slightly keeled, margins more or less spiny, with less of a bristle at tip. Arranged in 4 closely overlapping ranks.

STROBILUS: ¼–1 ½ in. long. Distinctly square-sided strobilus grows at the ends of branches.

MEGASPORES: Yellowish white.

NOTES: Several characteristics (such as the shape of sporophylls) of this plant vary across its very wide range. Thus, several mostly overlapping "races" of the species have been identified and require further study to determine their evolutionary relationships.

MARGINALIA: *A. Sterile spikes. B. Strobilus. C. Sterile leaf. D. Sporophyll with sporangia.*

DIAGNOSTIC ARROWS: *1. Sterile leaf, with spiny margin and bristle tip. 2. Leaves all the same size, appressed to the stem, and keeled.*

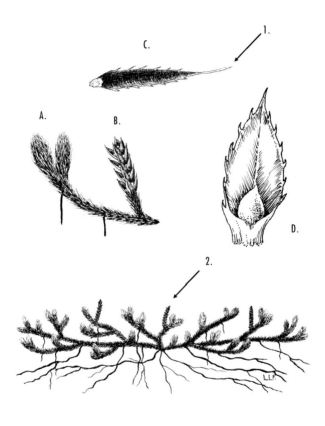

C.

1.

A.

B.

D.

2.

SELAGINELLA RUPESTRIS
ROCK SPIKEMOSS

NORTHERN SPIKEMOSS

Selaginella selaginoides (L.) Baeuv. ex Mart. & Schrank

HABIT: Mat-forming perennial plant of the north, with prostrate sterile stems, upright fertile stems with spreading sterile leaves, terminating in a long, almost cylindrical strobilus. Very distinctive species with only 1 close relative, the Hawaiian species *Selaginella deflexa.*

ECOLOGY: Mildly alkaline or calcareous soils of cold shores of lakes, bogs, and streams, spring-fed banks, talus slopes with moss, and serpentine barrens.

RANGE: Widespread but sporadic, occupying a boreal distribution across much of n. Canada (Nfld. and Lab. west to Man.) with a gap in the prairie provinces. Also Alaska, Yukon, Nunavut, south along mountains into Colo. and Nev. Reported in N.Y., n. Me., and Mich. Also Eurasia, nw. Africa, Canary Islands.

STEMS: Creeping, forming paired, stout branches that turn upright and stand 2–5 in. tall.

STERILE LEAVES: ¼ in. ± long (those on horizontal stems smaller than those on the upright stems). Green, narrow, spreading, coarsely and distinctly toothed with soft, spiny projections but not tipped with a long bristle; leaf becomes cuplike at juncture with the stem. Stomata (pores) scattered throughout underside of sterile leaves.

SPOROPHYLLS: ¼–½ in. long. Narrow to triangular, lacking ridges.

STROBILUS: Over 1 in. long. Cylindrical with only gentle angles.

MEGASPORES: Yellowish white with low rounded warts on the 3 flat surfaces. This species employs a unique "compression and slingshot" mechanism to eject megaspores.

MARGINALIA: *A. Close-up of strobilus with spreading sporophylls.*
DIAGNOSTIC ARROWS: *1. Upright strobilus-bearing stems. 2. Prostrate sterile stems.*

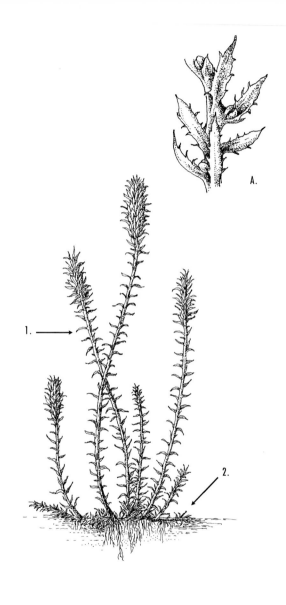

SELAGINELLA SELAGINOIDES
NORTHERN SPIKEMOSS

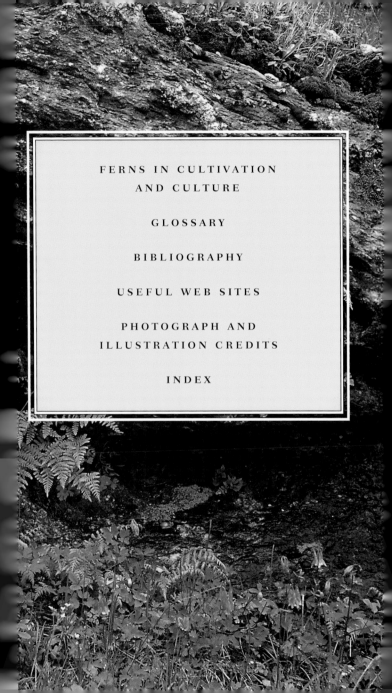

FERNS IN CULTIVATION AND CULTURE

Ferns and fern allies are more than just beautiful, wild plants of forest and field. They have long been used by human cultures in many fascinating ways, including medicine, animal bedding, food, photographic equipment, and artisanal tools. This Field Guide provides just a brief glimpse into the myriad traditional uses and gardening possibilities for ferns. The bibliography provides excellent references for those interested in more details about these topics.

CULTURAL HISTORY

Most people are familiar with the culinary uses of ferns. In the Northeast, three types of fern are edible in their fiddlehead stage—Ostrich Fern (*Matteuccia struthiopteris* var. *pensylvanica*), Cinnamon Fern (*Osmunda cinnamomea*), and Bracken Fern (*Pteridium aquilinum*). Of these three, only the Ostrich Fern is choice and commercially available. Although no fern is poisonous in the fiddlehead stage, some can be quite toxic after they have unfurled into fronds. The Bracken Fern, for example, contains known carcinogens, with trace amounts present even in the fiddleheads, so it is no longer harvested for consumption in this country.

Ferns are also used in traditional medicines of many cultures. Herbalists in other countries still use root extracts of the Male Fern (*Dryopteris filix-mas*) as a remedy for intestinal worms. Preparations from Maidenhair Ferns (*Adiantum* species) stimulate the function of the mucous membranes and are used to treat ailments such as asthma, coughs, and pleurisy. Other common herbal uses of ferns are as diuretics, blood coagulants, and treatments for bruises, burns, bites, and stings.

Clubmosses and Horsetails are also used in a variety of applications. Some violin makers still use Common Scouring Rush (*Eq-*

uisetum hymenale) for the final polishing of the instrument's veneer. They split open the Scouring Rush stems and polish the wood with the silica embedded in the inner stem lining, because it does not release sand particles and clog the wood's pores as fine sandpaper would do. In earlier centuries, Scouring Rushes were used to clean pots (the origin of its common name) and as a fine abrasive to burnish brass and other metals. Spores of Clubmosses (*Lycopodium* species) are highly flammable and were once used for fireworks and in early flash photography. Since they repel water, these spores were also used as a coating for pills and to prevent chafing (as we would use talcum powder).

Since ancient times, fronds of Bracken Fern (*Pteridium aquilinum*) have been used as animal bedding for livestock, and the rhizomes and young fiddleheads have been cooked and added to animal fodder. One of the most interesting uses of this species, though, is in glass-making. Ash of Bracken Fern is rich in alkali (hydrate of potassium), a substance that causes silica (the basic component of glass) to melt at a lower temperature. Several writings from medieval Europe, including Chaucer's *Canterbury Tales* (1388) and Vannoccio Biringuccio's *De la Pirotechnia* (1540), mention the use of ferns in glass-making.

FERNS IN THE GARDEN

Why do we include sections on gardening and propagating ferns in a field guide? Aren't field study and horticulture separate endeavors? In theory, perhaps. But growing ferns in a garden is a rich opportunity to appreciate the changing character of ferns over the seasons and to carefully study the splendid details of habit, growth, reproduction, and color. It affords the grower time to notice the intimate details of unfurling frond, soft downy hairs, or the golden colors of autumn foliage in certain species. Fern gardening brings a bit of nature into cultivated spaces and strengthens your identification skills in the field.

Ferns have long been desirable plants for the garden, and with good reason. In both garden and glade, ferns offer textures and forms that transform the character of a place in different seasons and changing light. In the cool, dark stillness of a forest floor, they blend into a quiet, lush mosaic of mosses, wildflowers, rocks, and fallen leaves under a sheltering canopy of trees. In early September, highlighted by shafts of early-morning or late-afternoon sunlight, delicate fronds resemble angel wings dancing in the slightest breeze.

In general, choice and arrangement of plants in the landscape is guided by two basic considerations: the pragmatic (well matched to the site's conditions, disease resistance, appropriate height and shape) and the emotive (evoking a feeling of place). On the practical side, many fern species are resilient, easy to grow, and resistant to both diseases and deer. They can be used with excellent effect to create a garden mood, associated as they often are with the serene, moist, shady floor of a mature forest, the rocky crevices of a cliff face, or an expansive, lush wetland.

A woodland wildflower garden would not be complete without ferns. At the New England Wild Flower Society's botanic garden, Garden in the Woods, Bloodroot (*Sanguinaria canadensis*), Spring Beauties (*Claytonia* spp.), Trillium (*Trillium* spp.), and Wild Blue Phlox (*Phlox divaricata*) take center stage in spring. As their flowers fade, however, fiddleheads unfurl and fill in the gaps where the spring bulbs and ephemeral wildflowers such as Squirrel Corn (*Dicentra canadensis*), Toothwort (*Cardamine diphylla*), and Dutchman's-breeches (*Dicentra cucullaria*) have gone dormant. Adding carefully placed boulders, undulating topography, and fallen logs strengthens the woodland feel.

Ferns extend the season in other ways. The Broad Beech Fern (*Phegopteris hexagonoptera*) makes a wonderful lush groundcover, for example, but since it is the last of the New England species to emerge, it is a poor choice for the gardener interested in showy spring displays. On the other hand, it continues to send up new fronds throughout much of the summer, giving a fresh, young look to the garden when other plants have long finished performing.

Wood Ferns (*Dryopteris* species), with their central crown and vase-shaped habit, are some of the best selections for gardens because they are tidy, easy to grow, and graceful. Goldie's Fern (*Dryopteris goldiana*) is the most magnificent of this group, with wide, sturdy, 4-foot fronds that are a rich, dark green at the base but often with a softer, pale green tip. Other *Dryopteris* species with leathery fronds but slightly smaller stature include Marginal Wood Fern, Male Fern, and Crested Wood Fern (*D. marginalis, D. filix-mas,* and *D. cristata,* respectively), each with distinctive variations in color, frond, and habit. The Spinulose Wood

Dryopteris goldiana (*Goldie's Fern*) provides a large, lush accent in the woodland garden. (Photo by Cheryl Lowe)

Fern (*D. carthusiana*) and Evergreen Wood Fern (*D. intermedia*) are a bit lacier and more delicate in character than other wood ferns.

Ferns such as the *Osmunda* species, Chain Ferns (*Woodwardia* spp.), and Marsh Fern (*Thelypteris palustris*) are primarily wetland species, well suited to naturalizing along the edge of a pond or wetland. Vigorous and lush, they quickly stabilize the soil, absorb nutrients, and fill gaps between shrubs or trees.

Although often associated with naturalistic woodland gardens and wetland plantings, ferns also belong in the formal garden. An expansive sweep of ferns can provide a visual resting place, a sense of abundant moisture, or the ambiance of a mature landscape. Ferns add variety to foundation plantings and along walls or fences. Taller, more vigorous ferns such as *Osmunda* species or Ostrich Fern (*Matteuccia struthiopteris* var. *pensylvanica*) provide bolder texture and substance, as well as vertical accent. A wonderful groundcover for the cooler, moist garden is the Narrow Beech Fern (*Phegopteris connectilis*) with its low growing habit and distinctive fronds. For gardeners willing to take on a challenge, Oak Fern (*Gymnocarpium dryopteris*) is another groundcover option, with its delicate triangular leaves and bright, spring green color that lasts through the season if the soil stays moist. For the shady mixed border, the fine texture and graceful habits of a moderate-sized fern such as Lady Fern (*Athyrium filix-femina*), Maidenhair Fern (*Adiantum pedatum*), or New York Fern (*Thelypteris noveboracensis*) stand in lovely contrast, yet comfortably transition from turf or path to the taller plantings of the beds. Maidenhair Fern, draped with miniature fans along graceful, curvy, wiry stems that quiver in the slightest breeze, is one of the best-loved of these.

Ferns do not usually inhabit the flashy end of the color spectrum. Fern aficionados speak of glorious textures and subtle, sophisticated shades of green, and they speak the truth. But ferns have other colors that can complement surrounding plantings: young fronds of Maidenhair and Chain Ferns (*Adiantum* and *Woodwardia* species) emerge in various shades of pink, maroon, and red; Hay-scented Fern (*Dennstaedtia*) dances on the yellow edge of green; and Cliffbrakes and Lip Ferns (*Pellaea* and *Cheilanthes*) are soft, downy, grayish green-blues.

Evergreen is a desirable character for Northeastern gardens. Christmas Fern (*Polystichum acrostichoides*) is adaptable, sturdy, and tidy, with leathery, dark green foliage. Green and upright through most of the winter, the old fronds are prostrate by spring, and turn brown by the time the new crosiers have unfurled. Several Wood Ferns (*Dryopteris marginalis*, *D. intermedia*, and others) are also green through the winter, but with stems weakened by snows and cold, the fronds lie prone for most of the winter. In the long winters of our northern states (especially those with little snow), it's still a treat to see green fronds, flattened though they may be.

Growing Ferns

Most ferns grow best in shade—not the deepest shade, but dappled light or open shade at the edge of a woodland. Seldom do you see ferns growing directly under a dense canopy of conifers unless the trees are young and moisture is abundant. Some species, such as Cinnamon Fern (*Osmunda cinnamomea*), Male Fern (*Dryopteris filix-mas*), or Marsh Fern (*Thelypteris palustris*), will also grow well in sunny conditions, but only if their feet stay moist and cool.

Most ferns prefer well-aerated, slightly acid soils with plenty of rich humus. Leaf mold, compost, decaying hardwood mulch, and chopped leaves can all be added to increase the soil's humus content. Most ferns have shallow roots, so mulching with those same materials is important for retaining moisture and keeping the root zone cool. Although most ferns are relatively care-free, as with other perennials, newly planted ferns should be kept moist during their first year in the garden. They need time for new roots to spread into the surrounding soil, so they can support themselves during the dry times. For consistently dry sites, select species such as Lip Ferns (*Cheilanthes*) or Hay-scented Fern (*Dennstaedtia*), which are more tolerant of dry conditions once established.

Some ferns are native denizens of rocky cliffs and best grown tucked between rocks or amid the well-drained gravel of the rock garden. Many of these species have distinctive preferences for calcareous or acidic conditions. Lip Ferns and Polypody Ferns (*Cheilanthes* and *Polypodium*) are good choices for acidic to almost neutral rock. Fragile and Bulblet Ferns (*Cystopteris fragilis* and *C. bulbifera*), along with Maidenhair Spleenwort (*Asplenium trichomanes* ssp. *quadrivalens*), Walking Fern (*A. rhizophyllum*), and Cliffbrakes (*Pellaea*), are found more often in calcareous sites. Some species, such as Blunt-lobed or Rusty Woodsias (*Woodsia ilvensis* and *W. obtusa*), seem to be less particular about soil pH, as long as it is well drained. Not all rocky cliffs are dry, however; in nature, dripping moisture from seeps or drifting mist from nearby streams and waterfalls might keep the substrate moist. In particular, Walking Fern, Maidenhair Spleenwort, and the *Cystopteris* species mentioned above prefer these moister sites.

Once you have provided the proper light, soil conditions, and moisture, garden maintenance is easy. A light application of fertilizer in the spring is useful but not necessary. More important is a mulch of compost or shredded leaves to keep the soil moist and prevent weed seeds from germinating. Occasional weeding may be necessary. One of the most vulnerable times for ferns is when the fiddleheads first emerge in the spring—avoid raking the beds then. You can cut down old fronds in the fall and remove or leave them as mulch, but resist the temptation to cut off the fronds of evergreen ferns until the new fiddleheads are about to emerge. On warmer days in the late fall and early spring (as long as the temperature is in the high 40°s F), they continue to photosynthesize, providing sustenance to the roots.

Some ferns, such as Sensitive Fern (*Onoclea*) and Bracken Fern (*Pteridium*), can be weedy in a garden. They are best left to naturalize in the uncultivated areas of your garden. Even Hay-scented Fern (*Dennstaedtia*) is best placed where it will not intrude into more formal, mixed plantings. Other species, such as Walking Fern (*Asplenium rhizophyllum*), Wall Rue (*A. ruta-muraria*), and Climbing Fern (*Lygodium palmatum*), are particularly challenging for the gardener; they require special site conditions, care, and a bit of good luck. Most of the the succulent ferns and Clubmosses are almost impossible to cultivate and best enjoyed in their natural habitats.

Obtaining Ferns for the Garden

In the early to mid-1900s, ferns and their relatives were important components of the floral trade, both as Christmas greens and

(Above) *Some ferns, such as* Os-munda regalis (*Royal Fern*) *are vigorous and easy to grow.* (*Photo by Cheryl Lowe*) (Right) *Others, such as* Lygodium palmatum (*Climbing Fern*), *are more challenging.* (*Photo courtesy of NEWFS*)

throughout the year, and they were collected extensively from the wild. Although this is no longer true to the same extent, ferns are still wild-collected to sell in both the floral and nursery trades. The New England Wild Flower Society encourages gardeners to purchase only nursery-propagated plants.

An increasing number and diversity of fern species can be purchased from reputable commercial nurseries that sell nursery-propagated plants. In addition, many ferns are easily divided from a friend's garden by cutting off a section of rhizome with both roots and dormant crosiers and replanting it. This is best done in early spring just before the crosiers unfurl. Ferns can be grown from spores, collected or obtained through plant society seed or plant exchanges, or from plantlets on species like the Bulblet Fern (*Cystopteris bulbifera*).

If a species is not readily available, many gardeners ask about the ethics of collecting plants from wild populations. Although not illegal if the landowner gives permission and the species is not protected under rare or endangered species regulations, this practice is not encouraged. It is probably not harmful if only a few plants are taken from a large, healthy population, but how do we track the number of people who collect from that patch or monitor the site for continued health? Without assurances, we cannot condone such practices.

A few ferns and most fern relatives are very difficult to grow or transplant, so although they are often desirable garden plants, transplanting is not recommended for any of the fern allies. If these plants are offered by a nursery supplier, ask the supplier about their propagation methods. Nurseries are beginning to propagate these species, but they are often wild-collected as well.

Cystopteris protrusa (*Southern Bladder Fern*) forms dense patches when grown in rich, moist soil in light shade. (*Photo by Cheryl Lowe*)

Glossary

ACUMINATE: Gradually tapering to a distinct, pointed tip.

ACUTE: Forming a distinct angle of less than 90° but more than 30°, such as the tip of a pinna or leaf.

ALTERNATE: Referring to structures (usually leaves) that are positioned in a staggered pattern offset from each other along a stem, rachis, or costa.

ANGIOSPERM: A member of the widespread group of seed plants whose ovules are enclosed in ovaries.

ANNUAL CONSTRICTION: A narrowed section of stem with smaller, sometimes more congested leaves (on certain Clubmosses). These indentations mark the start (and end) of seasonal growth.

ANNULUS: A ring or band of special, thickened cells that runs most of the way around the spherical sporangium.

ANTHERIDIUM (PLURAL, ANTHERIDIA): Short, bulbous, sperm-producing organ borne on the underside of the gametophyte.

APEX: Terminal (end or top) portion of a structure such as a frond or tip of pinna.

APICAL: Toward the top or outermost growing tip.

APOGAMY: Vegetative reproduction of a fern from a gametophyte without fertilization.

APPRESSED: Tightly pressed together, usually along a stem.

ARCHEGONIUM (PLURAL, ARCHEGONIA): The egg-bearing structure borne on the gametophyte.

AREOLE: A small, clearly defined area bounded by the netted veins on certain types of pinnae.

ASCENDING: Pointing upward or toward the end of a stem.

ASYMMETRICAL: With dissimilarly shaped or sized structures on either side of a central axis.

AXIL: The point of juncture between a leaf and a stem.

AXIS: A central line or structure (such as a midrib) along which parts of a plant are arrayed (e.g., pinnae along the rachis or pinnules along the costa).

BARREN: A habitat characterized by low levels of nutrients, water, or other resources, usually with sparse coverage of plants.

BASE: Bottom of a structure, usually where it joins another structure, such as a frond where it meets the rhizome, or a pinna where it meets the rachis.

BIPINNATE: A frond with pinnae that are cut all the way to the costa into pinnules.

BLADE: The leafy part of the frond.

BOREAL: Northern.

BULBLET: A spherical plantlet that is produced asexually and is capable of growing into a new plant upon release from its genetically identical parent plant.

CALCAREOUS: Rich in the mineral calcium (lime), referring to bedrock or soil.

CIRCINATE VERNATION: Uncoiling from a fiddlehead at the beginning of the growing season.

CIRCUMBOREAL: Distributed around the world in the northern latitudes.

CIRCUMNEUTRAL: With a pH of nearly 7, usually referring to soil.

CLATHRATE SCALES: Scales that are partly translucent, with a lattice of thicker cells, resembling stained-glass windows.

CONE: In Horsetails (*Equisetum* spp.), an upright structure at the top of fertile stems, resembling an armored, erect catkin composed of tight-fitting, hexagonal, highly modified leaves called sporangiophores that bear the sporangia.

CORM: In the Quillworts (*Isoëtes* spp.), the fleshy underground stem that bears the leaves and roots.

COSTA (PLURAL, COSTAE): Midvein of a pinna.

COSTULE: Midvein of a pinnule.

CREEPING: Growing horizontally and low along the soil.

CRENATE: With small, rounded teeth; creates a wavy leaf margin.

CRISTATE: Covered with crests that only occasionally join together and do not form a honeycomb arrangement (usually referring to the megaspore ornamentation of *Isoëtes*).

CROSIER: The coiled, unfurling young fern frond. (Syn., fiddlehead.)

DECIDUOUS: Referring to fronds or other structures that die back or fall off at the end of the growing season.

DELTATE: Shaped like a triangle or delta.

DENTATE: With spreading, pointed teeth.

DIPLOID: With 2 full sets of chromosomes per cell.

DISJUNCT: A population that grows in an area widely separated from most other populations of the species.

DISTAL: At or toward the tip or far end.

EARED: With a base that has a large, asymmetrical lobe ("auricle") resembling an earlobe (usually referring to the shape of pinnae).

ECHINATE: Covered with separate and distinct spines (usually referring to the megaspore ornamentation of *Isoëtes*).

ENTIRE: With smooth margins that lack lobes or teeth (usually referring to pinnae or pinnules).

EPIDERMIS: The surface or outermost layer of plant cells.

ERECT: Growing upright, vertically from the ground.

EUSPORANGIATE FERNS: Ferns (*Ophioglossum* and *Botrychium* species) that produce large sporangia consisting of several layers of cells that contain many spores each and that spring up erect or bent from the ground rather than as fiddleheads.

EVERGREEN: Remaining green throughout the winter.

EXTANT: In existence (usually referring to species or populations). (Ant., extinct.)

FALSE INDUSIUM: A flap of tissue, usually formed by the margin of the pinna or pinnule, that folds over to enclose the sori.

FERTILE: Capable of sexual reproduction (e.g., certain hybrids).

FIDDLEHEAD: The unfurling young frond of true ferns, which loosely resembles the ornate, curled end of a fiddle. (Syn., crosier.)

FILAMENTOUS: Threadlike.

FLORA: The collective group of plant species recorded in a given region.

FREE VEINS: Veins (conducting vessels) that extend straight from the main midvein of the pinna or pinnule to the edges; they may fork but do not form networks.

FROND: The entire aboveground, visible fern "leaf," including both the blade and the stipe.

GAMETOPHYTE: A tiny body bearing the organs that produce gametes (eggs and sperm) that will join to form the sporophyte.

GEMMA (PLURAL, GEMMAE): A tiny plantlet produced by vegetative reproduction that is genetically identical to the parent plant; sometimes produced by Moonworts (*Botrychium* spp.), Firmosses (*Huperzia* spp.), and Filmy Ferns (*Trichomanes* spp.).

GLABROUS: Smooth, without hairs or scales.

GLANDULAR HAIRS: Hairs (usually on pinnae, costa, rachis, or stipe) with small appendages that secrete sticky, viscous, or sweet substances.

GLAUCOUS: With a waxy, whitish powder.

GYMNOSPERM: A group of plants with ovules not enclosed in an ovary.

HABITAT: The physical environment in which an organism lives.

HAIR: A thin projection, only 1 cell thick (sometimes with a glandular tip), growing out of the epidermis of various plant structures. Not as stiff or stout as a spine or bristle.

HYBRID: Offspring of the union of two different species, subspecies, or varieties, produced when the sperm of one fertilizes the egg of another. Most hybrids are sterile due to incompatibilities of chromosome numbers, etc., but some are fertile.

INCISED: Deeply and sharply cut.

INDUSIUM (PLURAL, INDUSIA): A specialized flap of tissue that covers and protects the sorus.

INTERNODE: The section of stem or branch between the nodes, as in *Equisetum* species.

KEELED: With a conspicuous longitudinal ridge, like the bottom of a boat hull.

LANCEOLATE: Lance-shaped, narrow, longer than wide, and tapering at both ends.

LATERAL: To the side.

LAX: Not firm or rigid; appearing drooping or prostrate.

LEPTOSPORANGIATE FERNS: The group of ferns that produce greatly reduced stalked sporangia with walls only 1 cell layer thick. Leptosporangiate ferns unfurl from coiled fiddleheads.

LIMEY: Containing a high concentration of limestone, usually referring to bedrock or soils.

LINEAR: Straight and narrow, with parallel sides.

LOBE: A projecting section of tissue, usually referring to the margin of a pinna, pinnule, or blade.

MARGIN: Edge (usually referring to pinnae or pinnules).

MEGASPORE: In species with two kinds of spore (e.g., *Isoëtes, Azolla, Marsilea, Selaginella*), the larger spore that produces the "female" (egg-producing) gametophyte.

MICROSPORE: In species with two kinds of spore (e.g., *Isoëtes, Azolla, Marsilea, Selaginella*), the smaller spore that produces the "male" (sperm-producing) gametophyte.

MIDRIB: The central, usually raised axis of a frond, pinna, or pinnule, often enclosing the main vein.

MYCORRHIZAE: Fungi that form biological associations with plants and transfer nutrients to them.

NETTED VEINS: Vascular tissues that form complex networks rather than extend freely from the midvein to the margin of the pinna or pinnule.

NODE: A juncture, usually where a leaf or branch has attached to a stem.

OBLONG: Longer than wide, usually with rounded or elliptical edges.

OPPOSITE: Referring to structures (usually leaves) that are positioned directly across from each other at the same point along a stem, rachis, or costa.

OVATE: Shaped like a silhouette of an egg, with the widest point near the base.

OVERWINTER (ADJECTIVE, OVERWINTERING): To persist with living, metabolically active tissue during the cold months.

PALMATE: Hand-shaped, with 3 or more segments radiating out from a central point.

PENDENT: Hanging or drooping.

PINNA (PLURAL, PINNAE): A distinct subdivision of the blade when the blade is fully divided to the rachis, not just lobed.

PINNATAFID: Deeply lobed, but not cut all the way to the rachis or costa, so that separate pinnae or pinnules are not formed.

PINNATE: A blade that is divided fully into separate pinnae.

PINNATE-PINNATIFID: The pinnae are themselves deeply lobed but not fully divided into pinnules.

PINNULE: A distinct subdivision of a pinna that is fully divided to the costa, not just lobed.

PINNULET: A distinct subdivision of a pinnule that is fully divided to the costule (midrib of a pinnule).

POLYPLOID: With more than 2 sets of chromosomes.

PROSTRATE: Lying horizontally or low on the ground.

PROXIMAL: Toward or at the base or closest to the ground.

PTERIDOLOGIST: One who studies ferns, usually professionally.

PUBESCENT: With hairs.

RACHIS (PLURAL, RACHISES, RACHIDES): The central axis of the blade that bears the pinnae.

RANGE: The entire geographic distribution of a taxon.

REFLEXED: Arching notably backward or downward.

RETICULATE: Forming a networked pattern, as in the honeycomb of crests on the megaspores of certain *Isoëtes* species or netted venation in pinnae of certain fern species.

RHIZOME: The stem of the fern, usually horizontal and creeping but sometimes vertical and erect, which produces roots below and the frond above; often functions as a perennial storage organ.

ROOTS: Nutrient-absorbing structures that grow from the rhizome.

RUGULATE: Covered with low, mounded ridges (wrinkles) that do not form a honeycomb pattern (usually referring to the megaspore ornamentation of *Isoëtes*).

SCALE: A small piece of thin, papery epidermal tissue that resembles a loose piece of skin.

SERPENTINE: (1) A type of bedrock unusually rich in magnesium and silica; the source of asbestos. (2) With a coiling, snakelike form.

SERRATE: With sharp, forward-pointing fine teeth on the edge (usually referring to the margin of leaves).

SESSILE: With a base attached directly to an axis, without a stalk.

SIMPLE: Not divided into pinnae or pinnules; not compound; unbranched.

SMOOTH: Without obvious ornamentation, hairs, or texture.

SORUS (PLURAL, SORI): A cluster of sporangia, usually borne on the underside or margins of the pinnae or pinnules; its shape is often diagnostic of species or genus.

SPATULATE: Spoon-shaped.

SPORANGIOPHORE: Modified, scalelike plates of *Equisetum* cones that enclose the sporangia.

SPORANGIUM (PLURAL, SPORANGIA): A small, thin-walled, usually stalked case that bears the spores.

SPORE: The tiny offspring of a sporophyte, which gives rise to the gametophyte.

SPOROCARP: A specialized container that houses the sporangia, found in *Azolla* and *Marsilea* species.

SPOROPHORE: A fertile leaf that bears sporangia of *Botrychium* and *Ophioglossum* species.

SPOROPHYLL: A highly modified, reduced leaf that bears sporangia at its base (in species of the genus *Selaginella* and the Clubmosses and Firmosses).

SPOROPHYTE: The spore-bearing stage of the life cycle of ferns or fern allies; usually the familiar, leafy form of the species in the field.

SPREADING: Extending outward from vertical (as in spreading fronds) or outward from the stem (as in leaves of *Huperzia* spp.); intermediate between appressed and reflexed.

STERILE: Without sporangia; referring to the unfertile fronds of certain ferns or stems of fern allies without strobili.

STIPE: The stalked portion of the frond arising from the rhizome, below the point where the leafy blade is produced.

STROBILUS (PLURAL, STROBILI): A localized region of the stem, usually upright and found at the top; bears only sporophylls (such as in *Selaginella* spp. and the Clubmosses and Firmosses).

SUBOPPOSITE: Referring to structures (usually leaves) that are positioned somewhat offset from each other relative to a point along a central axis.

SUBSPECIES (ABBREVIATION, SSP.): A subdivision of a species; a population of a particular region genetically distinguishable from other such populations but capable of interbreeding with them.

SYMMETRICAL: Of similar shape and size on both sides of a central axis. (When folded along this axis, the forms of the sides match exactly.)

TALUS: A large pile of rock debris deposited by erosion, usually at the base of a cliff.

TAXON (PLURAL, TAXA): A generic term for a named group of organisms, such as a variety, subspecies, species, or genus.

TAXONOMY: The scientific process of classifying and naming groups of organisms.

TERMINAL: Toward the end or apex.

TETRAPLOID: With 4 sets of chromosomes.

TRICHOME: Hair.

TRIPINNATE: A blade with pinnae divided into pinnules that are divided fully into pinnulets.

TROPHOPHORE: The sterile blade of *Botrychium* and *Ophioglossum* species that does not bear reproductive structures.

TROPHOPHYLL: In species of the genus *Selaginella* and the Clubmosses and Firmosses, sterile leaves not associated with sporangia.

TUBERCULATE: Covered with low, rounded tubercles or bumps (usually referring to the megaspore ornamentation of *Isoëtes*).

VASCULAR: Referring to tissues (vessels) that conduct nutrients, sugars, and water through a plant.

VEIN: A type of vessel visible in a leaf.

VELUM: A thin membrane that covers the sporangium of *Isoëtes* (Quill-wort) species.

VESSEL: A tubular strand of tissue that conducts water or other substances throughout the plant.

WAVY MARGIN: An edge (of a blade, pinna, or pinnule) that appears scalloped or undulating when viewed from the side.

WINGED: With a flap or extension of tissue (think of webbed feet); if along the rachis, a wing creates a connection between pinnae.

XERIC: Exceedingly dry; a habitat subject to drought.

BIBLIOGRAPHY

Abbe, E. 1981. *The Fern Herbal, including the Ferns, the Horsetails and the Club Mosses.* Comstock Publishing Associates, a division of Cornell University Press, Ithaca, New York.

Angelo, R., and D. E. Boufford. 1996. Atlas of the Flora of New England: Pteridophytes and gymnosperms. *Rhodora* 98: 1–79.

Birdseye, Clarence, and Eleanor G. Birdseye. 1951. *Growing Woodland Plants.* Oxford University Press, New York, New York.

Brunton, D. F., D. M. Britton, and T. F. Wieboldt. 1996. Taxonomy, identity, and status of *Isoëtes virginica* (Isoetaceae). *Castanea* 61: 145–160.

Caplen, C. A., and C. R. Werth. 2000. Isozymes of the *Isoëtes riparia* complex. I. Genetic variation and relatedness of diploid species. *Systematic Botany* 25: 235–259.

Clute, W. N. 1938. *Our Ferns: Their Haunts, Habits and Folklore.* Second Edition. Frederick A. Stokes Company, New York, New York.

Cody, W. J., and D. M. Britton. 1989. *Ferns and Fern Allies of Canada.* Research Branch, Agriculture Canada, Publication 1829/E, Ottawa, Ontario.

Crow, G. E., and C. B. Hellquist. 2000. *Aquatic and Wetland Plants of Northeastern North America. Volume I: Pteridophytes, Gymnosperms, and Angiosperms: Dicotyledons.* The University of Wisconsin Press, Madison, Wisconsin.

Davenport, G. 1901. A plea for the preservation of our ferns. Society for the Protection of Native Plants, Leaflet No. 3. Boston Society of Natural History, Boston, Massachusetts.

de la Cretaz, A., and M. J. Kelty. 1999. Establishment and control of hay-scented fern: A native invasive species. *Biological Invasions* 1: 223–236.

Dunbar, L. 1989. *Ferns of the Coastal Plain: Their Lore, Legends, and Uses.* University of South Carolina Press, Columbia, South Carolina.

Farrar, D. R. 1992. *Trichomanes intricatum:* The independent *Trichomanes* gametophyte in the eastern United States. *American Fern Journal* 82: 68–74.

Farrar, D. R., and J. T. Mickel. 1991. *Vittaria appalachiana:* A name for the "Appalachian gametophyte." *American Fern Journal* 81: 69–75.

Fernald, M. L. 1950. *Gray's Manual of Botany: A Handbook of the Flowering Plants and Ferns of the Central and Northeastern United States and Adjacent Canada.* Eighth Edition. American Book Co., New York, New York.

Flora of North America Editorial Committee. 1993. *Flora of North America North of Mexico. Volume 2: Pteridophytes and Gymnosperms.* Oxford University Press, New York, New York.

Foster, F. G. 1984. *Ferns to Know and Grow.* (1995 revision) Timber Press, Portland, Oregon.

Gensel, P. G., and C. M. Berry. 2001. Early *Lycophyte* evolution. *American Fern Journal* 91: 74–98.

George, L., and F. A. Bazzaz. 1999. The fern understory as an ecological filter: Emergence and establishment of canopy-tree seedlings. *Ecology* 80: 833–845.

Gilman, A. V. 2002. *Ophioglossaceae of Vermont.* V. F. Thomas Company, Bar Harbor, Maine.

Gleason, H. A., and A. Cronquist. 1991. *Manual of Vascular Plants of Northeastern United States and Adjacent Canada.* Second Edition. New York Botanical Garden, Bronx, New York.

Haines, A. 2003. *The Families Huperziaceae and Lycopodiaceae of New England: A Taxonomic and Ecological Reference.* V. F. Thomas Company, Bowdoin, Maine.

Hallowell, A. C., and B. G. Hallowell. 2001. *Fern Finder.* Second Edition. Rochester, New York: Nature Study Guild Publishers.

Haufler, C. H. 2002. Homospory 2002: An odyssey of progress in pteridophyte genetics and evolutionary biology. *BioScience* 52: 1081–1093.

Holsinger, K. E. 1990. Population genetics of mating system evolution in homosporous ferns. *American Fern Journal* 80: 153–160.

Hoshizaki, B., and R. Moran. 2001. *Fern Growers Manual.* Timber Press. Portland, Oregon.

Jermy, A. C., and J. Camus. 1991. *The Illustrated Field Guide to Ferns and Allied Plants of the British Isles.* British Natural History Museum, London, United Kingdom.

Keller, H. W., P. G. Davison, C. H. Haufler, and D. B. Lesmeister. 2003. *Polypodium appalachianum:* An unusual tree canopy epiphyte in the Great Smoky Mountains National Park. *American Fern Journal* 93: 36–41.

Klekowski, E. J., and E. L. Davis. 1977. Genetic damage to a fern population growing in a polluted environment: Segregation and description on gametophyte mutants. *Canadian Journal of Botany* 55: 542–548.

Korall, P., and P. Kenrick. 2002. Phylogenetic relationships in Selaginellaceae based on rbcL sequences. *American Journal of Botany* 89: 506–517.

Kott, L., and D. M. Britton. 1983. Spore morphology and taxonomy of *Isoëtes* in northeastern North America. *Canadian Journal of Botany* 61: 3140–3163.

Lamont, E. E. 1998. Status of *Schizaea pusilla* in New York, with notes on some early collections. *American Fern Journal* 88: 158–164.

Lellinger, D. B. 1985. *A Field Manual of the Ferns and Fern-Allies of the United States and Canada*. Smithsonian Institution Press, Washington, D.C.

Li, J., and C. H. Haufler. 1994. Phylogeny, biogeography, and population biology of *Osmunda* species: Insights from enzymes. *American Fern Journal* 84: 105–114.

Little, D. P., and D. S. Barrington. 2003. Major evolutionary events in the origin and diversification of the fern genus *Polystichum* (Dryopteridaceae). *American Journal of Botany* 90: 508.

Luebke, N. T. 1992. Three new species of *Isoëtes* for the southeastern United States. *American Fern Journal* 82: 23–26.

Merryweather, J. W., and M. H. Hill. 1995. *The Fern Guide*. Second Edition. Field Studies Council, Shrewsbury, United Kingdom.

Mickel, J. 1994. *Ferns for American Gardens*. Macmillan Publishing Company, New York.

Mickel, J. T. 1979. *How to Know the Ferns and Fern Allies*. WCB McGraw-Hill, Boston, Massachusetts.

Mitchell, R. S., L. Danaher, and G. Steeves. 1998. *Northeastern Fern Identifier* (on CD-ROM). New York State Museum, Albany, New York.

Montgomery, J. D., and D. E. Fairbrothers. 1993. *New Jersey Ferns and Fern Allies*. Rutgers University Press, Elizabeth, New Jersey.

Moran, R. C. 2004. *A Natural History of Ferns*. Timber Press, Portland, Oregon.

Ogden, E. B. 1948. *The Ferns of Maine*. Thorndike Press, Thorndike, Maine.

Ogden, E. C. 1981. *Field Guide to Northeastern Ferns*. The University of New York, the State Education Department, Albany, New York.

Page, C. N. 1997. *The Ferns of Britain and Ireland*. Second Edition. Cambridge University Press, Cambridge, United Kingdom.

Peck, J. H. 1982. *Ferns and Fern Allies of the Driftless Area of Illinois, Iowa, Minnesota, and Wisconsin*. Milwaukee Public Museum Press, Milwaukee, Wisconsin.

Pryer, K. M., E. Schuettplez, P. G. Wolf, H. Schneider, A. R. Smith, and R. Cranfill. 2004. Phylogeny and evolution of ferns (Monilophytes) with a focus on the early leptosporangiate divergence. *American Journal of Botany* 91 : 1582–1598.

Pryer, K. M., H. Schneider, A. R. Smith, R. Cranfill, P. G. Wolf, J. S. Hunt, and S. D. Sipes. 2001. Horsetails and ferns are a monophyletic group and the closest living relatives to seed plants. *Nature* 409: 618–622.

Roberts, E. A., and J. R. Lawrence. 1935. *American Ferns: How to Know, Grow and Use Them.* Macmillan Company, New York, New York.

Schneider, E. L., and S. Carlquist. 2000. SEM studies on vessels in ferns. 19. *Marsilea. American Fern Journal* 90: 32–41.

Schneider, H., E. Schuettpelz, K. M. Pryer, R. Cranfill, S. Magallón, and R. Lupla. 2004. Ferns diversified in the shadow of angiosperms. *Nature* 428: 553–557.

Slosson, M. 1906. *How Ferns Grow.* Henry Holt and Company, New York, New York.

Smith, A. R., and R. B. Cranfill. 2002. Intrafamilial relationships of the *Thelypteroid* ferns. *American Fern Journal* 92: 131–149.

Snyder, L. H., Jr., and J. G. Bruce. 1986. *Field Guide to the Ferns and Other Pteridophytes of Georgia.* University of Georgia, Athens, Georgia.

Soltis, P. S., and D. E. Soltis. 1990. Genetic variation within and among populations of ferns. *American Fern Journal* 80: 161–172.

Sorrie, B. A., and P. Somers. 1999. *The Vascular Plants of Massachusetts: A County Checklist.* Massachusetts Division of Fisheries and Wildlife, Westborough, Massachusetts.

Svenson, H. K. 1944. The New World species of *Azolla. American Fern Journal* 34: 69–84.

Thorne, F., and L. Thomas. 1989. *Henry Potter's Field Guide to the Hybrid Ferns of the Northeast.* Vermont Institute of Natural Sciences, Woodstock, Vermont.

Tryon, A. F., and R. C. Moran. 1997. *The Ferns and Allied Plants of New England.* Massachusetts Audubon Society, Lincoln, Massachusetts.

van Hove, C., and A. LeJeune. 2002. The *Azolla-Anabaena* symbiosis. *Biology and Environment: Proceedings of the Royal Irish Academy* 102B: 23–26.

Verdoorn, F., in collaboration with others. 1938. *Manual of Pteridology.* Martinus Nijhoff, The Hague.

Wagner, F. S. 1993. Chromosomes of North American grapeferns and moonworts. *Contributions of the University of Michigan Herbarium* 19: 83–92.

Wagner, W. H., Jr., and F. S. Wagner. 1994. Another widely disjunct, rare and local North American moonwort (Ophioglossaceae: *Botrychium* subg. *Botrychium*). *American Fern Journal* 84: 5–10.

Waters, C. E. 1903. *Ferns: A Manual for the Northeastern States with Analytical Keys Based on the Stalks and on the Fructification*. Henry Holt & Company, New York, New York.

Werth, C. R., S. I. Guttman, and W. H. Eshbaugh. 1985. Electrophoretic evidence of reticulate evolution in the Appalachian *Asplenium* complex. *Systematic Botany* 10: 184–192.

Wherry, E. T. 1961. *The Fern Guide: Northeastern and Midland U.S. and Adjacent Canada*. Doubleday & Company, Incorporated, New York, New York.

Wiley, F. A. 1936, rev. 1948. *Ferns of Northeastern United States*. American Museum of Natural History, New York, New York.

Wolf, P. G., E. Sheffield, and C. H. Haufler. 1991. Estimates of gene flow, genetic substructure and population heterogeneity in bracken (*Pteridium aquilinum*). *Biological Journal of the Linnaean Society* 42: 407–423.

USEFUL WEB SITES

American Fern Society
www.amerfernsoc.org

Fern ID: The Ferns Identification Database
www.midwales.com/westhill/mydbfern

Flora of North America
www. fna.org

Hardy Fern Foundation
www.hardyferns.org

British Pteridological Society
www.nhm.ac.uk/hosted_sites/bps

The Delaware Valley Fern and Wildflower Society
www.dvfws.org

Hassler, M. and B. Swale. Checklist of World Ferns
www.homepages.caverock.net.nz/~bj/fern

Lubin, D. Ferns et al. of New England
www.world.std.com/~donlubin

Rook, E. J. S. Ferns and fern allies of the Northwoods
www.rook.org/earl/bwca/nature/ferns/index.html

Taylor, W. C. Our Fine, Feathery Ferns: a Sight for Sori. Milwaukee Public Museum www.mpm.edu/collect/botany/ferns.html

Thomas, P. A. and M. P. Garber. Growing Ferns
www.ces.uga.edu/pubcd/B737-w.htm

Tree of Life Project: Leptosporangiate Ferns
www.tolweb.org/tree?group=Leptosporangiate_Ferns&contgroup=
Filicopsida

USDA NRCS National Plants Database
www.plants.usda.gov/

Haines, A. Synonimized Checklist of the New England Tracheophytes.
www.arthurhaines.com/checklist.htm

PHOTOGRAPH AND
ILLUSTRATION CREDITS

Photographer credits can be found in the photo captions running with the text. Credits for uncaptioned photographs are as follows:

JEAN BAXTER/NEWFS: 52–53
FRANK BRAMLEY/NEWFS: 9, 384, 391, 398
WILLIAM CULLINA: ii–iii
ARTHUR HAINES: 16 top, 240, 280, 404
WILLIAM LARKIN/NEWFS: 21
CHERYL LOWE: xvi–1, 278–79
JOHN LYNCH/NEWFS: vii, 3, 29, 403
ADELAIDE PRATT/NEWFS: ix
DAVID STONE/NEWFS: xi, 405
ARIEH TAL: 382–383

Drawings on the following pages are by Elizabeth Farnsworth: 22; 25 top; 35, 2nd row center; 51, 2nd row left; 51, bottom row right; 57 A.; 62 bottom; 98 right; 109 A.; 111 whole plant, 111 C.; 113; 131; 137 C.; 145 whole plant, 145 B.; 149 right; 154 top; 183; 193; 202; 205 B.; 208 right; 223; 251 right; 257; 261; 271; 272; 275; 287 B.; 289; 291 A.; 295 A.; 297; 299; 301 A.; 302 right; 303; 307; 309 A.; 311 A.; 312; 317; 320; 325; 332; 355 B.; 359; 361 A., 361 B.; 363 top left, 363 top center, 363 top right, 363 bottom right; 366 top; 368 top, 368 center; 369; 370; 375 D.; 377; 379 D.; 381.

All other drawings are by Laura Louise Foster.

INDEX

Page references in **boldface** refer to illustrations.

THE PETERSON SERIES®

PETERSON FIELD GUIDES®

BIRDS

FISH

INSECTS

MAMMALS

PETERSON FIELD GUIDES®

PETERSON FIELD GUIDES® continued

REPTILES AND AMPHIBIANS

EASTERN REPTILES AND AMPHIBIANS Eastern and
  central North America 90452-8
WESTERN REPTILES AND AMPHIBIANS Western North
  America, including Baja California 93611-x

SEASHORE

SHELLS OF THE ATLANTIC Atlantic and Gulf coasts
  and the West Indies 0-618-16439-1
PACIFIC COAST SHELLS North American Pacific coast, including
  Hawaii and the Gulf of California 18322-7
ATLANTIC SEASHORE Bay of Fundy to Cape Hatteras 0-618-00209-x
CORAL REEFS Caribbean and Florida 0-618-00211-1
SOUTHEAST AND CARIBBEAN SEASHORES Cape Hatteras to the Gulf
  Coast, Florida, and the Caribbean 97516-6

PETERSON FIRST GUIDES®

ASTRONOMY	93542-3
BIRDS	90666-0
BUTTERFLIES AND MOTHS	90665-2
CATERPILLARS	91184-2
CLOUDS AND WEATHER	90993-6
DINOSAURS	97196-9
FISHES	91179-6
INSECTS	90664-4
MAMMALS	91181-8
REPTILES AND AMPHIBIANS	97195-0
ROCKS AND MINERALS	93543-1
SEASHORES	91180-x
SHELLS	91182-6
SOLAR SYSTEM	97194-2
TREES	91183-4
URBAN WILDLIFE	93544-x
WILDFLOWERS	90667-9
FORESTS	97197-7

PETERSON FIELD GUIDE AUDIOS

EASTERN BIRDING BY EAR
cassettes 0-618-22591-9
CD 0-618-22590-0

EASTERN MORE BIRDING BY EAR
cassettes 97529-8
CD 97530-1

WESTERN BIRDING BY EAR
cassettes 97526-3
CD 97525-5

BACKYARD BIRDSONG
cassettes 0-618-22593-5
CD 0-618-22592-7

EASTERN BIRD SONGS, Revised
CD 0-618-22594-3

WESTERN BIRD SONGS, Revised
CD 97519-0

PETERSON FIELD GUIDE COLOR-IN BOOKS

BIRDS 0-618-30722-2

BUTTERFLIES 0-618-30723-0

REPTILES AND AMPHIBIANS 0-618-30737-0

WILDFLOWERS 0-618-30735-4

MAMMALS 0-618-30736-2

DINOSAURS 0-618-54224-8

PETERSON FLASHGUIDES™

ATLANTIC COASTAL BIRDS 79286-x
PACIFIC COASTAL BIRDS 79287-8
EASTERN TRAILSIDE BIRDS 79288-6
WESTERN TRAILSIDE BIRDS 79289-4
HAWKS 79291-6
BACKYARD BIRDS 79290-8
TREES 82998-4
ANIMAL TRACKS 82997-6
BUTTERFLIES 82996-8
ROADSIDE WILDFLOWERS 82995-x
BIRDS OF THE MIDWEST 86733-9
WATERFOWL 86734-7

PETERSON FIELD GUIDES can be purchased at your local bookstore or by calling our toll-free number, (800) 225-3362. Visit **www.petersononline.com** for more information.

When referring to title by corresponding ISBN number, preface with 0-395, unless title is listed with 0-618.